Understanding
Old Testament Ethics

Understanding
Old Testament Ethics

Approaches and Explorations

John Barton

Westminster John Knox Press
LOUISVILLE • LONDON

© 2003 John Barton

Scripture quotations from the New Revised Standard Version of the Bible are copyright © 1989 by the Division of Christian Education of the National Council of the Churches of Christ in the U.S.A. and are used by permission.

Scripture quotations from the Revised Standard Version of the Bible are copyright © 1946, 1952, 1971, and 1973 by the Division of Christian Education of the National Council of the Churches of Christ in the U.S.A. and are used by permission.

Book design by Sharon Adams
Cover design by Mark Abrams

First edition
Published by Westminster John Knox Press
Louisville, Kentucky

This book is printed on acid-free paper that meets the American National Standards Institute Z39.48 standard. ⊗

PRINTED IN THE UNITED STATES OF AMERICA

03 04 05 06 07 08 09 10 11 12 — 10 9 8 7 6 5 4 3 2 1

Library of Congress Cataloging-in-Publication Data

Barton, John, 1948–
    Understanding Old Testament ethics : approaches and explorations / John Barton.
      p. cm.
  Includes the author's Amos's oracles against the nations, which was originally published in 1980.
  Includes bibliographical references and index.
  1. Ethics in the Bible. 2. Bible. O.T.—Theology. I. Barton, John, 1948– Amos's oracles against the nations. II. Title.

BS1199.E8 B375 2003
241—dc21

2002028065

Contents

Preface

Over the last twenty-five years I have published a number of studies concerned with biblical, and especially Old Testament, ethics. They have appeared in a variety of journals. This volume brings some of them together in a more easily accessible form and also gives me an opportunity to republish my monograph, *Amos's Oracles against the Nations*, which has long been out of print.

I have not attempted any full-scale updating of these pieces, which in most respects appear as they were originally published. The earlier ones are often not expressed exactly as I might express them today, but taken together they present positions I remain committed to. In two respects, however, I have modified them. I have 'inclusivized' the language: the conventions of 2002 no longer allow one, as those of 1980 did, to speak of 'all right-minded men' and be understood to mean 'all right-minded people'! And I have added a short bibliography of more recent works at the end of the older articles. I am very grateful to Dr. Anselm Hagedorn for help in preparing these. It would have been possible to undertake more extensive revision, but that would not have served the purpose of presenting articles no longer easily accessible to all readers in more or less the form they would encounter them if they looked up the relevant periodicals. (For the same reason, I have retained biblical quotations from the Revised Standard Version in the older articles, though I have used the New Revised Standard Version in more recent ones.) I hope to write further on Old Testament ethics, and would rather do so by producing a fresh book than by reworking material that belongs to the history of my thinking about this subject. It may be a bit presumptuous to think that students of the Bible still want to read material that in some cases is twenty-five years old, but our discipline is not one in which there is simple linear progress, and I hope there is still something of interest in these studies. In the Conclusion I look at some recent work and assess the prospects for Old Testament ethics over the coming years.

I am grateful to Sheila Vincent, who very accurately retyped all the material reproduced here, much of it of course originally produced on manual typewriters and therefore unavailable to my computer. Warm thanks to my commissioning editor, Philip Law, for agreeing to republish my work in this form.

John Barton
Oriel College, Oxford
May 2002

Acknowledgements

The introduction was a previously unpublished paper delivered as the Ethel M. Wood Lecture for 2000 before the University of London in the Senate House. I am grateful to many members of the audience for constructive comment and criticism.

Chapter 1 was originally published in the *Journal for the Study of the Old Testament* (vol. 9, 1978, pp. 44–64).

Chapter 2 was originally published in the *Journal of Theological Studies* (vol. 30, 1979, pp. 1–14).

Chapter 3 was originally published in *Ethics and Politics in the Hebrew Bible* (ed. D. A. Knight, Semeia 66 (1995): 11–22).

Chapter 4 was originally published in *The Bible in Ethics: The Second Sheffield Colloquium* (JSOTSup 207; ed. J. W. Rogerson, M. Davies, and M. D. Carroll R.; Sheffield: Sheffield Academic Press, 1996), 66–76.

Chapter 5 was originally published in *Studies in Christian Ethics* (vol. 12, 1999, pp. 12–22).

Chapter 6 was originally published as SOTS Monograph 6 (Cambridge: Cambridge University Press, 1980). It is an expanded form of one chapter of my 1974 Oxford doctoral dissertation, 'The Relation of God to Ethics in the Eighth-Century Prophets', written under the supervision of John Austin Baker, to whom I am deeply indebted.

Chapter 7 was originally published in the *Journal of Theological Studies* (vol. 32, 1981, pp. 1–18).

Chapter 8 was originally published as 'Ethics in the Book of Isaiah' in *Reading and Writing the Scroll of Isaiah: Studies of an Interpretive Tradition* (ed. C. C. Broyles and C. A. Evans; Supplements to *Vetus Testamentum* 70:1 & 2; Leiden, 1997, 1:67–77).

Chapter 9 was originally published in *The Book of Daniel: Composition and Reception* (ed. J. J. Collins and P. W. Flint; Leiden, 2001, 661–70).

Abbreviations

AB	Anchor Bible
AfO	*Archiv für Orientforschung*
ANET	*Ancient Near Eastern Texts relating to the Old Testament*, ed. J. B. Pritchard, 2d ed., Princeton 1955.
AO	*Der alte Orient*
ARMT	Archives Royales de Mari:
	Vol. I: G. Dossin (ed.), *Correspondance de Šamši-Addu*, Paris 1946.
	Vol. II: C. F. Jean (ed.), *Lettres diverses*, Paris 1941.
	Vol. V: G. Dossin (ed.), *Correspondance de Iašmaḫ-Addu*, Paris 1946.
	Vol. VI: J. R. Kupper (ed.), *Correspondance de Baḫdi-Lim*, Paris 1953.
ATD	Das Alte Testament Deutsch, ed. A. Weiser, Göttingen.
AThR	*Anglican Theological Review*
BASOR	*Bulletin of the American Schools of Oriental Research*
BeiEvTh	Beiheft zu *Evangelische Theologie*
BKAT	Biblischer Kommentar, ed. M. Noth and H. W. Wolff, Neukirchen-Vluyn
BoTU	*Die Boghazköi-Texte in Umschrift*, ed. E. Forrer, WVDOG 41 and 42, Leipzig 1922 and 1926.
BWA(N)T	Beiträge zur Wissenschaft vom Alten (und Neuen) Testament, Leipzig
BZ	*Biblische Zeitschrift*
BZAW	Beihefte zur Zeitschrift für die alttestamentliche Wissenschaft
CBQ	*Catholic Biblical Quarterly*
CH	Codex Hammurabi

EA	El-Amarna tablets: J. Knudtzon, *Die el-Amarna Tafeln*. Leipzig, 1907–08
ExpTim	*Expository Times*
EvT	*Evangelische Theologie*
FAT	Forschungen zum Alten Testament
HAT	Handbuch zum Alten Testament, ed. O. Eissfeldt, Tübingen
HUCA	*Hebrew Union College Annual*
IB	*Interpreter's Bible*
ICC	International Critical Commentary
IEJ	*Israel Exploration Journal*
JAOS	*Journal of the American Oriental Society*
JB	Jerusalem Bible
JBL	*Journal of Biblical Literature*
JNSL	*Journal of Northwest Semitic Languages*
JSOT	*Journal for the Study of the Old Testament*
JSOTSup	Supplements to *Journal for the Study of the Old Testament*
JTS	*Journal of Theological Studies*
KAI	H. Donner and W. Röllig, *Kanaanäische und aramäische Inschriften*, 2d ed., Wiesbaden 1966.
KBo	*Keilschrifttexte aus Boghazköi*, 28 vols., Berlin 1921–44
KUB	*Keilschrifturkundun aus Boghazköi*
MT	Masoretic Text
MVAG	Mitteilungen der vorderasiatisch-ägyptischen Gesellschaft, Leipzig
NEB	New English Bible
NIB	*The New Interpreter's Bible*
OBT	Overtures to Biblical Theology
OtSt	*Oudtestamentische Studiën*
OTG	Old Testament Guides
OTL	Old Testament Library
PEQ	*Palestine Exploration Quarterly*
PJ	*Palästina-jahrbuch des deutschen evangelischen Instituts für Altertumswissenschaft des Heiligen Landes zu Jerusalem*
RGG	*Die Religion in Geschichte und Gegenwart*
RV	Revised Version
SBT	Studies in Biblical Theology, London

ST	*Studia theologica*
ThSt	Theologische Studien
TLZ	*Theologische Literaturzeitung*
TRE	*Theologische Realenzyklopädie*
TZ	*Theologische Zeitschrift*
VF	*Verkündigung und Forschung*
VT	*Vetus Testamentum*
VTE	D. J. Wiseman, 'The Vassal Treaties of Esarhaddon', *Iraq* 20, 1958.
VTSup	Supplements to *Vetus Testamentum*
WBC	Word Biblical Commentary
WMANT	Wissenschaftliche Monographien zum Alten und Neuen Testament, Neukirchen-Vluyn
WVDOG	Wissenschaftliche Veröffentlichungen der deutschen Orientgesellschaft, Leipzig
ZAW	*Zeitschrift für die alttestamentliche Wissenschaft*
ZDPV	*Zeitschrift des deutschen Palästina-Vereins*
ZEE	*Zeitschrift für evangelische Ethik*
ZTK	*Zeitschrift für Theologie und Kirche*

Introduction

The Moral Vision of the Old Testament

> In Mesopotamian tradition man was created from the blood of a god who represents chaos and guilt, and thus bears within himself elements of a life bound to failure. This negative anthropology is linked to a pessimistic idea of the aim of human life, whose purpose is to relieve gods who have become guilty of the burden of work. Work as the object of human life is seen as a punishment for the guilt of the gods. How different things are in Genesis!

This quotation is from the important recent study by Eckart Otto, *Theologische Ethik des Alten Testaments*.[1] Otto goes on to argue that, in the Old Testament, human beings, so far from being the slaves of the gods and burdened with their guilt, are seen as the partners and collaborators of the one God who created them out of pleasure in their companionship. Whereas in Mesopotamia the human race was an afterthought—the solution to an unpleasant problem—in ancient Israel it was seen as the pinnacle of God's creative work and thus endowed with a dignity that even human sin could not remove. This attitude is summed up in Psalm 8, where human beings are 'a little lower than God' (or 'the gods'), 'crowned with glory and honour', and arguably also in the priestly creation story (Gen. 1:1–2:4a), where they seem to be the climax of God's creation.

It would be surprising if such a radically fresh appreciation of human dignity did not have consequences for understanding the moral life of human beings, and Otto seeks to illustrate these consequences by an exhaustive analysis of the two major Old Testament sources for moral teaching: law and wisdom. Examining these blocks of material against their ancient Near Eastern background, he has little difficulty in showing that the Old Testament writers have made a fresh and original use of material shared with their contemporaries in other cultures. There are two sides to this. On the one hand, laws which threaten human dignity tend to be modified: class distinctions are largely removed (though slavery remains); the sexes, though not equal, are at least not treated as different species; what makes for true human community is fostered and protected. On the other hand, human wrongdoing is in some ways taken more seriously than in the environing cultures, with murder treated always as a capital offence, and the exploitation of weaker members of society deplored and, so far as might be, punished. In a world where there are no evil gods on whom to place the burden of the world's wickedness, human responsibility is necessarily more marked.

So the dignity of the human person, and of human beings in society, is seen both in the treatment of all humans as of equal value—in principle even if they are non-Israelites—and in a greater emphasis on retributive justice when there is moral failure. Despite the sense all readers have that Old Testament law and wisdom are focused on God, in another sense they could be said to be more *anthropocentric* than their counterparts in other ancient cultures. There is no world of the gods about which to spin myths or on which to blame suffering and failure: human beings move to centre stage. If the Old Testament is a book about God, it is also a book about humanity, its duties and its failings. Old Testament legal and sapiential material may thus be said to have a distinctive *moral vision*. The vision is not uniform throughout, nor is it wholly lacking in other cultures: Otto is not making a claim for utter distinctiveness or complete consistency in the Old Testament. But he has, to my mind, demonstrated that there are major ethical themes that are rare elsewhere but strongly accentuated in Hebrew culture. The traditionally neglected sphere of Old Testament ethics has thus received a major new contribution.[2]

But Law and Wisdom, even if we include psalmody in the latter, makes up less than half of the Old Testament. It puzzles me that Otto says almost nothing about the Prophets, who have traditionally figured largely in discussion of biblical ethics, or about narrative. But I shall myself leave the Prophets largely unmentioned, important though they are, because I want to focus on the narrative books of the Old Testament, which in the Hebrew canon constitute the whole of the Torah and Former Prophets and a substantial part of the Writings, and in the New Revised Standard Version occupy 463 pages of the English Bible—not too easy to overlook.[3] If there is a moral vision in the Old Testament, then surely we might expect to find it there. How did Otto come to leave it out of his account?

There are three problems in turning to the narrative books for ethical insight. First, ordinary readers, not inured to these stories by constant attention as biblical scholars are, notice the very obvious point that they are often far from morally edifying. Joshua and Judges are probably the place where the shoe pinches worst, but in general Old Testament narratives have had a bad press. Here is one of A. S. Byatt's characters on the subject:

> I'm sure all those Scripture stories we did at the age of nine and ten are the reason I find religion not only incredible, but disgusting and dangerous. At that stage, you're already doing bits of Shakespeare, at least at the kind of segregated high-powered school I was at, and even if you say, or believe, you're bored or indifferent, there are all those passionate people, all those complicated motives, all that singing language, all the power, and, later, you know it changed you for ever. But the Scriptures were both dead and nasty.[4]

Second, though Old Testament stories are usually about what we might call 'moral issues', it is often not easy to decide what is being commended, what deplored. Readers of Genesis have often wondered whether Jacob's trickery, for example, is being held up for imitation or for disapproval.[5] The laconic style of Hebrew narrative makes this peculiarly hard to decide. The Deuteronomistic literature—many stories in Kings, for example—operates with a clear moral calculus, and we are told whether kings were good or bad. But the greater part of the biblical narrative refrains from direct comment. Later generations of Jews and Christians have often used the biblical tales as *exempla* for sermons or catechesis, but the texts themselves generally keep their own counsel. In the appalling story in Judges 19, we still do not know whether the Levite did right to cut up his dead concubine and send a piece of her to each of the tribes as a summons to war against the Benjaminites of Gibeah; and although, since the rape is plainly deplored, he cannot have been right to let it happen, the author does not say so in as many words.

Third, there is a general problem about describing what may be called the moral world of biblical narrative, akin to that of describing the moral world of, say, the Homeric epics. Are we talking about the real world of which the narratives are a later reflection, or about the imagined world of the stories considered as literary fiction? Old Testament scholars have tended to elide that question. Thus, in his fine discussion of morality in the Old Testament, Eichrodt routinely treats the stories in Genesis, Judges, and Samuel as evidence for moral perceptions in 'early Israel', which seems to mean roughly the age of the judges and of the early monarchy.[6] Especially now that late datings for biblical narrative are beginning to be popular, that seems a precarious operation. Recent scholarship is more inclined to think of the world of these tales as a literary world, imagined for the purpose. That still leaves us with the question of whether the writers thought of the moral ideas exemplified in the stories they were writing as normative for their own world or as operative in a kind of fairy-tale past. Such a distinction might be important, for example, in the case of the stories of Jacob, where the writer may think that Jacob's trickery was appropriate within a story of ancient times but may not be commending it to his contemporaries for imitation.

All this makes it easy to understand why a writer on Old Testament ethics might think it best to leave the biblical narratives out of his account, as Otto does. Nevertheless, it is hard not to feel that an important source is being wasted, and my own aim is to make a few observations about the moral vision of some Old Testament narrative and thus hint at ways in which a fuller study might be fruitful. It is impossible to do this without taking sides on some of the critical issues under discussion at the moment, but I shall deal with those summarily in the present context. I continue to believe that there is a large pool of pre-Deuteronomistic narrative material in the Old Testament, which can be found especially in the J source of the Pentateuch and in Joshua, Judges, and Samuel, and I am attracted to, though not yet wholly convinced by, Richard Elliott Friedman's recent argument that it constitutes a single work which later editors have broken up and interpolated and which runs from the creation story in Genesis 2 to the accession of Solomon in 1 Kings 2.[7] At any rate it seems to me that there are many shared approaches to moral issues in this material which differentiate it from the more obviously moralistic attitude of Deuteronomistic and, later still, chronistic works, and that consequently it makes sense to handle it all together. For our present purposes, however, I am going to concentrate on just two portions of this corpus, the stories of David and of Joseph, and especially the former.

There are, I suggest, two ways in which these stories inform us about the moral vision of their writers. First, they deal with moral issues that are not the subject of legal or wisdom texts, about which there is not or perhaps cannot be actual legislation, and that are too complex for aphoristic literature—which is the characteristic form of Wisdom—to handle. And second, moral insights are conveyed by the way the stories are plotted, by the shape of the narrative, and by the interplay of characters in the story they tell. As I have indicated elsewhere, I have been interested in Martha Nussbaum's work on the way narrative texts and drama can be vehicles for the elucidation of moral issues in ways that are not possible through other, more discursive genres; and I believe that the Old Testament is particularly rich in such examples.[8]

First, then, moral values that do not appear in law and wisdom. There are two speeches in the story of David that convey important moral attitudes. One is the speech of Nathan, when he confronts David with the murder of Uriah the Hittite after David's adultery with Bathsheba, in which Nathan presents the famous parable of the poor man and his single ewe-lamb which a rich neighbour steals in order to give dinner to an unexpected visitor (2 Sam. 12:1–6). Discussions of legal principles in ancient Israel have sometimes tried to bring the parable into line with explicit laws, but the problem here is that the penalty proposed by David, involving both fourfold restitution and the death penalty, is quite unrelated to laws about theft. Such discussions overlook the fact that what Nathan presents is an extreme case designed to evince not the king's judicial abilities but the king's moral indignation and anger. David is properly furious at the case presented to him because it involves not simply theft but the exploitation of the poor man by his rich neighbour. The parable will work only if Nathan can take it for granted that the king, like any other right-thinking person, will be outraged by a man who has all he needs and yet exploits the poor. The depiction of the lamb as 'like a daughter' to the poor man is not a mere literary flourish but an essential part of the moral case being put: this is a lamb which is not merely the rightful possession of the poor man but one which is dear to him. The parable presupposes that possession is not simply a matter of legal entitlement but may involve emotional attachment, and that this attachment has a moral value. Similarly, the rich man's offence is not simply theft: he deserves to die 'because he had no pity'.

Only by this means can Nathan bring home to David that, in his own adultery and murder, he has not merely broken a law but has offended against humanity. Like Amnon when he rapes his sister Tamar, David has done something which 'is not done in Israel', and committed an act of 'folly'—the strongly charged term for moral misconduct familiar from the wisdom literature. There is no problem here about possible ambiguity as to the narrator's approval or disapproval: the whole way the story is told implies that the narrator aligns himself with Nathan, and indeed that God does so, too, for it is God who sends Nathan to the king. Uriah has been treated as a nonperson who can be elbowed out of the way with impunity, but it takes the construction of a moral case about a wholly different set of events to bring this home to David. An analogy from a different sphere is more powerful than a frontal attack on his wrongdoing. Certainly Nathan's speech endorses two legal principles, the prohibitions of murder and adultery, which we find in the Decalogue; but it goes much beyond this to tease out a vision of the way human beings should relate to one another in society. Nathan assumes that a well-ordered society will be one in which ties of affection are respected by others, even the rich, even rulers, even the king. The poor and the subordinates of those in power are to be treated as human, not as pieces on a chessboard to be moved around at will.

The second speech that reveals a moral agenda is that of the wise woman of Tekoa in 2 Samuel 14. She has been put up by Joab to persuade David to bring back from exile his son Absalom, who had fled from Judah after killing his brother Amnon in revenge for his rape of Tamar, and she too goes about her task by constructing an analogous case. This time the circumstances are

closer to the events being referred to because she tells a tale of a blood-feud
in her own family arising from the murder of one of her two sons by the other,
and the application to David's family follows smoothly: '[I]n giving this decision [that is, to prevent the surviving son being executed for his murder] the
king convicts himself, inasmuch as the king does not bring his banished one
home again' (14:13).

But again we can learn much about the author's moral perceptions, and perhaps those of his social environment, from looking closely at the speech. The
woman accepts the general legal principle that murder should be punished
with the death penalty, but she argues that in this case strict justice will 'quench
my one remaining ember, and leave to my husband neither name nor remnant
on the face of the earth' (14:7). The need to have a line of descendants is a
good which, she believes, should override the claims of retributive justice; and
the king is competent to intervene in such a case to prevent the evil which a
strict application of legal principles would entail. Furthermore, the moral
claims of mercy in her (fictitious) case, as in the case of Absalom, can be under-
pinned by the general observation that 'we must all die; we are like water
spilled on the ground, which cannot be gathered up. But God will not take
away a life; he will devise plans so as not to keep an outcast banished for ever
from his presence' (14:14; the latter part of this verse is quite obscure in the
Hebrew, but the NRSV translation quoted here makes sense of it). In keeping
Absalom in banishment, David is honouring one moral principle, the sanctity
of life, but suppressing another, the importance of family continuity and sur-
vival in a world where no one lives forever and where, therefore, it is to the
good of all that strict justice shall not always be enforced. The particular circumstances of the case require creativity in interpreting the law, and they invite
mercy and forbearance. Perhaps we are also meant to remember that mercy
has just been shown to David himself: God forgave him when he repented of
his sin, and it is fitting that he should show the same forgiveness to his own
son, Absalom. And, as in the case of the fictitious story told by the woman of
Tekoa, the fact that he loves Absalom as she claims to love her son is not
morally irrelevant. His love for Absalom should point the way to the right
action to take and lead him to relent.

Forgiveness as a moral good is also, and preeminently, in evidence in the
story of Joseph. As Friedman remarks of the entire narrative work of which,
in his view, it forms a part, the story 'conveys that deception and cruelty in a
family fester and spread'—the same point exactly can be made of the story of
David—'and that the most likely way to stop it all is for one member of the
family who is entitled to recompense to choose not to take it—and forgive'.[9]
The story could not have the happy ending it has if Joseph did not voluntarily refrain from exacting vengeance for the wrongs done him. Throughout the

story, in fact, magnanimity is a striking facet of his personality, and here, as in the cases we have looked at in the story of David, there seems no doubt that the narrator approves of him and commends the way he acts. What is striking, as David Reimer has shown, is that the Old Testament has very little overt teaching on the need for forgiveness between human persons; forgiveness is nearly always a characteristic of God alone.[10] But the narratives, though they rarely use the term, are clear about the concept, and the Joseph story is possibly the clearest example of all. Joseph forgives his brothers, though not without playing a sardonic game with them first to bring their wrongdoing home to them. His forgiveness clears the way to the reunion of the family and its safe preservation in Egypt until the time appointed for the exodus. Joseph does not believe in insisting on his right to vengeance, and this abstention from revenge enables his family to blossom again after the danger of complete collapse. Forgiveness is thus a theme in the Old Testament, even though nothing is said about it in law or wisdom (at least, not within the Hebrew canon; but see Sir. 28:2–7).

So much for the first major contribution of narrative texts to our theme of moral vision: they embody and commend a range of virtues and good actions which must have been a part of the culture from which the texts come, even though they find little echo in legal or sapiential teaching. The narratives exemplify what Otto describes as *Ethos* rather than simply *Ethik*, a distinction that we might convey in English by saying that they breathe a particular moral atmosphere rather than merely laying down the law. We have concentrated on particular points within certain biblical narratives, though in discussing the Joseph story I have already moved on to think a little about the overall outworking of the plot, which I should now like to analyse in more detail as the second major contribution of narrative to the Old Testament's moral vision.

The plot of the early or classic Hebrew narratives that I have been discussing—that is, the pre-Deuteronomistic narratives—does not characteristically involve divine intervention to bring about its dénouement. God may indeed intervene, as he does in the story of David to bring about the death of David and Bathsheba's first child, or the defeat of the good advice given to Absalom by Ahithophel, but there is usually also, or often instead, a chain of human causation involved. In the part of David's story usually called the Succession Narrative (2 Sam. 9–20, 1 Kgs. 1–2), there is a sense of two parallel plots, the divine determination that Solomon shall eventually sit on the throne of Israel and the human interplay of good and bad (mostly bad) actions, which mysteriously have the same end result. From a narratological point of view, the divine determination can be seen simply as a theological interpretation of the fact that the plot is well formed, that is, that it ends with the result the reader has suspected all along. The peculiar skill of this narrative is that, as in a good

novel, each individual human action is presented as unforced, yet all move in
the same direction: the elimination of all the claimants to the throne who stand
in the way of the wholly passive Solomon. But because the human actions are
unforced, they are susceptible to moral analysis. The characters do not have
to act as they do; they can respond freely to changing circumstances, and—as
we saw in the case of Nathan's parable and the speech of the woman of Tekoa—
they can be influenced by others and persuaded into courses of action they
would not have adopted for themselves. Such stories exemplify that respect for
the dignity of human action which, according to Otto, is an important part of
the Old Testament's moral vision, as they make their decisions in freedom with
the divine hand, if present at all, hidden behind the natural processes of human
history.

All this is part of the Old Testament's assumption that human beings are
responsible agents, not the playthings of God or the gods. The consequences
of human action are not presented as random and unpredictable but as following certain moral patterns, most often a pattern involving just deserts. Yet
in a longer perspective there is also considerable moral ambiguity in what happens. The fact that David committed adultery with Bathsheba and then mur-
dered her husband does not constrain the actions of his children: Amnon's rape
of Tamar is an act for which he is entirely to blame, not one that is David's
fault, and his subsequent murder by Absalom is seen by the latter as just retribution, not as an act of random violence, and one for which he takes full
responsibility. Yet it is impossible for the reader not to feel a sense that family
history is repeating itself in a new form: these are the kinds of action we might
expect from David's sons. The next scene in the drama is morally more con-
voluted. David brings Absalom back from exile at the bidding of Joab via the
wise woman of Tekoa: surely a good action, certainly presented as such by her.
Yet it is because he comes back from exile that he is able to build up a following and thus, in due course, to rebel against David, an act that results in his
own death. From the point of view of the narrative structure, this death may
be seen both as a delayed punishment for his murder of Amnon—by pardon-
ing him David sets in train events which in fact lead to the revenge David
refrains from taking!—and also as one of the mechanisms which enables the
plot to end with the accession of Solomon, in whose path he might otherwise
have stood. Just deserts here mingle inextricably with inscrutable divine prov-
idence and with the unintended bad consequences of good acts. Though each
individual action is susceptible to moral analysis as right or wrong, the combination of many such actions produces an unreadable and complex web of
good and evil. The moral simplicities of the Chronicler, for whom good people do good things and are rewarded with good fortune, and bad people do bad
things and are duly punished, is lacking from these earlier narratives.

The Old Testament's moral vision is thus more complicated than it might appear, certainly more complicated than most people think it is. Basic to it, I have argued with Otto, is a certain concept of human dignity, in which the choices human beings make really matter. They are not God's puppets in a theatre whose audience is other divine beings, with their own concerns to which humans are irrelevant; they are instead partners with the single God in the only drama God is interested in, the drama played out on earth by created beings. This concept gives the human race both a greater glory and a greater responsibility than it usually had in the cultures that surrounded Israel. It is not subject to random divine acts and hence need not live fatalistically; on the other hand, it is accountable for its own sins, which cannot be laid at the door of some malevolent divine power. Hence both the hope and the fear we encounter in the Prophets: hope, because good moral choices are worth making; they are not nullified by an indifferent universe containing malign powers who snuff us out at will; but also fear, because wrong choices ensure bad consequences and the anger of a God who cannot be bought off. But alongside its high moral tone the Old Testament is also aware of the ways in which even good human actions can go sour, as reflected in the realism of its classic narrative texts. These texts achieve a certain tour de force, combining a belief in God's moral government of the world and the importance of good human judgement with Ecclesiastes's awareness that 'time and chance happen to all'. Both Judaism and Christianity have inherited that combination, and neither finds it easy to live with.

One of the commonplaces of biblical study is that the Old Testament lacks anything that could be called moral philosophy, and if by moral philosophy we mean the kind of theoretical discussion of ethics to be found in, say, Aristotle's *Nicomachean Ethics* or the dialogues of Plato, then the point is obviously correct. There can, however, be what may be called philosophical narratives—narratives, that is, which are a means of handling moral themes. Martha Nussbaum has shown that the novels of Henry James fall into this category, and earlier critics had said the same of Jane Austen.[11] A more obvious example would be Voltaire's *Candide*. In these very diverse cases the object is not only to entertain, though it is that, but to engage the reader in the narrative in such a way that moral or philosophical issues which might otherwise remain abstract or unfocused present themselves much more sharply and call forth a response. My suggestion is that the Old Testament stories I have been discussing fall into a similar category. Certainly they were told as entertainment: they are full of subtly developed characters, interesting incident, well-shaped plots. Certainly also some may contain historical recollection: I do not suppose that the story of David is composed out of whole cloth, for surely the incidents it relates are rooted in actual events of the early monarchic period. But the author's purpose in each case is to explore human moral choices and thus to illuminate the moral life of his or her readers. If we want to name a genre to which the stories of Joseph and David belong, Voltaire's expression *conte philosophique* has much to commend it: not exactly 'philosophical tale', but 'story with a serious purpose'.

We tend to take it for granted that the Old Testament is largely about theological and ethical matters; that is what we expect of a work that has become canonical within Jewish and Christian tradition. We also take it for granted that it contains large tracts of prose narrative, though comparison with other cultures may remind us that this does not really go without saying: prose narration of this degree of sophistication is not easily found in the eastern Mediterranean world at such an early period. The narrative, however, is quite varied in character and ranges all the way from conveying historical information by mere lists (genealogies and the like) to presenting human persons in the rounded and interesting way that marks the stories in Genesis and the books of Samuel. My suggestion is that the latter kind of narrative, at least, was conceived as a vehicle for presenting insights into the moral life of human subjects in such a way that the reader would be challenged and stimulated to thought and action. Simply put, the function of the completed stories of David and Joseph is to present the reader with the same existential challenge that the stories-within-a-story told by Nathan and the woman of Tekoa present to David himself.[12] These little stories and the effect they have on David show clearly that the literary culture of the time was one in which storytelling as a way of provoking moral response did indeed exist, and they give us a clue that the whole long narrative of which they form a part may have been intended to function in the same way for their readers. At both the 'micro' level of those two parables within the story and at the 'macro' level of the framing narrative, the object is to lead the reader or hearer to find analogies between the story and his or her own life and to draw appropriate conclusions. Narrative thus becomes a prime locus for moral discourse, though—characteristically for the Old Testament—at a practical rather than a theoretical level.

Can we use moral reflection expressed in this oblique style in our own constructions of moral obligation and reactions to moral dilemmas? The temptation for preachers in both Jewish and Christian traditions has been to reduce the narratives to a series of moral *exempla*, stories with 'a moral' in the manner of Aesop's fables. But this is really an attempt to neutralize the fact that a narrative structure was preferred by the writers, as though what they had to say by that means could be replaced by a moral platitude. It ignores the complexity we have seen to characterize the stories. The challenge of a story like that of David is to live with integrity in a world in which it is not possible to predict the exact outcome of moral or immoral action because there are so many other factors involved: chance or luck, the presence or absence of other persons who are also moral agents, and perhaps also the involvement of a God who is a free agent, not merely the guarantor of a moral calculus.

Legal texts lay down what is to be done to a person who commits certain prohibited acts; and though in a way it is a simple matter to list and categorize such material, a great deal more insight into the moral system of ancient Israel can be gained, as Otto has shown so well, by trying to grasp the underlying principles of legal codes, what we have been calling their moral vision. The aphorisms that comprise the wisdom literature are often more slippery, but even so it is possible to build up a profile of the good and wise person they envisage by contrast with the sinner or the fool. The task is harder with narrative texts, which allow the complexities of human motivation and conduct to become apparent and resist any reductionistic treatment. Nevertheless, I believe that we come away from reading such narratives as the stories of David or Joseph with a clear picture of what it is to be a moral agent, one that is more nuanced than we could acquire by any other means. I believe that among those who wrote the narrative literature of ancient Israel were some who had realized that human ethical enquiry needs to be anchored in specific cases, and that it is only through the richness of storytelling that we come to understand what it is to be human and to make informed choices in a world which is only partly predictable.

PART ONE

Morality and Justice in the Hebrew Bible

1

Understanding Old Testament Ethics

Few aspects of biblical theology have proved so intractable as the ethics of the Old Testament[1]. The only major work devoted to the subject is J. Hempel's *Das Ethos des Alten Testaments*[2], which appeared in 1938, and which was extensively supplemented for a new edition in 1964 but was not thoroughly revised. My purpose in this paper is to examine some of the shortcomings of this great work, along with related works of somewhat more limited scope, and to suggest that the picture of Old Testament ethics which the reader is likely to carry away from it is a rather artificial construct, which purchases coherence and system at the price of historical objectivity and verifiability. I shall try in the second part of the paper to examine some of the problems with which I believe any comprehensive treatment of Old Testament ethics would have to deal, and in a sketchy way to suggest how access might be had to some of them while erecting a few 'No Entry' signs against others. My overall purpose is to argue that there would be little point in trying to write *The Ethics of the Old Testament* but that, on the other hand, the treatment of particular areas of Old Testament morality might actually be made easier by removing this ideal from the field of study.

I

Apart from Hempel's major work, distinguished discussions of Old Testament ethics may be found in his monograph *Gott und Mensch im Alten Testament*[3] and in two works of Eichrodt: volume 2 of his *Theology*[4] and his monograph *Man in the Old Testament*.[5] Despite important differences, there is enough in common between the work of these two scholars for us to consider their positions together. I would suggest three reasons why neither has said the last word on our subject though it goes without saying that their work remains both inherently of great value and fundamental for modern study of Old Testament ethics.

1. The work of both scholars (though of Eichrodt more than Hempel) is marked by a tendency to systematize that sometimes forces recalcitrant materials into a predesigned mould or bases conclusions on too little evidence. In many ways the problems raised by an 'Ethics of the Old Testament' are the same as those raised by a 'Theology of the Old Testament': the title itself will tend to beg the question how much of a unity of approach is to be found in the Old Testament—whether it has a 'core' or a unifying principle. This is an obvious objection to any work that tends to systematize, and it reflects, of course, the recent trend against great systems in biblical theology. Eichrodt, in particular, takes it that there is an Old Testament ethic which takes on a different colouring in different parts of the Old Testament but which can be traced historically as a development from the covenant ethic of Sinai variously refracted through the differently furnished minds that it passed through. Given that there is such a basically single ethic, it is allowable to cite evidence almost irrespective of date, although at times it will be held that at an early period in Israel's history the true ethics of Yahwism were being restrained by more popular ideas. Eichrodt speaks of 'a struggle for the profounder comprehension of the ethical norms. It should . . . occasion no surprise that at points in the early Israelite tradition it becomes apparent that struggle was denied full success, and that popular morality refused to accept the progressive influence of the divine revelation'.[6] Hempel pays much more attention to the diversity of moral norms at different times and among different groups, but he too stresses that these are, as it were, variations within something called 'the ethics of the Old Testament' and often points to an underlying unity masked by transient differences.[7]

What is fatal here, I think, is a confusion about the proper *subject* for propositions about the ethical beliefs held in ancient Israel. We must distinguish three types of assertions about ethics: (a) all or most ancient Israelites held that X; (b) certain Old Testament authors held that X; (c) the Old Testament taken as a canonical text may be taken to support the view that X. When we speak of 'Old Testament attitudes' to slavery, marriage, social justice, and so on, it is all too easy not to be clear which of these types is meant. It is evident from the prophets, if indeed it is not obvious from common sense, that not all Israelites can have thought the same about at least some ethical issues; and it is very hard to know what sort of status to accord to such a formulation as the following, from Eichrodt:

> How vitally Israel's opinion of herself was affected by the detachment
> from egoistic possession or enjoyment in her relationship with God is

shown by the fact that the outward fortunes of the nation were vividly
felt as obstructing or furthering the mission entrusted to them as God's
people.[8]

Who is 'Israel' here? It would seem to be a true core or 'remnant' of those
whose beliefs went to make up what might be called (begging a good many
questions) 'orthodox Yahwism'. It can hardly mean 'Israelites at large', who
surely either did not have so clear a picture of their corporate relationship with
God, or (at least in some periods, if the prophets are to be believed) did not
think of themselves as entrusted by God with any 'mission'. But there is difficulty even in accepting this description as applying to 'normative' Yahwism in
a particular period; for it is far from clear whether Eichrodt thinks that such
beliefs were *in fact* held by whatever group in Israel we can plausibly regard as
normative—for example, priests or other religious leaders—or whether he
sees them as beliefs that, whether or not anyone influential accepted them,
represented the true expression of the nation's relationship to God *sub specie
aeternitatis*. Indeed, one might suspect that they are the beliefs that people
should have held if they had truly understood their position before God: almost,
that is to say, that they are an expression of 'Old Testament theology' in the
sense of a theology which *correctly* (from a modern Christian point of view?)
interprets the data of the corporate experiences of ancient Israelites.

Problems like these arise, of course, in every department of Old Testament
theology as presented by Eichrodt and have been commented on by others,[9]
but it is right to mention them here as a great source of confusion in understanding ancient Israelite culture, customs, and beliefs. The Old Testament is
evidence for, not conterminous with, the life and thought of ancient Israel; Old
Testament writers may at times state or imply positions which were the common currency of ancient Israelites, but they may also propound novel, or controversial, or minority positions.[10]

A further example may be adduced to show the essential incoherence of
Eichrodt's presentation. Once the demands of the God revealed at Sinai have
come to disturb the previously uncomplicated 'popular morality',

> a quite new stress [he writes] was bound to be laid on ethical norms,
> in so far as they were understood as expressing the will of the one
> divine Lord, who claimed to bring in subjection to himself the whole
> of human life in all its aspects. Because they were backed by the one
> absolute authority, these basic principles of human social life were
> lifted out of the sphere of the merely relative binding force which
> obtained within the framework and the limits of a particular historical
> situation, and acquired a share of the timeless and unconditional qual-
> ity of the holy. Now it was no longer possible to evade uncomfort-
> able obligations at the solicitation of more compelling interests. It was

precisely the concrete demand of the narrowest circle of the individual's life which laid hold on him with all the seriousness of a responsibility before God, and which gave the performance of his duty, even
in the most humble setting, the nobility of an act of worship.[11]

For *whom* was it 'no longer possible to evade uncomfortable obligations'? For
whom did the basic principles of social life 'acquire a share of the timeless and
unconditional quality of the holy'? The only adequate answer would seem to
be the normative Israelite who espoused the theological system adumbrated
in Eichrodt's *Theology*; and it is far from easy to track this person down. I
believe Eichrodt is *in practice* expounding what will follow for the modern
believer who takes seriously the idea of God and his relation to morality which
the Decalogue, in its present context in Exodus, implies; perhaps also what
ought to have followed or *might reasonably* have followed for a morally sensitive Israelite confronted with the same text or others like it; or again, what was
intended by the author or redactor of Exodus 20 and the surrounding material. But Eichrodt insists on making 'Israel' the subject of all this; and so long
as this is persisted in, we can make little progress in understanding those *real
people* who made up 'Israel' at various periods in the history of Palestine.

There is therefore a methodological difficulty about any view of ethics in
Israel which attempts to treat the actual expressions of ethical viewpoints in
the Old Testament as more or less typical examples of an 'Israelite' or 'Old
Testament' ethic. We shall return to this point and try to base on it a more pluralist approach to ethics in ancient Israel.

2. The second drawback to the work of Eichrodt and Hempel might be called
a lack of sociological depth. This may sound an odd charge to bring against
Hempel in particular, for he has most valuable material on the origins in different social groups of moral norms and systems, so I must explain what I mean
by this expression; it is bound up closely with the preceding objection. The sociological element in Hempel's work consists, first, in asking what obligations the
Old Testament ethic lays upon each social group—not the same as asking what
obligations each group thought were incumbent on itself; and second, in the
observation that some of Israel's ancestors were nomads, others city dwellers,
some shepherds, others farmers—hence the great diversity of laws in the Old
Testament, and some of the inconsistencies in the weight given to particular
offences. This means chiefly that different moral codes have been combined to
produce the Old Testament ethos. Now, this approach (which is certainly vital)
is basically historical or diachronic; it traces a linear development of morality as
the result of the mingling of different groups. But what it tends to ignore is the
contemporaneous existence of different social groups in any society. In the same
way, Eichrodt treats 'popular morality' as a set of merely human ethical conventions which obtained in early Israel and presented something of a challenge

to the theonomous code deriving from Yahweh's covenant; but this popular morality *gradually gave way* to the higher ideals of Yahwism. Yahwistic ethics did not wholly drive popular ideas out, but it reduced them increasingly to the status of hewers of wood and drawers of water. But this is really historically most improbable.[12] 'Popular morality' exists in all societies at all times: it is hard not to think that people were still vaguely saying, 'Such things are not done in Israel' even as the priestly author was putting the finishing touches to his perfectly theonomous Moses. If one is to attempt an analysis of ethics in ancient Israel, one cannot safely ignore 'popular morality' in any period.

In fact, the treatment of Old Testament ethics in both Hempel and Eichrodt tends to emphasize the diachronic axis and ignore the synchronic to the detriment of both. For, *first*, to discuss the ethical standards of one group, in a given period, as if they were the standards of the whole nation, inevitably distorts our understanding even of that group from which we draw our evidence. If prophetic ethics are treated as somehow normative for the eighth century, we shall find ourselves very much playing down the originality of the prophets themselves. Since our written evidence comes, inevitably, mostly from the more articulate and memorable representatives of particular periods, we shall run a considerable risk of exaggerating the degree of sophistication attained by the period in question if we treat our sources as normative rather than as at least possibly atypical.

Second, there is a great risk of compounding the error by tracing a historical development through the ethical 'systems' thus reconstructed for the various periods of Israel's history. Thus we may take an ethical system extrapolated from tenth-century historiography (?J), ninth-century saga (?Elijah and Elisha stories), eighth-century prophecy (Amos and Hosea), and seventh-century law (?Deuteronomy), and trace through it a line of development in Israel's ethical consciousness. A moment's thought will convince one that this must be an unsound way to proceed; but this is, in fact, the method pursued by both Hempel and Eichrodt, though (of course) with such sophistication and delicacy, and with so many insights which, taken piecemeal, are profound and important, that neither the reader nor they themselves are very likely to see the sleight-of-hand involved except with the benefit of hindsight. The mistake is, in any case, very easy to fall into in pursuing the history of ideas—to assume that *extant* evidence is also *typical* or *complete* evidence; and when the extant evidence has also the sanction of forming a canon, one is almost bound at some stage to slip into it. Nevertheless there are a number of issues in ethics where it has almost certainly introduced a distortion.

Two examples are as follows:

(a) We have already noted the tendency to locate 'popular morality' in the period of the judges and early monarchy, for which material of a folk-tale or saga type happens to be available, and to see it as retreating before more overtly theological ethics with the rise of prophecy. Now, in a similar way Eichrodt takes the priestly document as the source for much of his material about the postexilic age, without raising the question of whether its highly sophisticated system can fairly be supposed to reflect the understanding of the average person, and so be usefully compared with the *popular* ideas of an earlier period.[13] Talk of development is idle when there are so many variables: we could (at a guess) get exactly opposite results by comparing the ethics of St. Thomas Aquinas with those of early nineteenth-century London, and then the popular morality of thirteenth-century France with that of Jane Austen.

(b) Again, most scholars would agree that the preexilic prophets reject the idea that Yahweh's election of Israel should lead her to pursue expansionist policies, annihilating the surrounding nations. Eichrodt comments:

> There now occurs an important shift within the moral norms themselves. Emphasis is laid on points quite different from those previously stressed, and, in conjunction with this, areas of conduct so far overlooked are brought within the realm of moral obligation. Much less value is attached to warlike virtues; the self-assertion of the sinful nation can no longer be regarded as the absolute purpose of God. . . . In these circumstances there was bound to be less and less justification for the warlike spirit in religion and ethics. Only in a very qualified way did military boldness and the courageous hazarding of life and limb against the enemies of the land, retain moral value.[14]

Now, the practical effect of this is to suggest to the reader that the outlook of 'Israel' was changed in the age of the prophets, so that 'she' no longer saw election in the old militarist way. The Israelite ethical consciousness has changed, has progressed. But there is, in fact, every reason to think that people at large did not accept this new message from the prophets: thus, for Eichrodt's developmental model to work, we should have to gloss 'Israel' in this period as 'those in Israel who represented the *true* development of Yahwism'. In other words, the only alternatives are either that Eichrodt's statements are not historical statements about what people in Israel actually believed, but statements in systematic theology about the truths actually implied in the prophets' preaching, or that they are descriptions of the beliefs of various groups falsely generalised to suggest a moral consensus within which one can speak of development, progress, or decline.

The fact is that for any given period we usually have evidence for the ethical tenets of only a few social groups within Israel, and these are often not the same groups whose beliefs are attested for other periods. Any presentation of the ethical tradition in Israel that starts from the assumption that the extant sources for each period allow one to read off a typical and fully representative

picture of the stage that tradition had then reached is certain to be seriously
faulty.

3. The third aspect of the work of Eichrodt and Hempel about which I feel
uneasy is their treatment of the underlying *rationale* of the particular moral
norms observed in Israel at various periods. Both tend to assume that the basis
of Old Testament morality is more or less obvious; thus Eichrodt:

> We would expect from our knowledge of the Israelite view of God that
> here above all the derivation of moral conduct from the all-ruling will
> of God would be pursued with especial vigour, and, as we turn the
> pages of the Old Testament, this expectation is completely confirmed.
> From the earliest to the latest period it is God's demand, which comes
> vested with absolute authority, which is the strongest and the domi-
> nating motive of human conduct.[15]

And his subsequent discussion of particular norms begins 'Nevertheless': even
to unpack the contents of the divine commands must be seen as a concession.
Hempel even more strikingly uses the phrase 'irrational obedience' to characterize the typically Israelite view of ethics.[16] Elsewhere he calls this system
'theonomy'.[17] Its essence is that well-doing consists in simple obedience to
whatever rules God sees fit to ordain, and that no reason can or need be given
for the moral rightness of such commands. Hence, if the law is wrong, it can
only be because its guardians have falsified it: thus in Jer. 8:8. Eichrodt puts
this very clearly:

> The divine will keeps its secret; in its secret hiddenness it remains
> impenetrable and does not yield itself to his creatures as the ground of
> being which is accessible to the human spirit. . . . This excludes the
> possibility of deriving the law of one's being from universal law, or of
> understanding it as a special case within the general order. . . . Every
> attempt to spy out this Lord's plans, and to derive the reasonableness
> of the world's laws and the perfection of the lawgiver from the har-
> mony of the whole world as grasped by the human mind, is bound to
> come to grief on the absolute lordship of the Creator.[18]

He applies this emphasis on *irrationality* to the prophetic message in his article
"Vorsehungsglaube und Theodizee im Alten Testament."[19] The prophets, he
says, reject any attempt to construct a rational theodicy, even when their own
predictions are unfulfilled: they insist that humanity's only answer in face of the
incomprehensible will of God is to obey his laws and to trust him for the future.

Now, this kind of interpretation is plausible and obviously accords with the
preoccupations of important streams in twentieth-century theology, but I
think it should come as the conclusion to a detailed examination of Israelite
ethical codes, not as a presupposition which is to colour the whole investigation. We shall return to this question later and suggest that other models may

be found in the Old Testament than 'obedience to God' as the ground or basis for ethical conduct. Here our concern is simply to protest that both Hempel and Eichrodt seem to consider the question of whether there might be such models as not worth asking, since we already know that the basis for morality in the Old Testament (in the Bible?) is the expressed will of God.[20]

II

Having raised these objections to some of the work done by Hempel and Eichrodt on Old Testament ethics, let us now consider in more detail two matters that will need clarification if we are to understand more precisely the areas where we can and where we cannot usefully try to reconstruct ideas on morality in ancient Israel.

1. First, it will be profitable to take up some of the comments made in my second objection to Eichrodt and Hempel. I was there appealing for a greater attention to the *synchronic* existence of different social groups in Israel, each potentially capable of holding to a somewhat different set of moral norms, and (in particular) unequal in the degree of sophistication with which we may suppose them to have approached ethical problems. This does not at all mean that problems of dating can be avoided; rather, it means that we must plot our reconstructions of ethical notions adhered to by ancient Israelites on a chart with two axes, and each reconstruction, if it is to be useful, must be marked with two coordinates—we must indicate to which social group *and* to which period it belongs. It will not do to say, 'In early Israel the moral ideal was courage in battle, the end of morality was the possession of land, and the motivation was the belief that Yahweh was giving his people Palestine as a possession'.[21] We should need to ask, For which group of Israelites was this so? Equally, we must not say, 'Popular morality in Israel regarded the obligation of hospitality as overriding most other moral obligations'.[22] We ought to ask, In which period(s) was this true? Especially in the case of popular morality, it is very easy to think of the prophetic religion as suppressing its 'grosser' ideas of taboo, objective guilt, fate, and magic, and then, when these things 'reappear' in certain strands of postexilic popular piety and even in such works as P, to see this as a 'decline' into older ways of thought. I suppose all of us who learned to read the Old Testament from the point of view of the twin pillars of Wellhausen's system, the Pentateuchal four-document hypothesis and the pre-exilic prophets as the high point of Old Testament religion, have some such model of the development of Israelite thought in the back of our minds. But it rests on an inattention to the sociological dimension I mentioned in criticising Eichrodt, for its terms of comparison are incomparables—the religion of the

people at large in, say, the eleventh and fifth centuries, and the religion of the prophets in the eighth and seventh centuries. The mistake is, in essence, like that of the biblical theologians who, comparing the Hebrew-in-the-street with Plato and finding that Plato was more philosophical, concluded to a difference of mentality between the Greek and Hebrew races. We must always remember *both* axes with which we are operating.

What is immediately apparent, once this starting point is conceded, is that for certain pairs of coordinates we shall be able to provide no information. The *completeness* of the ethical maps produced by Hempel and Eichrodt is illusory, resulting from the generalisation of all periods from one period and of all social groups from one social group, in order to fill in the gaps in our knowledge. In fact, we have, it may be argued, no way of approaching popular morality in the fourth century, or priestly ethics in the tenth, or the ethics of the Judaean ruling classes in the ninth (assuming prevailing datings of Old Testament materials). The corpus of literature with which we work is far too small to provide us with a complete mapping of the ethical attitudes and practical morality of every group in every age. But any attempt to apply this principle of two coordinates with rigour will lead one to discover further areas of often-overlooked ignorance, such as the following.

(a) It may be granted that the morality of any reasonably complex nation can only be reconstructed by attending to differences of social group. But for ancient Israel we have only a partial insight into the social organisation of the people in any case. Neither Max Weber's *Ancient Judaism*[23] nor R. de Vaux's *Ancient Israel*[24] provides a definitive sociology of ancient Israel; and it is doubtful whether sufficient material exists from which one could be reconstructed. It is this problem which has made so many discussions of *wisdom* in particular so unsatisfactory and hard to check. Were 'the wise' a distinct social group, and, if so, in which periods? Were they 'civil servants'?[25] How was the didactic tradition which the Old Testament attests communicated—through schools of the Babylonian or Egyptian types or in a more domestic setting, in villages or only in the capital? How are didactic and liturgical traditions related, and can an accurate *Sitz im Leben* for works which betray their influence be reconstructed? (This last may be said to be one current form of the problem of Deuteronomy.)[26] It is difficult to think that these questions will ever be definitively resolved. With the material at our disposal we are unlikely to be able to improve much on Hempel's work on the sociological aspects of ancient Israelite ethics; but there is no doubt that the sociology of ancient Israel cries out for more detailed treatment than it has yet received, if students of biblical ethics are to know just where to set the limits of their possible knowledge.

(b) Second, the question arises regarding the *sort* of evidence that will justify us in proposing a particular set of norms or ideals as characteristic of particular groups in particular periods. I think it is fair to say that none of the work so far produced on Old Testament ethics has grasped this nettle firmly enough. Both Eichrodt and Hempel, for example, draw freely on Genesis, Judges, and 1 and 2 Samuel for evidence of attitudes to moral questions in 'early Israel', but it is, in general, unclear what criteria they apply in extracting the information they require. Eichrodt's section on 'popular morality' seems to work with approximately the following principle. If an attitude is expressed by a character in one of these books, that is probably an attitude prevalent in early Israel:

> Men know themselves to be bound also to a wider circle, in upholding the covenant of friendship (1), and in risking their lives for the national community, whether it be in peril from hostile armies (2) or from some other threat (3); and at such times all private feuds have to take second place (4).[27]

> (1) I Sam. 18.1–4; 19.2–7; 20.8 ('a covenant of Yahweh'); II Sam. 9.1; 21.7.
> (2) Judg. 3.27f.; 5.2, 9, 18, 23; 7.23f.; I Sam. 11.7; II Sam. 10.12, etc.
> (3) Judg. 21.1ff.; II Sam. 2.26ff.; 24.17.
> (4) II Sam. 1.18ff.

But again, if the storyteller (at which redactional stage is not discussed) allows an incident to be told without comment, he may be supposed to support the moral principle it involves—or perhaps, he shows that his contemporaries would have found the principle acceptable. This I take to be the logic of the following:

> Thus, the building up of the family with numerous offspring is of equal obligation on both man and woman, and in a crisis makes even bizarre measures seem justifiable, or at least excusable.[28]

The reference is to Gen. 19:32 (Lot's daughters). Presumably the *narrator* (J?) is here seen as early enough in date himself to provide evidence of attitudes in early Israel (for Eichrodt is clearly not claiming that this attitude is that of the 'patriarchal age'—'early Israel' for him means Israel after the settlement). Hempel explicitly stresses that we cannot read these stories with profit unless we are fully aware of the *redactor's* intention:

> It is a mistake to think that the story of Jacob can be understood without the highly critical (Yahwistic) judgment expressed in Gen 32.10f.[29]

But like Eichrodt he uses incidents in the stories of, say, the patriarchs as incidents believable in early Israel and hence evidential for the kind of ethical norms then widely accepted.[30]

Clearly some very complex problems are involved in using these stories as a source of ethical material. Even if we leave on one side the formidable difficulties raised by recent discussions of the dating of the Pentateuchal sources, the stories of the judges, and the 'Succession Narrative', and the state of turmoil in study of the historicity of the patriarchs, the fact that the ethical material is embedded in literary *narrative* is in itself a severe handicap. Redaction criticism is not yet, probably never can be, an exact tool, and where a writer as reticent as the 'Yahwist' is concerned, one can hardly say with assurance how he viewed the actions of his characters—whether with approval, disapproval, or benign indifference. So far from assuming his approval of what he reports without comment, we can hardly ignore the possibility that stories in Genesis, as also in Judges, are *stories of the remote past*, in which different ethical standards were believed to be appropriate from those that obtained in the author's own day. The characters may be meant neither as models to be imitated nor as awful warnings; rather, they may be larger-than-life figures in whom the reader is to see the great past of the nation, when the divine purposes were achieved through men and women who did things which would hardly be permissible or possible in the reader's own day. For one thing, they were in constant touch with the deity through dreams, oracles, and miracles (which is not the case now, in the Israel (say) of the court of Solomon or of Uzziah and Jeroboam II), and so were able to know when God intended to suspend the usual moral rules. Maybe, then, we can know extremely little of the ethical ideas prevalent in the writer's day by studying the stories he tells. But equally, of course, we may be able to learn no more about the true morals and manners of the ages of which the stories tell, for the writer may be concerned not with verisimilitude (which his readers had no means of judging) but with the presentation of a heroic age now long past.

It is true that many scholars think the patriarchal stories *do* reflect genuine customs of the second millennium B.C. in some of their details, and I am not here specially concerned to deny this possibility, despite the recent debate.[31] Where ethics are concerned, however, we shall normally find we are dealing with features of the narratives that are not amenable to being 'located' in a particular historical period. Whether, for instance, the 'ancestress in danger' story (Gen. 12, 20, and 26) is in any way related to the customs of half-sibling marriages in certain second-millennium texts, I do not know. It is quite clear, however, that the logic of the story as now told is that the patriarch is deliberately deceiving the foreign king, and if we are to use the story as evidence for ethics in the 'patriarchal age' or the age of the author or redactor, we are more likely to find ourselves asking questions about truth telling and lying than about marriage customs: Did Israelites in this period (or patriarchs in their age) regard lying as justified for the attainment of a good end? Now, the considerations I have already adduced suggest that this question is probably unanswerable from these narratives. What the patriarchs *actually* believed about deceit is surely lost beyond recall. As for the writer, he may mean us to approve of the deceit because of the excellent purpose it serves, or to disapprove of the deceit but marvel at the mystery of the God who can bring good out of evil, or to be amused and intrigued but pass no moral judgment, or to register the change in *mores* since the heroic age in which the nation began. We cannot say with confidence what is the author's intention, and how much less can we generalise from his work and draw conclusions about an ethical consensus in early Israel! The evidence simply will not stretch that far.

These two cautions should not be taken to mean, however, that we can have *no* knowledge of ethics in Israel at all, only that we need to examine our criteria much more rigorously. I have found a great deal of illumination in pursuing this matter (especially as it affects popular morality) in Sir Kenneth Dover's book *Greek Popular Morality in the Time of Plato and Aristotle*.[32] Dover's method is very carefully worked out, and his book contains some salutary warnings against overconfidence which seem to me as applicable to the Old Testament as to the texts he deals with (perhaps more so in view of the much smaller extent of the Old Testament evidence). He maintains that there are about six possible sources for reconstructing Greek popular morality in the fourth century:

1. Speeches in court (e.g., Demosthenes)
2. Plays
3. Epigrams and epitaphs
4. Statements in the philosophers about what 'most people' say and think
5. Plato's and Xenophon's portrayals of unphilosophical men talking to Socrates
6. Made-up speeches in the historians

Of these, he argues that one is on shaky ground with any of the last three. Explicit statements about popular morality in the philosophers may easily be simply mistaken or deliberately or unconsciously caricatured; Plato's unphilosophical men may also be figments of Plato's imagination, or they may be deliberately made to set up Aunt Sallys for Socrates to knock down; and the speeches that historians put into the mouths of their subjects are often less valuable as evidence than anecdotal reminiscences, which may well be more illuminating because less tendentious. Speeches, plays, epigrams, and epitaphs are generally more reliable. For example, an orator sets out a case in a matter of family dispute. Whether the case is true or not is neither here nor there for Dover's purposes; 'it is . . . evidence for what the speaker (a) wished the jury to believe and (b) judged that they would not find it hard to believe. Therein lies its importance for the study of Greek morality; if we knew it to be a truthful account of a sequence of negotiations within a particular family, it would actually be less important'[33]—because, after all, it might be atypical, whereas the orator's account is bound to be plausible and therefore typical.

Similarly, Dover quotes in illustration a speech of Demosthenes which includes the following assertion: 'We have *hetairai* for pleasure, concubines for our day-to-day physical well-being, and wives in order to beget legitimate children and have trustworthy guardians of our households'.[34] Now, says Dover, 'this gives us *not*, as has been alleged, "the fourth-century view" of women, but one view which was possible, was judged by the speaker unlikely to offend, and was absolutely necessary for the argument . . . which he is developing in that part of his speech'.[35]

These careful qualifications strike me as having a good deal to say to the student of popular morality in ancient Israel. Just as Dover cannot use historical narrative or overt presentations of popular morality at all readily because of the problems of simple mistake or tendentious distortion, so we cannot easily use narrative material or hortatory material like most of Deuteronomy. We do not know sufficiently what the author of such material is driving at to be able to distinguish what is commonplace from what forms his own contribution. Dover notes that in tragedy the purpose may often be to portray a morality *not* shared by the audience, but one which they had learned to associate with the heroic age to which tragedy relates,[36] and this idea led to the previous remarks about the patriarchal stories. Caution is therefore in order with many types of material.

But Dover's use of *speeches* suggests to me that a rather more hopeful place to start is with the prophets, who are addressing an audience which one might do something to reconstruct; and by this means it might be possible to fill in the eighth- to sixth-century portions of our popular morality chart, if only sketchily. Reconstructing the audience is still not easy, and we ought to beware of putting too much weight on apparent quotations of the people's attitude, such as Wolff has studied in his illuminating article 'Das Zitat im Prophetenspruch'.[37] Amos 3:2, Hos. 6:1–3, and Ezek. 18:1 *do* seem to record sayings popular in the prophet's day from which he dissents; but they may, of course, come into the category of 'the words of unphilosophical men talking to Socrates'— in other words, they may be caricatures, cited in a form easy to refute. I do think, however, that one may sometimes make modest progress in this area.

To take an example, I believe it is possible from Amos's oracles on the nations (1:3–2:5) to conclude that, at least as Amos saw it, popular morality in his day included the following points:[38]

(a) All nations were under an obligation to observe certain rules of conduct in warfare and eschew 'atrocities'. The idea that moral laws are binding on non-Israelites cannot very well be an innovation by the prophet, since, if it were, the surprise effect which the Israel oracle is generally supposed to be meant to evoke would be lost. The logic of the oracles requires that Amos is on common ground in rebuking the nations for their atrocities, before rounding on Israel itself.

(b) Infringements of social morality, such as Israelites can be shown to have committed (2:6–16), are not in the same class of atrociousness as war crimes. Amos clearly does not share this view but presents the social injustices within Israel as even worse than war crimes—evidently breaking new ground in doing so. The lack of prima facie plausibility in such a view seems to have been apparent to Amos's contemporaries as it might be to us.

(c) There is an obligation for Israelites not to practise certain abuses—afflicting the poor, taking bribes, and so on—even though these things may not seem as bad to most people as to the prophet. Whether these things come from the 'official' morality—viz. whether he knew them from 'the law'—I do not think it is easy to say for certain; but unless they were well known in popular morality, Amos's message will have been very obscure to his audience.

Now, of course, the prophet's assumption that his hearers shared these three moral notions may have been ill-founded, but I think it is reasonable to suppose that the prophets were fairly well aware of what their hearers would be likely to take as given. This kind of conclusion must seem very limited and perhaps unduly tentative, but it seems to me to be the kind of conclusion one ought to be aiming at in studying Old Testament ethics.

2. Second, we might look in more detail at the question of the rationale of ethics in the Old Testament. One of my objections to Hempel and Eichrodt was that they tended to assume that we know what this rationale is in advance: obedience to the declared will of Yahweh the lawgiver, in grateful response to his acts of mercy. If it is accepted that this ought rather to be regarded as an open question, and the possibility of a diversity of opinions admitted, are we likely to have any success in establishing what these might be? One of the likely consequences of our stress on the need to consider different social groups separately might be to remind us that people most of the time do not reflect on the underlying rationale of the ethical principles which guide their conduct and, therefore, that any interpretation of Old Testament material to mean that the average Israelite held a carefully worked-out view of the relation to God to ethics will be on the face of it rather implausible. The question of rationale can surely be raised most profitably in the case of individual Old Testament writers and individual figures like the classical prophets, rather than of ancient Israelites in the mass; though the subtle question of what kind of *unconscious* or *implicit* theology underlies certain expressions of worship or wisdom is also worth asking, even though it may be harder to discover satisfactory answers and a good deal of anthropological and sociological competence is likely to be needed for the investigation. At any rate, some relatively accessible material to which to put the question of the rationale of ethics might be found in the works of the prophets, in Deuteronomy, in some of the wisdom books, and perhaps in the priestly legislation, so far as this can

be delineated. Narrative material again presents peculiar difficulties because we are often ignorant about the degree of freedom enjoyed by the writer; but some of the postexilic tales—Esther, Ruth, Jonah, Judith, Daniel 1–6, and the additions to Daniel—have sufficient unity of conception for us to speak with reasonable confidence of their 'authors' and to enquire into their presuppositions about ethics. Among the possibilities that emerge from probing some of this literature in a preliminary way, three types seem to me to emerge fairly clearly:

(a) First, there is indeed *obedience to God's revealed will*. Though I do not believe that this should be regarded as 'normative' for the Old Testament, it is, of course, not difficult to find plentiful examples of it there. Deuteronomy provides some classic expressions of it (e.g. 10:12–15), and it is also probably normal in Hosea (4:6; 11:2),[39] while the stories in Daniel 1–6 in many cases concern the obedience and faithfulness of Jews to their God in the face of persecution. Hempel provides numerous other illustrations.[40]

(b) Second, there is *conformity to a pattern of natural order*—a vague phrase which is meant to be suggestive rather than defining. What is meant is something like certain senses of 'natural law': a belief that the creation somehow works according to moral principles, of which God as creator is in some sense the 'source' and guarantor, but which are not explicit 'commands' uttered by him and demanding obedience just because it is he who utters them. In this approach human ability to detect the moral norms by reason, rather than dependence on the revelation of God, is stressed. I have discussed some examples of 'natural law' in the Old Testament in 'Natural Law and Poetic Justice in the Old Testament',[41] with special reference to P, Amos, and Isaiah, and the question is there raised regarding how far this outlook can be said to 'derive' from the wisdom tradition, of which many scholars would probably regard it as characteristic.[42]

(c) Third, there is the notion of *imitation of God*. Good conduct for human beings consists in doing such things as one might suppose God would do, if God were human. What those things are can be worked out on a sort of principle of analogy from what God is known or believed to have done in fact. It might be argued that this principle is somehow reducible to one of the others, or that there is a common model that subsumes them all; but it is easy to see that one could regard it as basic, without raising the question of its reducibility. Few scholars find much trace of this idea in the Old Testament; there are, of course, places which regard the attempt to be 'as God' as a sin (Gen. 3!). Buber, however, has argued most enthusiastically for it:

> The imitation of God—not of a human image of God, but of the real God, nor of a mediator in human form, but of God himself—is the central paradox of Judaism[43]

—and a paradox well grounded in the Old Testament itself, he thinks. It could indeed be argued that the element of grateful response to God which often accompanies obedience in the Old Testament (and arguably reduces its 'irrationality') could more accurately be seen as an imitation of God. Thus to be kind to strangers and the helpless because Yahweh was kind to the helpless Israelites, sojourning as aliens in Egypt (Deut. 24:17–18), is an instance both of grateful response to the divine grace, issuing in obedience to God's laws, and also of an attempt to be like God, modelling one's own conduct on God's as it is seen in Israel's history. A number of other passages in Deuteronomy make similar points: for example, 5:15; 10:17–19; 15:15.

Eichrodt touches on this theme of the imitation of God in discussing the Holiness Code:

> The priestly law-teaching in the Holiness Code links submission to the unconditional will of God with conduct towards one's neighbour . . . by teaching men to understand the faultless regulation of life in accordance with God's commandment as a forming of human nature after the pattern of the divine. The holy God wills not only to separate his elect out of the world for his service by sanctifying them . . . but also to see the immaculate purity of his own nature, that which separates him from the sinful impurity of human living, reflected in a holy people. This signifies an advance from a fellowship of will with God to a fellowship of nature, thus transposing the ultimate motive of moral action into the desire to be modelled on the pattern of the divine, the only way in which Man can be fully incorporated into the divine world. This undoubtedly removes the last possibility of a conflict between the human and the divine will, and guarantees the unity and freedom of moral conduct.[44]

It seems to me that this idea of imitating God deserves a fuller investigation than it has so far received.

Thus I believe that there is plenty of scope for an examination of the basis of ethics in certain parts of the Old Testament literature, and it is my suspicion that the material will prove on detailed examination to be even more diverse and pluriform that this paper has suggested. Increasingly it seems that in Old Testament ethics, as in other aspects of Old Testament study, simple answers falsify; despite much that has been destructive in this paper, I hope to have suggested that the complexity which I have tried to point to is an invitation, not to horrified silence but to invigorating exploration.

Works on Biblical Ethics since 1978

Birch, B. C. 'Moral Agency, Community, and the Character of God in the Hebrew Bible'. In *Ethics and Politics in the Hebrew Bible*. Semeia 66. Ed. D. A. Knight. Atlanta: Scholars Press, 1995, 23ff.

Clements, R. E. 'Wisdom, Virtue, and the Human Condition'. In *The Bible in Human Society: Essays in Honour of John Rogerson*. JSOTSup 200. Ed. M. D. Carroll R., D. J. A. Clines, and P. R. Davies. Sheffield: Sheffield Academic Press, 1995, 139–57.

Crüsemann, F. 'Domination, Guilt, and Reconciliation: The Contribution of the Jacob Narrative in Genesis to Political Ethics'. Semeia 66. 1995, 67–78.

Davies, E. W. 'Ethics of the Hebrew Bible: The Problem of Methodology'. Semeia 66. 1995, 43–53.

Davies, P. R. 'Ethics and the Old Testament'. In *The Bible in Ethics: The Second Sheffield Colloquium*. JSOTSup 207. Ed. J. W. Rogerson, M. Davies, and M. Carroll R. Sheffield: Sheffield Academic Press, 1995, 164–73.

Demmer, K. 'Vernunftbegründung und biblische Begründung in der Ethik'. ZEE 37 (1993): 10–21.

Fabry, H. J. 'Deuteronomium 15: Gedanken zur Geschwister-Ethik im Alten Testament'. *Zeitschrift für die Altorientalische und Biblische Rechtsgeschichte* 3 (1997): 92–111.

Frey, C. 'The Biblical Tradition in the Perspective of Political Theology and Political Ethics'. In *Politics and Theopolitics in the Bible and Postbiblical Literature*. JSOTSup 171. Ed. H. Graf Reventlow, Y. Hoffman, and B. Uffenheimer. Sheffield: Sheffield Academic Press, 1994, 55–65.

Janzen, W. *Old Testament Ethics: A Paradigmatic Approach*. Louisville: Westminster John Knox Press, 1994.

Otto, E. *Theologische Ethik des Alten Testaments*. Stuttgart: Kohlhammer, 1994.

———. 'Of Aims and Methods in Hebrew Bible Ethics'. Semeia 66. 1995, 161–71.

———. 'Woher weiss der Mensch um Gut und Böse? Philosophische Annäherungen der ägyptischen und biblischen Weisheit an ein Grundproblem der Ethik'. In *Recht und Ethos im Alten Testament: Gestalt und Wirkung (FS. für Horst Seebass zum 65. Geburtstag*. Ed. S. Beyerle, G. Mayer, and H. Strauss. Neukirchen-Vluyn: Neukirchener, 1999, 207–31.

Paris, P. J. 'An Ethicist's Concern about Biblical Ethics'. Semeia 66. 1995, 173–82.

Pleins, J. D. *The Social Visions of the Hebrew Bible: A Theological Introduction*. Louisville and London: Westminster John Knox Press, 2000.

Rodd, C. S. *Glimpses of a Strange Land: Studies in Old Testament Ethics*. Edinburgh: T. & T. Clark, 2001.

Rogerson, J. W. 'Old Testament Ethics'. In *Text in Context: Essays by Members of the Society for Old Testament Study*. Ed. A. D. H. Mayes. Oxford: Oxford University Press, 2000, 116–37.

———. 'Discourse Ethics and Biblical Ethics'. In *The Bible in Ethics*. JSOTSup 207, 1995, 17–26.

Schmidt, W. H., H. Delkurt, and A. Graupner. *Die Zehn Gebote im Rahmen alttestamentlicher Ethik*. Erträge der Forschung 281. Darmstadt: Wissenschaftliche Buchgesellschaft, 1993.

2

Natural Law and Poetic Justice in the Old Testament

I

In the heyday of the biblical theology movement, it might have seemed absurd to suggest that the Old Testament contained any reference to 'natural law'—surely a Graeco-Latin idea if ever there was one. Perhaps that partly explains why Friedrich Horst's important paper on the subject in *Evangelische Theologie* for 1950[1] seems, despite its moderation, to have met with comparatively little response and not to have stimulated much further work on the subject. Now that the climate of Old Testament theology is markedly more pluralist, it may be easier to make a case for natural law as an important element in much Old Testament thinking about ethical obligation; not just in, say, the Wisdom books, where it might be readily accepted as part of the essentially non-Israelite concepts with which wisdom may be thought to function, but in the Prophets and perhaps even in some strands of the Pentateuch itself. It may, of course, be felt that this will be simply to jump on the anticovenant bandwagon which is already rolling at some speed, and no doubt there is some truth in that. This paper will attempt to examine this alternative model for understanding the relation of ethics to God in the Old Testament literature, though there will certainly be no suggestion that it is normative for, or even typical of, the Old Testament in the way that might be claimed for the covenant; indeed, part of my purpose is to question the existence of 'normative' concepts or systems in Old Testament theology.

In speaking of 'natural law' at all, one is faced with a jungle of possible definitions and implications. The term is meant to suggest a way of looking at ethics which stresses that certain moral norms are felt to be *natural*, in tune with the way things are, or likely to be held by everyone in virtue of some innate moral sense. The *Dictionary of Christian Ethics*[2] provides a useful, concise definition: natural law is 'the view that there are certain precepts or norms of right conduct, discernible by all men'. The author of the article goes on to suggest various subtypes, including (1) 'those rules of justice which may be found written in the hearts or consciences of men' and (2) 'a set of ethical judgments obtained by reflecting on man's ordinary experience, as contrasted with the divine laws that may be supernaturally revealed'. Horst similarly worked with a two-fold division of natural law, and we may usefully take his division as a guide for our own discussion. Natural law, he says, may be viewed under two aspects: according as one is attending mainly to the moral norms seen as 'natural' in themselves or to the moral agents who 'naturally' perceive them to be valid. It is clear that for most systems of natural law this distinction will be a methodological one rather than one of substance: the supposed universality of natural law rests on the notion that it is *inherent* to humankind, just as it is inherent in the world, not merely a matter of widely agreed convention—in Cicero's definition, 'ius naturae est quod non opinio genuit sed quaedam innata vis inseruit' (some innate force).[3] However, it is useful to preserve the distinction if one is looking for evidence of 'natural law' in the Old Testament, and to ask, as Horst does, *first*, 'Is the Old Testament aware of any moral norms embracing all humanity and existing over and above particular moral injunctions (either God-given or man-made)?'—norms, that is, applicable to human beings *qua* human; and *second*, 'Does the Old Testament acknowledge any moral norms or principles built into the nature of things?' Let us take these questions in turn.

1. As I hinted earlier, quite evidently one would think first of the wisdom tradition. A classic example of appeal to human nature as the basis for an ethical obligation is Job 31:13–15:

> If I have rejected the cause of my manservant, or my maidservant,
>   when they brought a complaint against me;
> what then shall I do when God rises up?
>   When he makes inquiry, what shall I answer him?
> Did not he who made me in the womb make him?
>   And did not one fashion us in the womb?

Here an appeal is made to the common origin of all people as a principle which should rule out injustice between them—in striking contrast to the Deuteronomic exhortations to be kind to slaves, which appeal rather to the Israelites' own experience of slavery in Egypt and to the response-evoking kindness of God in setting them free.[4] But far more interesting than this standard example is the case of the priestly work, as analysed by Horst. In the description of humankind as made in the image of God, Horst sees a general principle with far-reaching implications for morality, which are spelled out for the first time in God's words to Noah after the Flood: 'Whoever sheds the blood of man, by man shall his blood be shed; for God made man in his own image' (Gen. 9:6). Humans are so created as to be inherently sacrosanct: to take their life is to contradict the nature God has given them. Some support is given to this way of looking at Genesis 9 by its place within the overall framework of P, which makes the covenant with Noah the form of God's relationship with humankind in general, as against the specifically Israelite legislation on Sinai. It may, of course, be objected that God is seen as the source of the prohibition of murder in Genesis 9 just as much as of, say, the cultic laws of Exodus 24, and that consequently the rationale of the two sorts of law is really the same: God commands as God chooses, and the law is to be obeyed simply for that reason, not for any inherent qualities it might be thought to possess. But against this I believe Horst is right to argue that the prohibition of murder is not seen by the writer as a potentially arbitrary commandment—as perhaps are the cultic laws—but as simply an explicit statement of what is held to be evident in any case from the existence of humans as made in God's image, namely their essential sacrosanctity ('Unantastbarkeit'), their natural right to be immune from attack. God is indeed the 'source' of this sacrosanctity as of everything else, but it is misleading to see God's role in this connection as that of a lawgiver. Rather, God is our creator and has made us to have a certain character which must be respected.

To this example of Horst's we may add one more, which he mentions only in passing—an example from the prophets. The oracles on the nations of Amos 1 and 2 notoriously represent a difficulty for any view of the ethical tradition in ancient Israel which sees it as exclusively tied to law and covenant, since the nations here accused of war crimes cannot be thought of as standing in a covenant relationship with Yahweh such as would entail the acceptance of Israelite norms of conduct in war. But on the other hand, attempts to see these oracles as essentially like the many other oracles against the nations to be found in the prophetic books, which call down judgment on the enemies of Israel for the arrogance they have shown in opposing Yahweh's chosen people, have also failed, for it is not clear that all the crimes Amos condemns have been committed against Israel in any case, with the burning of the king of Edom's bones by the Moabites being the special stumbling block. Many recent commentators have therefore come round to the views stated carefully by Mays[5] in his commentary: that the nations are *assumed* to owe obligations to Yahweh by analogy with the obligations that Israel, in the law, is *known* to owe. Ethical obligation is here being *extended* to the nations, just as (on many interpretations) Yahweh's power is so extended by the prophets. The unsatisfactory feature of this understanding of the matter, briefly, is that it does not easily account for the element of surprise in the Israel oracle (2:6–16), which according to a consensus opinion is the ultimate aim of the oracles on the nations. For the surprise effect to work, we must suppose that Amos can safely assume his audience's acquiescence in the oracles against the nations—that the atrociousness of war crimes and their abhorrence to Yahweh seemed obvious to them; for it is the very obviousness of what Amos says that is meant to lull his hearers into that false sense of security from which the Israel oracle of 2:6–16 is to awaken them so rudely.

If this view is correct, then one cannot very well suppose that people in Amos's day thought foreign nations were under no obligation to eschew war crimes—in fact, a moment's thought will convince one that this is a very implausible idea about any culture; rather, we should have to say that the atrociousness of certain kinds of war crime was an established point which everyone could be assumed to agree about. Now, the only safe conclusion to be drawn is that in this area of morality there was, or was supposed by Amos to be, a consensus, an agreed convention in Israel. If one wished to speculate a little, however, one might very well suspect that the convention rested on some sort of feeling about the rights of human beings *qua* human, that is, on a kind of 'natural law' in the first sense that we are considering. I shall go on to suggest that Amos is also concerned with natural law in the second sense, and if that is so, then a good case can be made for seeing his prophecy as appealing largely to ideas of natural justice—rather more indeed than to what might be called the 'revealed' law, or even to law in the normal secular sense.

2. If we now turn to the other aspect of natural law, the notion that a certain kind of ethical system is somehow built into the world or to the nature of things, I suppose we should once again most naturally look to wisdom for examples. This source is so familiar, however, that I shall avoid going over it here and instead shall discuss a few examples from less obvious parts of the Old Testament. The first example comes again from Genesis, from Abraham's debate with God about the fate of Sodom, which was the subject of a most interesting short article in the *Expository Times* by C. S. Rodd.[6] Commenting on Abraham's question, 'Shall not the Judge of all the earth do what is just?', he asks, 'According to what standard can Abraham judge whether God is acting justly or not?'. He concludes, 'What seems to me to be inescapable is that Abraham sets up some standard over against God by which he dares to judge God's actions'. He then adds,

> If I am correct in my interpretation, we are presented with at least two views of the relationship between religion and ethics in the Old Testament. For most of it, those scholars are clearly correct, who point out that the Israelites viewed law and morality as God's will, command, or teaching. On the other hand, there are some Old Testament writers who dare to enter into a dispute with God, and their action is intelligible only if they are claiming to possess some moral standard which they can set up over against God's decrees.

I am less sure than Rodd that the case discussed is an exceptional one. On the positive side, however, he is surely correct in thinking that Abraham (the writer) is appealing to some kind of moral norm by which even God can in principle be judged, though, of course, the point of the argument is that God never deviates from this norm. But the very possibility of asking the question does seem to indicate that human beings may obtain their moral norms not just from what God chooses to reveal but from the perception of some ethical principle inherent in the way things are. From a sociological perspective, we might say that it is by the projection on to the universe of moral principles drawn from the consensus view of the society of which the storytellers form a part.

For other illustrations of this kind of natural law, we may turn again to the prophets. Isaiah, I believe, provides our strongest evidence. As is well known, attempts to show that Isaiah's moral strictures on his contemporaries rest on an appeal to the law are not very convincing, largely because of what they leave out. Condemnation of bribery, of idolatry, and of murder can readily be understood as an attack on the people for breaking 'the law' in some sense, perhaps even the Decalogue, if that is thought to antedate Isaiah. Always supposing, therefore, that the law was understood in the eighth century as a codification of Yahweh's demands on his people, Isaiah can be presented as here telling his audience that they have failed to obey their divine Lawgiver. But by far the greater part of Isaiah's references to the people's sin deals with matters which either were not in fact the subject of law (e.g., drunkenness) or could not be in the nature of the case. Into this second category must be put his criticisms of the political actions of his day: his attacks on the excessive luxury of the rulers of Judah, and especially the strictures on the women of Jerusalem in chapter 3; his continual references to folly and stupidity; and, perhaps above all, his condemnation of pride, whether seen in the pretensions of Shebna (22) or in the boasting of the king of Assyria (10). Scholars such as Fichtner[7] and Whedbee,[8] who have argued strongly for an alignment of Isaiah with the wisdom tradition, have relied extensively on just this kind of thing and have seen that the whole thrust of Isaiah's message is misunderstood if he is seen as appealing to a knowledge of the law as the basis for his attacks. Rather, somewhat in the manner of the compilers of Proverbs, he is concerned with false *attitudes*: a wrong and inflated sense of one's own importance, a selfish lack of concern for others, and (in the case of political alliances) a tendency to rely on the unreliable rather than on God, the source of true strength.

I am not specially concerned here to endorse the idea that 'wisdom' must lie at the back of such emphases, but simply to suggest that the attitude towards ethics which underlies them would seem to be like that of some parts of the wisdom tradition, in that they are most easily explained as a coherent whole if we see them as deriving from belief in a kind of cosmic order: an order which is God-given in the sense that God, after all, is the creator of the world but which has very little to do with what we might call the 'revealed religion' of law and covenant. This idea comes out clearly in the passages where Isaiah explicitly tells us what, in his view, lies at the root of some particular sin, or where he condemns some attitude of a general kind. Thus 1:3, 'The ox knows his owner, and the ass its master's crib; but Israel does not know', while it certainly implies a special relationship of Yahweh with Israel which we may call 'the covenant' if we choose, lays its primary emphasis on the *unnaturalness* of Israel's rebellion, which is seen as standing in sharp contrast with the purely instinctive 'natural' reactions of animals.

The woes, in chapter 5, contain several quite general indictments of those whose immoral conduct shows them to be out of true with the way things really are—those 'who call evil good, and good evil, who put darkness for light, and light for darkness, who put bitter for sweet, and sweet for bitter!' (5:20). If it is right with RSV to render the elliptical expression of 29:16 'You turn things upside down', then we have there an excellent summary of this way of looking at sin; and in any case the rest of the verse quite plainly makes the same point about the unnaturalness of sin when it asks, 'Shall the potter be regarded as the clay; that the thing made should say of its maker, "He did not make me"?'

Furthermore, this understanding of the basis of ethics in Isaiah allows one to see a coherence between his condemnation of social injustices and his political oracles, for in these, too, he stresses the perversity or blindness to an obvious order of priorities manifested by those who encourage the Egyptian alliance. He does not at all suggest, as is sometimes said, that foreign alliances entail apostasy, for example by requiring oaths to be sworn by gods other than Yahweh. On the contrary, he sees such alliances as wholly human expedients which ignore the difference between God and humanity—the Egyptians are human and not God—and between created and uncreated power—their horses are flesh and not spirit. The trouble with alliances is that they exalt human strength above its natural place: those who seek to win victories by allying themselves with Egypt are guilty of hubris in much the same way as the Assyrians, boasting of their own success and ignoring the plan of Yahweh.

Indeed, when idolatry *does* appear in Isaiah, it too is assimilated (oddly to our way of thinking) to the model of unnatural human self-assertion: idols are 'the work of [people's] hands, that which their own fingers have made' (2:8), so that to worship them is in some sense a kind of self-worship—we are already in the world of Deutero-Isaiah here. Rather than being a sign of unfaithfulness to, say, the covenant with Yahweh, idols are a symptom of a human desire to have the divine realm under one's own control. This no doubt is a misunderstanding of the use of images in worship, but its very oddness as a way of interpreting idolatry—which, after all, one might think was a confession of human *weakness*—may serve to show that idolatry, like other sins, is being pressed into a single mould: it is simply one more example of sin as what I would call a 'cosmic nonsense', a reversal of the same way of looking at the world which, according to Isaiah, would lead everyone to bow in humility before the true God.

If this is a plausible model for understanding ethics in Isaiah, there are a few indications that Amos, too, sees things in something of the same light: though with him, explicit statements about the nature of sin are proportionately much fewer in relation to simple denunciations of actual sins. But Amos 6:12 provides the classic description of a 'cosmic nonsense': 'Do horses run on rocks? Does one plough the sea with oxen? But you have turned justice into poison, and the fruit of righteousness into wormwood'. Just as, we argued, Amos is determined that the sins for which he condemns the nations shall be *obvious* sins, for which they can seek no excuse by saying that they did not realize they were wrong, so in the case of Israel he stresses the blatant character of her social injustices: their wrongness stares one in the face; they are an affront to nature itself. Again this suggests that the question of where Amos got his moral norms, whether from law or wisdom or folk morality, while interesting enough in itself, is strictly speaking irrelevant to a correct interpretation of his message. Never mind how people first came to see that these offences were wrong: their wrongness now is obvious; they contravene a law of nature just as would an attempt to plough the sea. However what we may call Amos's 'sources' may have viewed such sins, he himself sees them as breaches of an order which we can only call natural law.

Obviously it would take a far more detailed presentation of this case to demonstrate that Amos and Isaiah saw things as I have outlined them, but I hope to have suggested that this interpretation has a reasonable prima facie plausibility. I am specially concerned with the prophets as witnesses to natural law for the following reason. Horst, like some others who have written on natural law in the Old Testament, shows a perfect readiness to accept it as part of the ideas available in the ancient world on which Israel could draw, and even as present in some of the literary strata underlying the present books of the Old Testament. He is most unwilling, however, to allow that anyone we could reasonably call 'one of the Old Testament writers' held such a notion, since this seems to compromise the totally theonomous character of Old Testament morality and to threaten the centrality of law and covenant as the vehicles of the divine imperatives which alone can claim to be the basis for moral conduct in ancient Israel. Natural law thus belongs to the same realm as Eichrodt's 'popular morality',[9] to the pre-Yahwistic ethical consciousness of ancient Near-Eastern peoples which had to be thoroughly 'Yahwized' before it could become part of the thinking of those who produced the Old Testament. Its content, though accepted, had to be construed not as part of a world order but as part of the declared will of God; and human moral response to it had correspondingly to be understood as obedience to the covenant-God. The only strand of the Old Testament where it is allowed that this construal may not have happened in full is, as already suggested, the wisdom tradition. For this alleged fact, of course, explanation in terms of foreign influence or of the essentially peripheral character of wisdom within the Old Testament canon are readily available.

Now, if I am correct in thinking that Amos and Isaiah present a view of ethics which can fairly be described as 'natural law', then this restriction of natural law to the background or the periphery of thought in ancient Israel is mistaken. No doubt it might still be argued that in the final form of the Old Testament, at the level of canon, obedience to God's law is the only normative model for understanding ethics. But this will be a truth, if it is a truth, about late postexilic Judaism, or about the hermeneutical problem of the Old Testament, not about the thought of Israel's prophets in the eighth century nor even (if my earlier suggestions are right) about the priestly writer, say, at the end of the exilic age. And since Old Testament scholarship is still concerned with the thought of these individuals, that will presumably be an argument for a greater diversity within the Old Testament witness to the basis of ethics than has traditionally been allowed. If Amos, Isaiah, and P show not just an awareness of the idea of natural law but a positive acceptance and use of it, all sorts of consequences follow for any attempt to describe Old Testament ethics as a whole. It will be difficult to say that obedience to God's law is the main line of the Old Testament's ethical approach, if that line does not run through any of these three figures. Correspondingly, the peripheral character of wisdom would need some reassessment. Of course this kind of reassessment is well under way in other areas of Old Testament theology, such as the question of history as the medium revelation or the centrality of the covenant as the model for the relationship between God and humanity; this is simply a suggestion that it needs to extend to ethics as well.

II

In the second part of this paper I shall consider the question of how one is to establish the presence of a natural law approach in particular parts of the Old Testament. In the examples discussed so far, I have simply argued that the text makes better and more coherent sense if interpreted as resting on an idea of natural law than on any other model. In many passages of law, prophecy, and wisdom alike, however, nothing is said of an abstract-enough kind for one to deduce what is the underlying rationale of ethics for the writer in question—or indeed whether he is conscious of any general principles underlying particular moral norms at all. Are there, however, any clues which can fairly be used in trying to discover whether a writer is thinking in the categories of natural law? I think that, at least in the case of the Prophets, it may be possible to see such clues in passages where a divine judgment is declared in a way that stresses its *appropriateness* to the sin which has called it down: where, in English, we should speak of 'poetic justice'. A typical example would be this from Isaiah (5:8–9):

> Woe to those who join house to house,
>   who add field to field, until there is no room,
>   and you are made to dwell alone in the midst of the land.
> The LORD of hosts has sworn in my hearing:
>   Surely many houses shall be desolate,
>   large and beautiful houses, without inhabitant.
> For ten acres of vineyard shall yield but one bath,
>   and a homer of seed shall yield but an ephah.

Those who have driven the poor off their land so that they could increase their own crops will find in the judgement that they have only increased the scale of their disastrous harvest; those who have pushed others out of their houses to live in solitary splendour will see all their own houses wrecked and left uninhabited. This is what I would call poetic justice, and there is a lot of it in the Old Testament, especially in the Prophetic books.

Now, poetic justice became the subject of a heated controversy among German Old Testament scholars following the publication of Klaus Koch's article 'Gibt es ein Vergeltungsdogma im Alten Testament?',[10] until in 1972 a collection of essays centring on the same theme was published under the title *Um das Prinzip der Vergeltung in Religion und Recht des Alten Testaments*.[11] Koch, building on a suggestion of Fahlgren,[12] in turn inspired by Pedersen,[13] was interested in poetic justice as the expression of a particular worldview which, he claimed, was incompatible with the idea of retribution as commonly understood in the Old Testament—the idea that God from time to time steps into human history and acts as a judge, condemning the human sins and punishing them by a free act of will. According to Koch, one might sum up Old Testament thinking about retribution more accurately in a phrase such as 'Die Tat ist die Saat'—I suppose, 'The deed is the seed'. Human actions in the Old Testament have their repercussions for the agent built into them; there is no gap between act and consequence into which a wedge of divine retribution can be inserted. God's role is simply to oil the works and check the switches; he never needs to interfere to keep the machine going, and he would never dream of throwing a spanner in the works. Most strikingly, Koch adduced a number of Prophetic passages in support of this thesis, including, perhaps most curiously of all, from Hosea (8:7): 'They sow the wind, and they shall reap the whirlwind'. In sum, he postulates a mentality wholly foreign to the modern mind, in which the question 'Will God punish sin?' is an unaskable question; to raise it shows that we have not grasped the alien thought-world of the Old Testament.

There are clearly some similarities between the worldview that Koch postulates for all ancient Israelites and the 'act-consequence' relationship which von Rad[14] believes to be characteristic of wisdom as against some other Israelite traditions. But even if von Rad's moderate use of the idea is accepted, most people would perhaps judge that Koch takes the idea altogether too far. For an allegedly prerational view, it has some curious affinities with deism, and probably the anthropological assumptions on which it rests would not now be generally accepted. Its origins clearly lie in the 'synthetic view of life' postulated by Pedersen, propped up by some linguistic arguments of doubtful weight, for example, that the words for sin and punishment are sometimes the same in Hebrew, ʿawōn meaning both a sin and the penalty for sin, raʿ both moral evil and the physical evil with which it is rewarded (as in English, we might note with some discomfort). Plainly, in this linguistic appeal, as well as in the postulation of an essentially distinctive thought-world unlike that of the modern West, it has affinities with the biblical theology movement though these are of a paradoxical character, since Koch's theory leads on the whole to the conclusion that God does *not* act in history for the ancient Israelite and that the notions of law and covenant are far less to the fore in the prophets than is commonly supposed. Even if the existence of automatic or built-in retribution—the so-called 'schicksalswirkende Tatsphäre'—in the Old Testament were accepted, it could be objected, and it was by Reventlow,[15] that this was but a remnant of a more primitive level of thinking which the prophets themselves had left far behind—though I would not be very happy with this objection myself. Furthermore, this emphasis on the general Hebrew mentality supposed to lie behind such ideas was partly meant as a corrective to the view one finds, say, in Gunkel,[16] that the idea of retribution was one of the great prophetic contributions to Israelite thought. Consequently, a renewed awareness of the originality of the prophets, such as we have seen in more recent years, might tend to reduce its appeal and support Gunkel.

For all these reasons it is probably fair to regard Koch's interpretation of poetic justice in the Old Testament as largely unsuccessful.[17] But the facts he was trying to explain are still there, and I should like to suggest that we can make some headway in explaining them if we abandon attempts to treat them as evidence of how the 'mechanism' of retribution for sin was supposed to work—which I do not think we have any way of knowing—and instead investigate what they may imply about the nature of the moral norms for transgression of which such poetic justice is exacted, by whatever means. This approach has the advantage of attending to what Old Testament writers are actually saying rather than trying to reconstruct a subconscious worldview which they could not themselves conceptualize. The problem about such reconstruction attempts, after all, is common to all quests for a 'worldview' supposed to lie below the conscious level. We have already seen the shipwreck of attempts to make the message of the Old Testament inhere in the words it uses or in the structures of the Hebrew language rather than in the assertions made by means of them, and a similar fate seems likely to overtake the suggestion that the message inheres in the worldview to which the Old Testament bears witness rather than in the things it says. As with the appeal to peculiarities of biblical language, so with appeals to an Israelite worldview; one obvious danger is that actual assertions in the Old Testament become tautological or vacuous. If it is built into the mentality of ancient Israelites that deeds carry their own nemesis within themselves, then the question 'Will I suffer if I sin?' becomes, as Koch indeed suggests, a nonsense question: if asked, an ancient Israelite would presumably give us a blank stare or ask us to repeat or rephrase the question. The vivid images in which the prophets show the congruence of sin and punishment become pointless, utterly banal platitudes. So far from helping us to understand the prophets by showing them as belonging to their own age and culture, this interpretation makes it difficult to see why they should have met with anything but bored acquiescence. It does not explain the prophetic references to poetic justice; it explains them away.

Perhaps it would be better, then, to see them not as expressions of a worldview, to which there was no conceivable alternative, but rather as the expression of a conscious point of view, as positive assertions of a definite theological position. And this position, it seems to me, concerns not the mechanics of retribution for sin but the moral character of the God who, by whatever mechanism, inflicts it. To say that the sinner is punished in a way that fits the sin is to say that God is consistent and rational in his dealings with us as one would expect a human judge to be; he gives people *what they deserve*, pays them back in their own coin, makes the punishment fit the crime. Scharbert[18] makes the point that the 'poetic justice' texts show us a God 'who is directly touched by human actions in the ethical sphere and reacts to them in an appropriate way'; whose punishment is understood in terms of 'a sense of justice which demands an appropriate "reward" for a good or evil deed'. The ethical consistency of God, rather than the method by which retribution is effected, is the point at issue: God's judgment is never capricious, but wholly consistent, and he acts according to moral principles which are essentially the same as those recognized among human beings. His justice is not simply a matter of definition, as in a wholly theonomous ethical system in which justice simply means 'what God does or commands', but is a matter of empirical experience when judged by the standards which human beings use in assessing the conduct of other people. And this, I would suggest, means that the prophets who use the notion of poetic justice are implicitly appealing to a human consensus about what sort of acts are just and unjust—a consensus which is not logically derived from the revelation of moral norms by God but rests on ideas about ethics formed by reason, and one which one might conveniently refer to as natural law. The object, then, of prophetic references to sinners getting their just deserts is essentially to appeal to the reason of the audience: surely they can see that God will not be less just than a human being would be, but will react with total consistency to sins that they themselves ought to be able to see the wickedness of. For the moral principles which rational people can recognize are not other than the principles on which God works when judging human actions.

If this is a fruitful explanation of the important data which Koch's hypothesis of a synthetic view of life did not, perhaps, adequately explain, then we would have a useful tool for detecting traces of natural law in the Old Testament. Again, it should be stressed, appeal to something like natural law is not operating at a level of consciousness lying far beneath the actual intention of the prophets; it is in large measure the essence of the point they are making. The prophetic emphasis on the justice of God requires that the audience have some agreed moral standards by which even Yahweh can be judged, and it is the function of the prophet to ensure that people have no excuse for misinterpreting his actions as unjust or capricious. The culminating example is perhaps the dispute over God's justice in Ezekiel 18, where it is stressed that God respects the principle of the nontransmissibility of guilt just as much as those who falsely accuse him of having breached it. God really is as just as people would like God to be—just according to human standards of justice. The prophetic task is to show that this is not a consoling fact but a cause for fear and for repentance. But unless they are operating with something like a concept of natural law, a moral criterion by which God too can be assessed, the prophetic arguments on this point make no coherent sense.

To sum up: I have tried in this paper to suggest that the somewhat monolithic character of Old Testament ethics as it is presented in standard works will not stand up to examination. Ethics as obedience to God's expressed will certainly does occur in Old Testament literature, but it is by no means the exclusive view. Natural law, both in the weaker sense of moral principles supposed to be common to all and in the stronger sense of principles built into the structure of things, is also present, not just at the primitive or early stages of Israelite thought, not just in peripheral literature, not just in material influenced by foreign sources, but at the conscious level of the arguments presented by the prophets, and probably also in some parts of the Pentateuch. In particular, texts which speak of poetic justice may probably be seen as making appeal to the idea of natural law, and as attempts to argue that God's justice is analogous to ours and observes much the same principles—principles available to human reason, not inscrutable and unaccountable. If this is correct then Old Testament ethics are due for the same pluralizing treatment that is currently being accorded to other aspects of Old Testament theology.

Works on Natural Law and the Bible since 1979

Biggar, N. J. and R. Black, eds., *The Revival of Natural Law: Philosophical, Theological and Ethical Responses to the Finnis-Grisez School*. Ashgate: 2000.

Curran, C. E. 'Natural Law in Moral Theology'. *Readings in Moral Theology* 7 (1991): 247–95.

George, R. P. *Natural Law Theory: Contemporary Essays*. Oxford: Clarendon Press, 1992.

Hauerwas, S. 'Nature, Reason, and the Task of Theological Ethics'. *Readings in Moral Theology* 7 (1991): 43–71.

Novak, D. *Natural Law in Judaism*. Cambridge: Cambridge University Press, 1998.

Rodd, C. S. *Glimpses of a Strange Land: Studies in Old Testament Ethics*. Edinburgh: T. & T. Clark, 2001.

Rogerson, J. W. 'Old Testament Ethics'. In *Text in Context: Essays by Members of the Society for Old Testament Study*. Ed. A. D. H. Mayes. Oxford: Oxford University Press, 2000, 116–37.

3

The Basis of Ethics
in the Hebrew Bible

It has become something of a cliché in biblical studies that ethics in the Hebrew Bible is a neglected field. This cliché could be called the opposite of a self-fulfilling prophecy—we might call it a self-negating truism. For the more often people say it, the more apparent it is that the ethics of the Hebrew Bible is not quite so neglected as it once was. The recent invaluable survey of the subject by Eckart Otto in *Verkündigung und Forschung* contains six pages of bibliography in small type and prompts the editor, Werner H. Schmidt, to comment that Otto has been able to point to 'considerable research activity on this ostensibly neglected theme' ('eine reiche Forschungstätigkeit . . . zu dem scheinbar vernachlässigten Thema').[1] Perhaps ethics is indeed no longer quite the Cinderella of Hebrew Bible study that it once was.

This is not uniformly true, however, of all aspects of the subject. In this paper I should like to draw attention to certain questions within the general sphere of ethics that biblical scholars could perhaps usefully give more thought to, under the umbrella title 'the basis of ethics'. I have in mind two particular issues that in modern Western culture would be thought of as belonging to the sphere of moral philosophy. The first asks why—on what grounds—the ethical norms acknowledged in the biblical text, or observed in ancient Israel, were regarded as binding. The second asks what *kind* of moral system is represented in the Hebrew Bible. Is it, for example, an ethic of obligation or duty, on the one hand, or of goal-directed conduct on the other—deontological or teleological, to use terms sometimes found in moral philosophy? Otto notes that such questions about what he usefully calls 'metaethics' are indeed seldom raised in the secondary literature. Whereas in Old Testament theology questions of structure, systematic form, and central theme are firmly on the agenda, he says, 'in the realm of Old Testament ethics this discussion is entirely lacking' ('im Bereich der alttestamentlichen Ethik fehlt diese Diskussion vollständig').[2]

Otto suggests that the study of Old Testament ethics could provide a considerable impetus to moral discussion in the wider theological and philosophical world, but it has tended not to engage with these large-scale questions. Of course, it is right to point out, as does Smend,[3] that ancient Israel was a prephilosophical culture. In the Hebrew Bible there is no coherent reflection on what is prescribed or proscribed in the manner of Western philosophical thought, and there is no unity such as would justify us in speaking of 'an ethic', in the singular. Nevertheless, most biblical specialists (including Smend himself) would probably agree that the Hebrew Bible, whether at the level of individual books and sections of books or at the redactional and even canonical level, is more than just a jumble of isolated precepts with no underlying rationale. The surface details of the ethical system or systems in the Hebrew Bible are generated by deeper and more fundamental structures of ethical thinking, even if these are relatively inarticulate by comparison with those of Western moral philosophy.

Where this point is denied by biblical scholars, it may be because of their own theological views about the true origins of ethics rather than because of any empirical examination of the biblical text. When I was first thinking about biblical ethics more than twenty years ago, I noticed that many scholars claimed there was no 'philosophical' thinking in the Hebrew Bible and hence also no moral philosophy. (This position was centrally important to much in the 'biblical theology movement', though it perhaps seems less vital now.) These same scholars, however, commonly made remarks about the centrality of the *covenant* in Israel's moral life and stressed that all ethical conduct was to be understood as obedience to the will of the God of Israel as laid down in the covenant stipulations. Whether that is true or not, it seemed to me then (and still seems now) to be just as 'metaethical' as any other high-level analysis of what holds an ethical system together. To say that ethical obligation is obedience to the declared will of the national God is to say that it is not, for example, the observance of custom or of allegedly universal human norms. Once distinctions like that are possible, we are in the realm of moral philosophy— though no doubt of a fairly primitive kind—whether we like it or not. Better to acknowledge this and try to be sensitive to such systematisation and metaethics as there may be in the Hebrew Bible than to ignore it and uncritically accept one model—usually that of ethics as obedience—as if it were self-evidently the only model with which Israelite thinkers operated.

It was with this conviction that I wrote a short article in 1978 called 'Understanding Old Testament Ethics',[4] which was a tentative beginning in a quest for the basis or bases of the ethics of the Hebrew Bible. I should like to suggest some changes of emphasis that may be helpful for the future. It still seems to me that we can identify three basic models in the Hebrew Bible: obedience to God's declared will, 'natural law', and imitation of God. But all three models need closer definition and more subtle analysis.

OBEDIENCE TO GOD'S DECLARED WILL

Obedience to the declared will of God is probably the strongest model for ethical obligation in most books of the Hebrew Scriptures. It is methodologically important to distinguish between 'ethics in ancient Israel' and 'ethics of the Hebrew Bible/Old Testament'. But where the obedience model is concerned, I suspect it would appear under both headings in any systematic account of biblical ethics. Many *people* in ancient Israel in various periods seem to have thought (or perhaps better: assumed) that human beings, and Israelites especially, should do as God told them; and many of the *texts* they produced, which now form our Bible, operate with the same assumption. On this issue that particular methodological distinction may matter less than it does elsewhere. Ordinary Israelites and those who wrote the biblical books alike regarded 'the good' as that way of life which God enjoined. There were no doubt different levels of sophistication in thinking about the matter, but there was no essential disagreement.

At the same time there is another distinction which is perhaps more important in this case than in some others. That is the distinction between, on the one hand, what the text shows or implies about either ancient Israel or the compilers of Scripture and, on the other hand, how modern Jews or Christians suppose ethics to be grounded. When important writers on Hebrew Bible ethics such as Eichrodt or Hempel emphasized the 'theonomy' of biblical ethics, almost to the exclusion of other models, they were, of course, drawing on much solid evidence from the texts. But they were also surely motivated partly by a dogmatic scheme in which the true theological account of ethics is viewed as divine command. Similarly, when Karl Barth maintained that in placing ourselves under the obligations laid down in biblical ethics we are taking on the obligation to obey God, the divine Commander,[5] he was not primarily saying that an obedience ethic happens to predominate, as a matter of historical fact, in the biblical documents. He was saying that, seen from the perspective of systematic theology, ethics is obedience to God, and whatever norms are to be found in the Bible should be appropriated (by *us*) on that basis. Although it would look odd in practice, it would not have been inconsistent in theory if any of these writers had found that ancient Israelites in general, or the writers of the Hebrew Bible in particular, did *not* see ethics as a matter of obedience yet had still argued that we should now accept biblical moral teaching within a framework of obedience. (In a moment I want to mention a case where Barth does argue in something like this way.) But, for the most part, Hempel and Eichrodt, at least, presented their reading of the texts as correct historically, not just as desirable theologically. And it is possible that they here failed to see how far their own theological preferences might be distorting their judgement about the historical facts.

'Obedience' perhaps suggests to a modern person *blind* obedience. Hempel, in particular, made much of the secret of the divine will and saw theonomy as a subtype of heteronomy, a system in which the human subject may not question but must simply submit, being in no way autonomous: 'He has told you, O mortal, what is good'.[6] However, in his presentation of Hempel, Otto stresses that this can be exaggerated. According to Hempel, Otto notes, 'die alttestamentliche Ethik sei nicht die Ethik der Unterwerfung unter eine blanke Gotteswillkür' ('Old Testament ethics is not an ethic of submission to pure divine whim').[7] And this is because Yahweh's own action towards Israel is not arbitrary but manifests the same moral character that God demands of them: 'Spezifikum dieser Ethik sei eine Zusammenbindung von JHWHs mit der vom Menschen geforderten Sittlichkeit' ('Yahweh's own ethical behaviour is bound together with that demanded of human beings').[8] We shall return later to this equation of divine ethics with human ethics.

NATURAL LAW

The second ethical model that has concerned me I usually call, for convenience, 'natural law'. The term, as I use it, is meant to point us in a certain general direction, to draw attention to places in the Bible where ethics is not obedience to revealed or 'positive' law but rather an accommodation of human action to principles seen as inherent in the way things are. It is 'a vague phrase which is meant to be suggestive rather than defining'.[9] It is *not* meant to imply, absurdly, that ancient Israelite culture knew about the later Western natural law tradition in all its refinements.

Provided we adopt a fairly loose definition, I do not think a 'natural law' model for some biblical ethics should be ruled out in principle. Of course, it is still possible that it does not actually occur, but I sense that the climate of biblical study is a bit more favourable to such interpretations now than it was in the late 1970s. Factors here are the enhanced respect for Wisdom literature, in which appeals to the natural order are most at home; the work of H. H. Schmid on 'world order', presenting creation rather than *Heilsgeschichte* or covenant as the primary focal point of Hebrew Bible thought and theology; and the development of 'green' concerns among biblical scholars, with an attendant interest in a 'creation ethic' relevant to ecology.[10]

One small example of this shift might be the currently increased interest in what Christian theology has traditionally called the 'ceremonial' laws—laws about festivals, diet, and rituals. Writers like Eichrodt and Hempel follow classical Christian interpretations of these as the very epitome of 'theonomous' laws, just as, indeed, much Jewish tradition has also done. There are sayings in the rabbinic literature that make precisely the point that these laws do *not* make sense to any 'natural' human understanding; they are given for the very purpose of reminding Israel that, in Eichrodt's words, the 'divine will keeps its secret; in its secret hiddenness it remains impenetrable and does not yield itself to his creatures as the ground of being which is accessible to the human spirit'.[11] But a theology which centres more on creation and the natural order is likely to find laws about the relation of human beings to the animal world and to the cycles of the seasons far less opaque and to trace them back to something which might, at least as an interim measure, be called a natural law ethic. Greenberg and Finkelstein have both pursued this from a Jewish perspective, and some impulses in the same direction may be found in the work of social anthropologists, primarily Mary Douglas.[12]

Natural law may also be seen as an aspect of 'natural theology', the belief that there can be knowledge of God not dependent on direct revelation. This is the subject of James Barr's book *Biblical Faith and Natural Theology*,[13] which is hospitable to the idea that there is natural theology and also natural law within the biblical text. Without developing Barr's themes in detail, we may point to his extended discussion of Karl Barth, who is rather the villain of the piece in this work. Barr suggests that Barth was disturbed by the presence in the Bible of passages friendly to the idea of natural law—above all Romans 1 and Acts 17, but also some texts in the Wisdom books and the Prophets. He presents Barth as wriggling furiously to try to suppress all the 'natural' elements in such places. He does, however, also point out that Barth had a theory that could accommodate them, implausible though it looks to anyone who is not already a convinced Barthian. Barth argued that the possibility of a natural knowledge of God and of ethical standards, such as these passages support, is here being made known to us *precisely in passages which are part of Scripture*, that is, part of revelation. It is God who tells us that we have a natural knowledge of the things of God, and to that extent such knowledge is natural only in a rather specialized and, indeed, paradoxical sense.

As one would expect, Barr clearly regards this somewhat contorted line of argument as an unworthy ruse. But whether that is so or not in this particular case, it does remind us how important are the methodological distinctions referred to earlier. We can distinguish *within the biblical text itself* between the plain sense of passages taken in isolation and their meaning as parts of a larger whole: chapters, books, sections of the canon, Scripture as a complete work.

There may well be passages which originally reflected a 'natural law' ethic but have now been subordinated to a model of obedience. The texts that were a problem for Barth may or may not be examples of this, but others certainly are. In Proverbs, ethical reflections originally based on observation and 'natural' reasoning appear, in the final form of the text, as essentially divine revelation about the will of God. 'Natural' law thus became a subdivision of 'revealed' law. The canonizers of Scripture had succeeded in treating 'natural law' elements in the materials they had inherited in a manner not unlike that of Barth. Thus it was with no sense of incongruity that the compilers of the Mishnah were able, in due course, to quote more often from Proverbs than from any other biblical book outside the Torah when they wanted to give divine sanction to the rulings they had made.

Finally, on the question of natural law, it is important to see that the term is not intended to imply an ethic which allows no place for God. There are indeed a few places in the Hebrew Bible where we can point to pure human convention as possibly the source of moral conduct. This is a possibility for the oracles against the nations in Amos 1–2,[14] and it is certainly a plausible way of interpreting some wisdom sayings, for instance those that belong in manuals of etiquette. No one in ancient Israel is very likely to have thought that the advice to avoid bad table manners when your host can influence your career (e.g., Prov. 23:1–3) was a divine injunction, not even when this idea was expressed in the imperative form we find in Ben Sira ('Be ashamed of leaning on your elbow at meals'; Sir. 41:19). But my own impression is that little genuinely conventional morality has survived in our texts. Otto rightly argues that the more we study the redaction of the legal, wisdom, and prophetic books, the more we find that ethical norms, however 'natural' in origin, have been 'theologized'.[15] But—and this is my point—this is not necessarily the same as saying that they have been incorporated into an obedience model. Natural law can perfectly well be theological. It normally was so in the Western legal and ethical tradition until very recent times. Natural law and positive law, in classical theory, are two ways by which ethics flows from God: they are not to be opposed as respectively human and divine. But since this misconception is so common, it may well be that the term 'natural law' is often misleading, and a fresh term might be useful.[16]

IMITATION OF GOD

In my 1978 article I mentioned a third possible model for theological ethics in ancient Israel: the imitation of God. I had put this forward with little conviction, but thought it should at least be considered, mainly because Martin

Buber had made so much of it. But subsequently I have begun to think that it is more common, and more important, than I then allowed. It is particularly visible in Deuteronomy: 'The LORD your God is God of gods and Lord of lords, the great God, mighty and awesome, who is not partial and takes no bribe, who executes justice for the orphan and the widow, and loves the strangers, providing them food and clothing. You shall also love the stranger' (10:17–19); or, classically, 'You shall be holy, for I the LORD your God am holy' (Lev. 19:2). Although in one sense the desire to be 'as God' is reprehensible according to Genesis 3, in another the task of human beings, and especially of Israelites, is to do as God does: to take God's character as the pattern of their character and God's deeds as the model for theirs. This is far less generally recognized as a basis for ethics in the Hebrew Bible than the corresponding ideal of the *imitatio Christi* is in the New Testament and in Christian tradition, but it is there all the same.

Otto notes that Hempel already gave the imitation of God some prominence within his obedience ethic.[17] As we saw earlier, one reason why obedience to Yahweh is not to be seen as *blind* obedience is that Yahweh is, in fact, perceived as having a moral character. Yahweh is bound (perhaps voluntarily so) by at least some of the ethical constraints imposed on Israel. As the passage just quoted from Deuteronomy makes clear, the God who enjoins care for the needy cares for them also: Yahweh asks of human agents nothing that is not also self-imposed. 'JHWH lege sich Regel und Richtschnur auf, wie er den Menschen an Regel und Richtschnur binde' ('Yahweh applies a rule and measure to himself, just as he binds human beings to a rule and measure').[18] 'Das Handeln Gottes mit dem Menschen kann Modell dafür sein, wie der Mensch mit dem Menschen handeln soll und darin ist dieses Zeugnis Kern einer alttestamentlichen Ethik' ('God's dealings with humans can be a model for the way humans should deal with each other; this testimony is the core of an Old Testament ethics').[19] Otto himself thinks that this insight of Hempel's could be fruitful in the quest for *the* ethics of the Hebrew Bible, which he sees as the ultimate goal of study in this general area. Let me explore this possibility a little.

At the moment I am not sure how many concrete examples of imitation ethics can really be found in the Hebrew Bible. But Otto has pointed to one central aspect of this way of thinking, namely, its insistence that God is bound by moral laws just as human beings are, even though some of the things God does in the Bible show clearly that the parallelism is not complete. Many texts certainly attest the conviction that God does *not* act like a human agent. David said to Saul, 'If it is the LORD who has stirred you up against me, may he accept an offering; but if it is mortals, may they be cursed before the LORD' (1 Sam. 26:19). God may persecute David if God chooses, even through the agency of Saul; humans following their own volition may not. Yet in general there is an assumption that God acts according to moral standards that human beings also share. That is why God can be upbraided for failure to do so, as we see so often in the Psalms, in Job, and in Abraham's famous insistence (Gen. 18) that the Judge of all the earth should 'do right'—that is, should do the kind of thing Abraham would think himself obliged to do in similar circumstances.[20]

This sense of a community of moral perception between God and humanity, which seems inherent in the idea of imitating God, takes us well beyond the few texts which in so many words tell their readers to behave as God does. I think Otto may well be right to see in it a potentially unifying theme for much that the Hebrew Bible has to say about ethics.[21] In a way it can hold together both obedience and natural law models. Hempel proposed that we should follow Luther in seeing the divine commands in the Decalogue as really not arbitrary laws but rather an expression of natural law, spelling out how natural law is to be applied in practice.[22] He suggested that the same could be said of the ethical message of the prophets, which similarly gives concrete expression to the basic relationships in which men and women need to live. Perhaps we may add to this the idea that the God who utters or underwrites these laws, these ethical principles, is somehow bound by them equally. Yahweh is a *good* God, a designation which is not incompatible with what people in Israel would have meant by good; thus it made sense for them to try to imitate God. This might be one of the many possible senses of being made 'in the image of God': that Yahweh and humanity share a common ethical perception, so that God is not only the commander but also the paradigm of all moral conduct.[23] Edmond Jacob was already making fruitful suggestions along these lines in 1960.[24]

Perhaps the 'imitation' model can gain some support if we ask our second 'metaethical' question about biblical morality. Moral philosophers commonly distinguish deontological systems, the ethics of duty, from teleological systems, the ethics of goal. Applying such terms to the Hebrew Bible once again runs up against the prephilosophical character of Israelite culture. Yet we may make some progress—and see that this is not just an exercise in anachronism— by noticing ways in which the biblical text seems on inspection to be rather different from its popular image. Intuitively we expect the Hebrew Bible to be primarily about obeying God, and the discovery of natural law and imitation models comes as a surprise. In the same way, we perhaps expect it to be heavily deontological, with Eichrodt's 'unconditional ought', *das absolute Sollen*, greatly predominating.[25] (This, incidentally, is a hard concept to express in biblical Hebrew!) But closer acquaintance with the biblical material shows that there is also a strongly teleological character to much of the moral teaching in the Hebrew Bible. Something like this is perhaps implied when we remind ourselves that *torah* is not exactly 'law'—directives sent down from on high— but 'teaching', advice on how to follow the path that will take the hearer or the reader to the goal God has in mind. The Wisdom literature, similarly, is strongly teleological: 'Do not forget my teaching, but let your heart keep my commandments; for length of days and years of life and abundant welfare they will give you' (Prov. 3:1–2). The possibility of moral conduct with no goal in view is, arguably, hardly envisaged before Job; at any rate it is clear that asking where a course of action would lead was normal in Hebrew culture. Laws, where one might most expect to find mere divine commands, are, in fact, richly provided with motive clauses, many of them orientated towards the future prosperity of the person who is being encouraged to obey the law.

Thus the moral life is envisaged, it seems, as a cooperative venture between God and humanity. Its commonest image is that of a path, leading to the place where it will converge with the highway trodden by God. And if the teleological character of ethics is clear for Israelites in general, it is even more apparent in the case of those special people who are singled out as having 'walked with' God, as Genesis says of Enoch. Any comprehensive treatment of ethics in the Hebrew Bible would need to give some account of the idea of *vocation*, the singling out of people to be God's agents. Such a calling gives them special obligations, which we can certainly understand on an obedience model— hardly, perhaps, on any other model. But it also gives them a special way of life and an insight into the intentions and character of God, and it empowers them to be in the place of God for the people at large. The mysteriously godlike character of those with such a vocation, as we see it, for example, in Moses, Samuel, or other prophets, speaks of the possibility of the divine life and human life running in parallel; and this may be connected with the idea of the imitation of God. To imitate God in *this* sense is not the role of the ordinary person but is a quite special vocation. Nevertheless, it implies an affinity between the divine and the human; it implies that the human is *capax dei*. And thus it suggests that the imitation of God may indeed lie near the heart of what the Hebrew Bible has to say about human morality.

This paper has presented various partial answers to the quasi-philosophical questions that can be put to the Hebrew Bible. The presentation has made no attempt at completeness, either in the material surveyed or in the questions asked. At best I hope to have suggested fruitful avenues for further investigation. Two methodological points, however, may be made on the basis of our discussion. Scholars inevitably differ over their detailed findings, but they also differ about which questions it is sensible to ask of a given corpus of texts. I have suggested that the study of Old Testament ethics has sometimes suffered from an unwillingness on the part of scholars to contemplate 'philosophical' questions at all, on the grounds that the people of ancient Israel simply were not interested in, or could not have understood, questions of such a kind. A case could undoubtedly be made in favour of such a belief, but it *needs* to be made; it should not be asserted as though it were obvious. Second, among those who accept that we can ask about the basis of ethics in the Hebrew Bible, some assume that the answer to the question is already known and indeed is obvious: ethics is obedience to God. Again, a case can be made for this, and indeed we have seen that it is undoubtedly true for many biblical texts. But the case is not self-evident. I hope to have convinced the reader that these are at least real questions, and that they can be tackled, even if not always answered, by empirical investigation of the texts. As in many areas of academic inquiry, nothing blocks the way to answering a question so effectively as the belief that the answer is already common knowledge.

4

Reading for Life

The Use of the Bible in Ethics

One of the central tenets of the biblical theology movement was the idea of an enormous gulf between biblical thinking and philosophical thought—between Hebrew and classical culture. This applied as much to ethical as to metaphysical questions. It was regarded as simply obvious that the two cultures were utterly different in their approach to morality. One reason that this was superficially so plausible is that it worked by comparing two unlike things. In essence, it said that the narrative material in the Hebrew Bible was not much like Greek philosophy; put like that, the contrast is true but unsurprising. The difference is a generic one, and to make it the basis of a contrast between the whole of the two cultures involved is a category mistake.

Nevertheless, the contrast is not completely empty. For we could ask *why* there is so much narrative in the Hebrew Bible and so little reflective or speculative writing. Such quasi-philosophical literature as ancient Israelite culture produced is to be found not in narrative but in the Wisdom literature; but that in many ways supports the idea of a Greek-Hebrew contrast. With the exception of Ecclesiastes, a book from the Hellenistic age which may well show the influence of the Sceptics, the biblical Wisdom literature belongs generically not with philosophy but with a work such as Hesiod's *Works and Days*: aphoristic wisdom, practical advice on living, with an absence of metaphysical speculation and any attempt to systematize knowledge or to challenge received wisdom. Though it was unreasonable to contrast Greek philosophy with Hebrew narrative, it was entirely sensible to note the relative importance of speculative literature and of narrative writing within the corpus of Greek and Hebrew literature, respectively. The 'biblical theologians' had some sense that one or the other type of writing was somehow characteristic of the peculiar genius of the two cultures—and this was reasonable in itself, though they overplayed their hand. Though Greek literature is certainly not characterized by an absence of narrative, the biblical writings just as certainly do lack any real philosophy, and any reader of the Old Testament sees at once that there are types of question this literature simply is not equipped to tackle—precisely those we now normally call philosophical. Despite the fact that it changes much in what it receives, rabbinic literature is a real continuation of the Old Testament's distinctive style of thinking. If you ask an abstract question about a piece of biblical narrative, the Rabbis are likely to reward you with another narrative. This is not the way we do philosophy, nor the way Greeks in the classical period did it.

Thus the sense of a difference between Israel and Greece is well-enough grounded in the literature, even if it was crudely expressed in biblical theology. Nevertheless, it ought somehow to be possible to discuss both cultures without falling into category mistakes at every turn. Greek tragedy may offer a bridge. Tragedy is no more philosophy than narrative or historiography is, yet through it many profound questions are addressed. And some of the narrative texts in the Old Testament have this same kind of profundity, which cannot be called philosophy, yet they deal, in their own way, with some of the issues that concern, or have concerned, philosophers. But the problem of genre does still raise its head: How can one extract philosophical or ethical truth from texts that work with narrative, drama, and poetry rather than constructing that analysis in plain prose, which is what we have come to think of as philosophy?

This question is a central concern of Martha C. Nussbaum. Her first book, *The Fragility of Goodness: Luck and Ethics in Greek Tragedy and Philosophy*,[1] engages profoundly with Greek tragedy from this distinctive point of view. My purpose in this chapter is to consider how her work might help the student of the Old Testament—which, like Greek tragedy, is unphilosophical yet profound—to show the fruitfulness of the Bible in the human ethical enterprise. But since I have not progressed very far towards making her classical key turn in the biblical lock, I shall spend most of it presenting her ideas on their own terms, in the hope that others may also find them a stimulus to their own work on biblical ethics.

I

Nussbaum's study begins from an observation lacking in the work of most biblical theologians: it is not only that Greek culture differs from Hebrew in having philosophical writings as well as historiography, poetry, and so on, but also that Greek culture has great variations within itself and ought not to be treated as a monolith. One major distinction is that between Plato and Aristotle. To put the contrast crudely, Plato works on ethical problems from first principles whereas Aristotle's method is empirical, based on the minute observation of particular cases and of what commends itself to the average person (the average person, at least, of Aristotle's own sex and class). Aristotle attends to the concrete and particular rather than to the general and abstract. At the very beginning of the *Nicomachean Ethics* (1.3), the principle is enunciated that in every intellectual pursuit the kind and degree of certainty that can be achieved is that appropriate to the subject matter being studied. Where ethics is concerned, we do not attain to *epistēmē*—a theoretical body of certain knowledge—but rather to practical wisdom. To put it in modern terms, ethics is not a science but an art. Here is Nussbaum's account of Aristotle:

> First, Aristotle says two things about the ultimate criterion of correctness in ethical choice that tell strongly in favour of the non-scientific picture. He says that the standard of excellence is determined with reference to the decisions of the person of practical wisdom: what is appropriate in each case is what such a judge would select. And he says that the 'judgment' or 'discrimination' in ethical matters rests with, or is 'in', something which he calls perception (*aisthēsis*), a faculty of discrimination that is concerned with the apprehending of concrete particulars, rather than universals. The context of this claim makes it clear that he wishes to express grave reservations about universal principles as arbiters of ethical correctness: 'The person who diverges only slightly from the correct is not blameworthy, whether he errs in the direction of the more or the less; but the person who diverges *more* is blamed: for this is evident. But to say to what point and how much someone is blameworthy is not easy to determine by a principle (*tōi logōi aphorisai*): nor in fact is this the case with any other perceptible item. For things of this sort are among the concrete particulars, and the discrimination lies in perception.' (*NE* 1109b.18–23) Principles, then, fail to capture the fine detail of the concrete particular, which is the subject matter of ethical choice. This must be seized in a confrontation with the situation itself, by a faculty that is suited to confront it as a complex whole. General rules are being criticized here both for lack of concreteness and for lack of flexibility. 'Perception' can respond to nuance and fine shading, adapting its judgment to the matter in hand in a way that principles set up in advance have a hard time doing.
>
> These two principles are pressed repeatedly by Aristotle in order to show that universal statements are posterior in ethical value to concrete descriptions, universal rules to particular judgments. 'Among statements (*logoi*) about conduct,' he writes in nearby passage, 'those that are universal (*katholou*) are more general (*koinoteroi*), but the particular are more true—for action is concerned with particulars (*ta kath' hekasta*), and statements must harmonize with these' (*NE* 1107a 29–32). Rules are authoritative only insofar as they are correct; but

they are correct only insofar as they do not err with regard to the particulars. And it is not possible for a simple universal formulation, intended to cover many different particulars, to achieve a high degree of correctness. Therefore, in his discussion of justice Aristotle insists that the wise judgment of the agent must both correct and supplement the universal formulations of law:

> All law is universal; but about some things it is not possible for a universal statement to be correct. Then in those matters in which it is necessary to speak universally, but not possible to do so correctly, the law takes the usual case, though without ignoring the possibility of missing the mark. . . . When, then, the law speaks universally, and something comes up that is not covered by the universal, then it is correct, insofar as the legislator has been deficient or gone wrong in speaking simply, to correct his omission, saying what he would have said himself had he been present and would have legislated if he had known (*NE* 1137b 13ff.).

> The law is here regarded as a summary of wise decisions. It is therefore appropriate to supplement it with new wise decisions made on the spot; and it is also appropriate to correct it where it does not correctly summarize what a good judge would do. Good judgment, once again, supplies both a superior concreteness and a superior responsiveness or flexibility.[2]

Now, a method of ethical enquiry which places so much emphasis on particulars, and is so suspicious of universal rules, is well adapted to take account of fictional narrative, historiography, and drama. You could hardly read Greek tragedy in order to feed a Platonic understanding of ethics. For one thing, Plato was famously opposed to tragedy anyway, so that would go against the grain. But for another, the constant examination of particular people in their ethical life would be at best superfluous, at worst intolerable, for a theory that is always looking to generalize as much as possible. For an Aristotelian approach, however, these kinds of literature are eminently suitable for ethical investigation, alongside the lives of real people in all their particularity and concreteness. For Aristotle, the plots and characters of the tragedians are ideal material for the ethicist—rather as the particularities of biblical narrative function in this way for traditional Jewish ethics.

Having established that reading tragedy may be as fruitful for the ethicist as reading moral philosophy, Nussbaum moves on to a second stage, in which she tries to show what picture of ethics, in fact, emerges from this kind of investigation. For the tragedians, the moral life is not a matter of the human will alone, as on a Kantian model, but is made up of the interplay between the will and the actions it causes, on the one hand, and on the other the effects of chance, fortune, luck—*tyche*. The poet's task is not simply to judge people by a standard of

conduct to which they ought to adhere, but to register and reflect nonjudge-
mentally on their lives as a whole: on the aspects resulting from birth and accident, as well as on those for which they can be held accountable. Using a
quotation from Pindar, she argues that, for the poets and tragedians, a human life
is not simply an artefact—what a person has made of him- or herself—but a plant:

> Human excellence
> grows like a vine tree
> fed by the green dew.[3]

One might recall the righteous man of Psalm 1, who is 'like a tree, planted by
streams of water'—planted by someone else, that is, not by himself. Too much
is *given* in our lives for us to think of them as something we ourselves have made.
And these nonvoluntary elements—constitution, psychological makeup, social
background—are relevant ethically; they are not elements that the moralist
ought to disregard because they do not proceed from the person's will.

The detachment from harsh judgement and the compassion towards frail
human beings that the poet should exercise is well captured when in another
book she quotes Walt Whitman:

> Of these States the poet is the equable man . . .
> He bestows on every object its fit proportion, neither more nor less . . .
> He judges not as the judge judges, but as the sun falling round a
>   helpless thing . . .
> He sees eternity in men and women, he does not see men and women
>   as dreams or dots.[4]

From this humane point of view, the poets and tragedians made it their task,
above all, to *observe*—to observe the particularity of individual lives and to
rehearse them for readers and audiences so as to evoke not praise or blame but
those two great Aristotelian reactions: terror and pity. These are supremely
ethical qualities since they rest on recognizing our human affinities with those
represented in tragedies or poems, and hence our vulnerability to the same
mixture of wrong intention and bad luck that brings them low.

For us to learn about ethics from Greek tragedy it is necessary, above all, to
be open to the uniqueness and complexity of each character we meet there.
Even if we want eventually to extract general principles from the actions and
fate of those characters, we should delay this until we have them sharply in
focus. As Nussbaum says, this goes well beyond the standard ethical or philosophical device of using a model or example of a particular moral virtue. Valid
though that may be, it is very different from the tragedian's characters, who are
not devised to illustrate a principle but conceived as complete human beings
woven out of many elements. They cannot be measured, says Nussbaum, with

a straight and rigid ruler but only with what Aristotle refers to as 'the Lesbian rule'. This is a flexible metal ruler, invented on Lesbos, with which it is possible to measure the curved bits of buildings. The rule has a certain objectivity—its calibration, for example—but it adapts to what it is measuring; and that is how philosophers must be if they go, for ethical teaching, not to fellow philosophers but to the dramatists.

Nussbaum provides a worked example of how an Aristotelian ethicist might read a tragedy. It is in the form of a commentary on a long speech of Hecuba in Euripides' *Trojan Women* (1158–1207). The speech is Hecuba's response to her grandson's death at the hand of the Greeks who have sacked the city:

> As a person of practical wisdom, Hecuba brings to the concrete situation of choice a disparate plurality of attachments and commitments, many of which have been nourished by early moral training, long before reflective adulthood. She also brings her *prima facie* reflections about what, for her, will count as a good life for a human being. She brings her love of her son, of her grandson; her love of Troy; her attachment to religious duties and duties to the family; a conception of proper courage, both in battle and in politics; a conception of proper reasonableness. She brings her view that a good life for a human being involves growing up in a family and a city and serving both the city's good and that of one's loved ones in it; that it involves going on to the end of life performing these excellent activities and receiving, at the end of life, a pious burial; that it is a better thing, nonetheless, to die prematurely for these values than to make cowardly compromises. Training in these values has evidently made her well acquainted with her 'target', so that in this new situation she knows what to look for; the intentionality of her desires has a focus. As a result she is adept at sorting out the new situation before her, singling out without hesitation the features of ethical relevance.
>
> Each of the features in the situation is seen by Hecuba as a distinct item with its own separate nature, generating its own separate claims. She does not offer definitions of the values she prizes; but this does not mean that she does not implicitly conceive of each of them as having a distinctive nature. She has a pretty good idea of what piety is, what courage and cowardice are; and it is clear from what she says about them that she takes them to be distinct and incommensurable items. There is not the slightest sign of a measuring scale, or any other reductive device.[5]

To draw any parallels here with the Bible may seem odd. It is generally assumed that the Bible does not concern itself with how to live a human life within human limits but with how to be obedient to the commands that God has laid on human beings. I have myself argued that, at the level of what may be called the Bible's ethical theory, this is not a wholly fair account.[6] But Martha Nussbaum's work suggests the thought that even the actual narratives

in the Bible, in which people are presented as ethical agents yet also as victims
of circumstance, do not really support such a view either. Old Testament narrative clearly has little in common with Plato, and hence with Greek philosophy, *if*, that is, we take Plato as somehow the Greek philosophical norm: this
was correctly seen by the biblical theology movement. But it does, on the other
hand, have a good deal in common with Aristotle and with the tragedians who,
before Aristotle, had already expressed their ethical thought through that
minute attention to the particulars of given human lives which would later
come to be thought of as Aristotelian. There are little cameos in the Old Testament of characters who would not be at all out of place in a Greek tragedy,
and with whom the question of whether or not they obeyed the law of God
seems to be outside the centre of interest. Some of them have been studied in
Jonathan Magonet's book *Bible Lives*.[7] Jephthah and his daughter form such an
example, as does Palti son of Laish, in a masterpiece of laconic narration:

> David sent messengers to Ish-bosheth, Saul's son, saying, 'Give me my
> wife Michal, whom I betrothed at the price of a hundred foreskins of
> the Philistines.' And Ish-bosheth sent, and took her from her husband
> Paltiel, the son of Laish. But her husband went with her, weeping after
> her all the way to Bahurim. Then Abner said to him, 'Go, return'; and
> he returned. (2 Sam. 3:14–16)

Indeed, most of the narrative in the books of Samuel could be read with an eye
to the complexity of human ethical dilemmas and to the need for ethical conduct even in the midst of far too many constraints on human freedom. Commentators have sometimes noted that much of 1 and 2 Samuel seems rather
'secular' in tone: God does not keep intervening here as he does in Judges or
Chronicles. But after noting this as an apparent problem, biblical scholars usually go on to deny it, saying that the stories are not as secular as they look, or
to excuse them on the grounds that they are ancient and understandably rather
primitive. Surely neither response is correct. It would be better to see that ethical concerns are represented in the plurality of characters in these narratives,
and that, if God is indeed in them, it is in the pity and terror they inspire in
the readers, not in general principles which they illustrate, as if they were
medieval (or modern) sermon illustrations.

II

In 1990 Martha Nussbaum published a further work, a collection of essays
titled *Love's Knowledge: Essays on Philosophy and Literature*.[8] Her enterprise here
is the same, but the literature studied is modern, with the novels of Henry

James as her primary subject. It is from this collection that I have taken the phrase 'Reading for Life', which Nussbaum in turn gets from Dickens's David Copperfield, who says that he spent his childhood with his father's books as his only companions, sitting in his room and 'reading as if for life'. I take it this means 'reading for dear life'—'reading as if life depended on it'—but Nussbaum uses the expression to sum up an attitude to literature already clear in *The Fragility of Goodness* but taken further in this more recent book. This attitude is that books, especially imaginative fiction, provide us with companions who will prepare our minds and hearts to cope with life. Against the formalism of, say, the New Criticism or early structuralism, this sounds extraordinarily naïve, far too lacking in suspicion about literature, prone to the pathetic fallacy, and somewhat Leavisite. But Nussbaum's programme is not concerned with great and edifying works portraying noble models for us to imitate; it is concerned with literature that offers us sharply delineated characters whose complexity and fragility are properly realized—modern literature, in fact, that has many of the characteristics of Greek tragedy. Again, her interest is in how ethics can be presented through fiction in a way that avoids what she thinks is the reductionism and thinness of cool philosophical prose.

The key value is perception: 'The discrimination lies in perception'. Fiction can train us in such perception, and the fact that fictional characters are not real is not a problem; for, as she perceptively observes, all human love is love of fictional characters anyway—men and women that we can only love by understanding them as something like ourselves, which is already in some measure to fictionalize them, to make them in our own image:

> The love of a fictional character can be love because it is an active and interactive relationship that sustains the reader for many hours of imagining, of fiction-making, beyond the time spent with the page itself; and because, in this relation, the mysterious and ineffable charm of interaction with a powerful presence can be experienced in much the way it is in life; because, too, the reader is at the same time a reader of his or her own life, bringing to the imagining the hopes and loves of real life. Of course this interaction takes place in fantasy. But David [Copperfield] insists upon the closeness of its links to love in life: its activation of the same generous, outgoing and erotic impulses, its power to transform the texture of the world. And he also indicates that the loves we find in life owe, themselves, a great deal to the storytelling imagination and to romantic projection. This does not mean that they are based upon *illusion* in any pejorative sense . . . the way one thing is associated with another, the richness of the intersection of one image with many others, all this is not mere deception, but part of the texture of life, and a part of life's excitement. Part, too, of our ability to endow a perceived form with a human life: in that sense, all sympathy, all morality, is based on a generous fantasy.[9]

Again Nussbaum illustrates her contention that narrative prose can be the ideal vehicle for moral reflection in extended examples from Henry James and Dickens, too long even to summarize here. It might be fair to say that the best ethical reflection is not just narrative, but narrative plus sensitive commentary, written in a style that is itself not a matter of abstracting from the particularities of fiction but rather of respecting them and drawing the reader's attention to them. Fiction requires rational analysis if it is to yield its powerful capacity for ethical insight, but analysis must not mean dissection nor reduction to generalities and rules of thumb. One of the things we owe to the various formalisms of the twentieth century is the insight that literature is irreducible; that it is not merely a 'way of saying' something other than what it does, in fact, say. Narrative texts are not 'all about' some abstract virtue or vice, and they are not there to teach us this or that lesson. This is precisely Nussbaum's point. Literature is important for ethics because literature is as complicated as life itself and cannot be decoded or boiled down. Ethical insight comes from reading it—first sequentially and then reflectively—*not* from trying to extract a 'message' from it. A sensitive commentary will unpack the complexity in a helpful way, and that is what literary criticism has to offer to the ethical enterprise.

It seems to me that some biblical narrative texts could well be analysed or commentated in the style Nussbaum proposes. In the Old Testament, such accounts as the story of David's adultery with Bathsheba, and the ensuing disasters in his family as one of his sons rapes his daughter and another son exacts revenge, are so told that, much as with a Greek tragedy, they uncover universal human tendencies through the presentation of very particular people and situations. The resemblances between Old Testament narrative and Greek tragedy have most recently been explored by Cheryl Exum;[10] without going into detail, it seems to me that her analyses would form a possible basis for a Nussbaum-type discussion.

In conclusion, though, I should like to suggest that such an enterprise would have the effect of redrawing, in a useful way, some of the lines of demarcation between the various things biblical scholars do. At the moment, battle lines are drawn between those who continue to practise what is commonly called historical criticism and those who study the biblical text as a literary artefact. It is generally assumed that the first group are interested wholly in historical and not at all in aesthetic questions, and vice versa. The second approach—a holistic, synchronic, literary reading—detaches the text wholly from its ancient moorings and reads it as *our* text; furthermore it sometimes does this in the context of an avowedly theological agenda, reading the biblical text as part of the Holy Scripture of Jews or Christians. Nussbaum's readings seem to me hard to place on the 'historical-critical versus literary-critical' map. She is, of course, saying that the text—whether of Euripides or of Henry James—is a literary one, susceptible to literary-critical analysis. At the same time, however, she is not making any attempt to detach it from its ancient setting. The commentary on Hecuba's speech quoted earlier, for example, is far from trying to modernize Hecuba, and is, on the contrary, determined to 'read' her as a character in a historical context very distant from our own. What unites us with the text is not a decision to read it as if it had just been written, but the conviction that it and we are both exercised by certain fundamental questions about human beings and the world they inhabit, chief among which is 'How ought we to live?' In the terms used by biblical scholars, Nussbaum is both a historical-critical and a literary critic: the two are held together without effort because she is, above all, concerned to seek in the texts the answer to that question—for then *and* now. One gets from her writing a sense that the great texts matter because they ask what is good for humankind and never rest till they have found an answer.

5

Virtue in the Bible

'Virtue ethics' has moved to the centre of interest in recent years.[1] For a biblical scholar such as myself, it is interesting to ask whether there are any anticipations of it in the Bible. But because the term is a slightly fuzzy one, there would be a danger if one began with a tight definition of it and tried to measure the Bible against that. It may be better, and safer, to start from a fairly loose specification of the area of discussion which 'virtue ethics' covers and to ask about virtue in the Bible against the background of a deliberately imprecise set of ideas about what virtue is in general. In that way it will be easier to avoid the typical danger of this kind of exercise, where one shows only what can surprise no one, namely, that an ancient text does not exactly fit into a modern category. I shall try, therefore, to assume a charitably wide definition of what we might mean by virtue ethics.

There seem to me at least four features that people have in mind when they talk of virtue ethics:

1. First, an ethics of virtue sometimes contrasts doing with being—ethics as a set of decisions with ethics as commitment to a particular lifestyle. Rather than being concerned with resolving difficult ethical cases, the ethicist who propounds a virtue ethic will be interested in the fixed and stable moral dispositions from which people's ethical decisions flow and will emphasise that the most interesting aspects of the moral life are not those in which difficult decisions are required in marginal cases, but rather those that relate to the general tenor of a person's day-to-day life.[2]
2. Linked with the idea of a stable disposition to virtue is the importance of moral formation and the development of the moral character over time. One may make progress, or alternatively one may regress, in one's virtuousness.[3]
3. If there is a place for moral rules, it is more as a distillation from many good decisions made by virtuous people than as laws operating in an abstract

way. There is an emphasis on the particularity of each person's moral life, which—while it by no means rules out moral laws, especially if these are seen as rules of thumb—does discourage one from seeing morality chiefly as a duty to perform a set of ethical rules and emphasises instead the importance of each individual, set in his or her own particular circumstances, as the focus of ethical interest. Martha Nussbaum has contributed much to this way of thinking,[4] and I shall return to her later.

4. To live a life of virtue one needs a moral *vision*, which means the ability to 'read' the successive situations one finds oneself in from an ethical point of view and to live consistently rather than in an unexamined way throughout the course of one's life.[5]

These are no more than pointers towards what might be meant by a virtue ethic, but I hope they will do for now as a sufficient definition for us to ask about ethics in the Bible. I shall concentrate chiefly on the Old Testament because that is what I know about, though with occasional sorties into New Testament territory. I want to argue that, at the level at which the Bible is explicit about ethics, virtue is not a very helpful model, but when we once ask about more implicit ethical notions, it may not be so bad after all. Thus my argument takes the form of a *sic et non*, or rather *non sed sic*.

I. EXPLICIT ETHICS

To begin, then, in the manner of Aquinas: It would seem that there is no virtue ethic in the Bible. The place one might immediately look for the first of our themes, that of fixed and stable moral dispositions, is the Wisdom literature, especially Proverbs and the Wisdom of Jesus ben Sira. Now, the Wisdom literature certainly concerns itself with people as moral types rather than with isolated moral decisions, and to that extent may seem a good quarry for a virtue ethic. Proverbs occupies itself with dividing people into two categories, variously the wise man and the fool or the righteous man and the sinner, and it assumes that there is a complete correspondence between these respective types: that is, all wise men are righteous; all fools are unrighteous. One is not allowed in Proverbs to offer one's folly as an excuse for sinning: that is rather like excusing one's bad driving on the grounds that one has been drinking. It is not a mitigation but rather an intensification of guilt. Folly is a *moral* category, meaning culpable ignorance or lack of ethical insight. It is taken for granted that people's actions are a reflection of their character as wise or foolish, and this may well remind us of virtue ethics. Moral decision making is not really on the agenda in Proverbs or Sirach: in any circumstances, the wise man instinctively chooses what is right; the fool what is wrong. As we read in the New Testament, a good tree produces good fruit, and a bad tree evil fruit;

therefore by their fruits you will know them. People do not come to a moral issue as a *tabula rasa*, so that they may choose either the good or the evil, as though it were in each case an open question how they would choose; they come with their character already formed, and the good infallibly choose the right way; the bad the evil way.

Yet on closer inspection I think the gulf between this and a modern virtue ethic may be wider than at first appears. Note that there are no Laodicean moralists in the Wisdom literature. Everyone is either good or bad, wise or foolish. Living the good life appears to be an absolute, with no gradations or variations. Proverbs operates in some ways with a similar pattern of thought to that in Deuteronomy, where Moses lays before the people of Israel as a whole a choice between good and evil, the way of life and the way of death (e.g., Deut. 30:15), a tradition that continues throughout the Old Testament and reemerges in the New Testament and other early Christian literature: one may think of the 'two ways' teaching in Barnabas and the Didache. Ethical choice is a once-for-all affair which sets one's feet either on the way to life or on the way to death: there are no half-measures. This does not seem to me very like what a virtue ethic is asserting about human character, despite superficial resemblances. And I think the same could be said, for example, of St. Paul. The Pauline epistles abound in the language of virtues and vices, but the subtlety which sees everyone as a mix of the two, or as living a life in which virtue is *cultivated* and vice therefore rooted out seems largely lacking. People belong in one of two camps. Nevertheless, in Paul there are of course more nuanced ideas, such as the way the indwelling Spirit shapes the believer, which may well be able to contribute to a virtue ethic. The Old Testament Wisdom literature, however, seems to me to inhabit a cruder world of thought, where character is indeed all important but is seen as fixed and unchanging, almost at times as predetermined.

This leads directly into the second aspect of virtue ethics, its emphasis on moral formation or the training of character. It may be that, though Proverbs presents good and evil as fixed and unnuanced choices, the actual purpose of the book taken as a whole was some kind of moral training: by reading about the wise and the fool one gradually learned to imitate one and avoid turning into the other. This idea would be implicit in the existence of the book rather than explicit within its text, and it takes us into the kind of area I want to explore in the second part of this paper. But there is no doubt that, taken at face value, Proverbs eschews most ideas of moral progress. Hebrew culture differs from Greek on precisely this issue: the Hebrew Bible does not operate with any idea that one can grow in virtue but sees virtue as something one either has or lacks. It is true that if you give instruction to a wise man, he will become wiser still (Prov. 9:9), but there is no point in giving instruction to a fool, because he will persist in his folly just as much as before.

What the Bible thinks about is not moral progress but *conversion*. Ezekiel is, of course, the classic exemplar. Chapter 18 explores various combinations of good and bad fathers, and good and bad sons, and states with absolute authority not only that the moral character of the father does not infect the son but also that the moral character one once had oneself is not determinative for the future. So far from being locked up in one's previous vice, it takes only the moment of conversion to leave vice behind forever and set off on the path of goodness. 'Turn, and live', says the prophet. True, he is talking primarily about the nation in exile, not about individuals, but his message can be applied also to the individual and only makes sense if it is true also in the individual case. What one has to do is to turn around and walk away from one's previous sin. Then one can become a righteous person, with no taint left from one's former life.

The same may be said of most New Testament teaching on morality. Paul is not telling his readers about how to advance in the moral life but describing the effects of conversion. What converts must not do is to revert to their earlier manner of life, but this is not the same as saying that they must make steady progress. One may say of the Bible, again at an explicit level, that it suffers from the failing some people find in evangelistic forms of Christianity. It tells us how to pass from darkness to light but is less good at nurturing us in the light and helping us to make progress. Formation is, I would argue, a largely postbiblical concept. The Bible can be *used* in it, no question; but it is not what the Bible is primarily about. The typical Old Testament situation, at any rate, is that of Saul, who is beloved by God and then suddenly forfeits God's pleasure and at once descends into the pit of sin and evil. There is little if any sense that his character can be shaped or formed: he begins good, and then becomes bad, and that is all there is to be said.

Last but not least, there is what may be called a Lutheran/Pauline argument which would actually appeal to the Bible *against* the possibility of virtue ethics, arguing not only that such an ethic is not there in the Bible but that the Bible, read through the eyes of Paul, actually opposes any such thing. It is surveyed by Gilbert Meilaender in *The Theory and Practice of Virtue*, in his chapter 'The Examined Life Is not Worth Living'. It regards all talk of moral progress as contrary to the principle of justification by faith and as a denial that a redeemed human being is *simul justus et peccator*. The argument will, I am sure, be familiar to most Christian ethicists, and I will not rehearse it in detail. I have a lot of sympathy with it but do not think it can be defended on strictly biblical grounds, because by no means all of the Bible or even of the New Testament is Pauline in its emphases, and the Old Testament, in particular, has no hesitation in speaking about people's conduct as simply good or bad, deserving or not deserving of divine favour. And in recent years it has been powerfully argued, for example by E. P. Sanders, that Paul himself is not always Pauline in the sense defined by Luther.[6] What a Lutheran critique does remind us of, however, is that being converted is by no means the same as making moral progress, and thus it undergirds the general argument of this section.

On the face of it much of the Old Testament seems as far as one could get from the idea of moral goodness as the distillation of the way good people actually live. On the contrary, moral goodness means taking decisions in accordance with a previously existing divine law. This could not be clearer, for example, in Deuteronomy, where Moses emphasises again and again that God has revealed his laws to Israel and that the good for them consists in obeying these laws. But the same is true even in the Wisdom books, for all that the 'law' there—seldom so called—is often more a natural than a positive law.[7] The rightness or wrongness of this or that kind of conduct is the given, and human action has to accord with it. People must do what the divine lawgiver or the human teacher sets before them as correct conduct, and there seems to be little space for what we might call moral improvisation. Classic texts here would be Psalm 119, or the second part of Psalm 19, where praise is heaped on the law of God as the norm to which all human conduct must conform. Once again, such texts can be *used* in moral training or formation, and there is good evidence that they were so used in both Judaism and Christianity from early times. But they do not themselves speak of the good for humankind as what flows from the right conduct of good people but rather as the explicitly expressed will of God.

It is important to remember that many areas of human conduct which will form a central part of any ethic of virtue are simply not mentioned in the Old Testament at all. To turn the Bible into a code for daily living, rabbinic Judaism had to produce the Mishnah, which elaborates many of the laws in the Pentateuch and principles stated in other biblical books until they become a guide for every part of life. Even then, areas that both we and they considered relevant to morality are left out: there is no guidance in Bible or Mishnah on many virtues such as humility, gentleness, or forbearance. And the morality of the Old Testament does not necessarily conform to what we should regard as a proper distillation of the conduct of good people: not only in the way it commends some things we no longer regard as virtues, such as implacable revenge, but also in that it permits lifestyles including such features as polygamy, resort to prostitutes, and material acquisitiveness. Thus some of the characteristic features of a virtue ethic are lacking because the emphasis lies on the divine lawgiver rather than on human moral character, while others are lacking simply because they are nowhere mentioned. It seems to me that the general style of Old Testament ethics is that in certain areas life is closely regulated by divine decree so that human freedom to explore moral possibilities is fiercely circumscribed; while in others there is no guidance at all—they are not seen as coming within the purview of moral discrimination—and no assumption that a good life will veer one way rather than another.

Finally, what of the importance of a moral vision? The Psalms, especially 19 and 119 already mentioned, do speak of a coherent way of seeing the moral world, though it is much more in terms of divine law than of human ethical insight. As we have just seen, much Old Testament ethics is norm-bound: in terms of modern ethical theory, it presents a deontological rather than a virtue-based ethic. But when it is not stressing moral obligation as obedience to law, this is equally not evidence of an attachment to a virtue ethic, but more of a eudaemonism that we should have to call, in our terms, teleological or conse-quentialist. This is clearly the case in much of the Wisdom literature, which is often advice on how to get on rather than training in the pursuit of the vir-tuous life. Without wholly accepting his idea that Wisdom represents the class ethic of the middle or bureaucratic class in monarchic Israel, I still believe that E. W. Heaton was right to emphasise how strongly it is orientated to success rather than to virtue. Here is an excerpt from his lengthy characterisation of the ideal man as defined by Proverbs:

> The man of Proverbs is a highly-motivated member of the lower mid-dle classes. . . . He identifies himself neither with the rich nor yet with the poor . . . and disapproves when men of different stations pretend to be what they are not. . . . He knows that money is not the be-all and end-all of life and he wants to get his priorities right. What is more, he has his home and family to think about, even though he is ambi-tious to give them security. . . . He is backed up by a devoted and extremely capable wife. Not only does she see to the meals and the children's clothes, but works all hours to earn a bit extra. A wife, he holds, makes a world of difference to a man in his position. He is one who sets great store by domestic peace and feels sorry for men with 'a nagging wife and a brawling household', where the sons are always contradicting their father and getting their mother upset. . . . That is why he believes in being strict with his boys and knocking some sense into them. . . . The man of Proverbs is an open, cheerful character, who speaks his mind and does everything in his power to promote neigh-bourliness in the community at large. . . . The way to deal with ene-mies, he believes, is not by revenge but by the same sort of generosity a man ought to show to everybody in need. He would not want to deny that he had his principles, but he prefers to think of himself as a prac-tical man, for whom getting results is all-important, even if sometimes it does mean compromise. There are occasions, for example, when a bribe works 'like a charm', and to turn a blind eye is the only sensible thing to do. . . . Such realism is the secret of his success. . . . What counts in the end is the 'know-how' which is born of experience and the rigorous use of a carefully-trained mind.[8]

II. IMPLICIT VIRTUE

Thus it seems to me that the language of 'virtue' may not be well adapted to describe the Old Testament's characteristic approaches to morality, which the old models of deontology and consequentialism are better at describing. Both can be found in the Old Testament more obviously than a virtue ethic. But against this is a widespread perception that a model which is helpful in thinking about Christian ethics might be expected also to be helpful in thinking about the text on which Christian ethics draw, namely, the Bible. So I have to ask whether there is any level at which a virtue ethic is nevertheless a useful approach to Scripture. Two possibilities occur to me.

1. One is that, although at the explicit level the Bible does not really operate with a virtue ethic, something like such an ethic may be implicit in places where morality is not directly under discussion. I have in mind principally the narrative texts of the Old Testament. Of these, some work with a very simple black-and-white scheme that has little to contribute to our discussion: one thinks of the judgements on the various kings of Israel and Judah in the books of Kings, for example, which simply designate them as 'good' or 'bad' (usually 'bad') and have no more to say. But there are other narrative texts in the Bible which have long been recognised as powerful works of art, and the recent emphasis on a literary reading of biblical texts has placed them in the centre of interest for biblical scholars and drawn attention to features which may, I believe, be of concern to ethicists too.

It has long been noticed that the Old Testament is often very reticent about drawing moral judgments in the way it narrates its stories. Both Jews and Christians have regularly turned to biblical narrative for ethical instruction just as if it had the form of law. Thus when St. Ambrose taught his catechumens in Holy Week he referred them, he tells us, to the sayings of the wise and the deeds of the patriarchs as dual sources of moral teaching;[9] and the rabbis similarly treated biblical stories as valuable primarily for their exemplary value, as illustrations of this or that moral obligation or of the consequences for the individual that would follow from observing or transgressing it. But the two types of material, teachings and narratives, are not really on a par, and it is far from clear that the biblical writers originally told the stories they did because moral obligations could be inferred from them. Indeed, it seems apparent that this was not their intention, for in many of the stories the message that emerges if one tries to extract a moral is quite obscure and seems at best tangential to the story being told. The Fathers had many problems particularly with the patriarchal stories for precisely this reason, that they are so poorly adapted to inculcate good moral practices. The stories of Jacob, for example, seem to take a certain delight in his trickery and double-dealing. Much the same may be said of many of the narratives in the books of Samuel, which have been a particular delight to modern literary critics of the Bible just because they cannot be turned into a series of moral fables.

While this might suggest that the narratives, too, are alien from anything like a virtue ethic, I would argue that the opposite could be the case. What we have in these stories is exactly that presentation of human beings in all their singularity which has been the subject of several virtue ethicists, among whom I would specially want to mention Martha Nussbaum. The characters in many of these stories might be analysed in much the way she analyses characters in Greek tragedies and in modern novels, not in order to reduce them to exemplifications of some general moral principles but in order to see what can be learned from them about the difficulties and merits of living a moral life or the problems of failing to do so. It may be suggested that those who recorded these stories, like the Greek tragedians, were in the business of presenting unvarnished and complex characters for the contemplation of the reader. This reader was being invited to see in them the moral difficulties, and especially the interplay of moral choice with luck or divinely engineered fate, which make human life the complicated thing it is. If one takes as an example the so-called Succession Narrative or Court History of David, one only has to survey the secondary literature quite cursorily to see that its purpose has been identified in a huge variety of incompatible ways, ranging from the suggestion that it was written as propaganda for Solomon to the opposed notion that it was intended to undermine all the claims of the monarchy.[10] David Gunn achieved wide approval with his designation of the Narrative as 'serious entertainment', not meant to sway the reader in some particular direction but rather to share the pleasure of laying bare human motivations and the interplay of human action and reaction in a well-known set of events.[11] But this, especially if we stress the word *serious*, makes the parallel with Greek tragedy or even the nineteenth-century novel far from fanciful.

One might, even so, insist that the biblical authors appeal in the end to norms of morality that do not come under the definition of virtue ethics. David is judged by God for adultery, which is absolutely forbidden in the Old Testament, not subject to nice weighings-up of advantage and disadvantage. Nevertheless his character as a whole is many-sided, and we have to set against his vices the obvious sense the narrator has that he was in certain ways admirable, and that God was (however obscurely) on his side and behind his actions. David's life is presented as deeply flawed, but it is also presented as an examined life, and one which manifests a concern for how one ought to live even when this runs clearly counter to the character's own moral insights. The same is true of many of the more minor characters in the story. They have their own moral vision, and this vision interacts with their luck to produce interesting moral possibilities. If there is anything in Nussbaum's approach to Greek tragedy, then similar things might well be said of these biblical stories, as I have argued elsewhere.[12] David is not an *exemplum* but a person like ourselves, who illustrates the difficulties of the moral life not by what he teaches but by what he does and is.

Now, it may be that the approach to ethics Nussbaum describes, and which I am trying to appropriate for biblical studies, is not correctly called a virtue ethic anyway. But if it is, then the Bible does seem to have at least some examples of it. Stanley Hauerwas writes that much moral debate 'has ignored the fact that much of our moral experience is a matter, not of judgment, but of how the agent forms himself and his actions from his particular perspective and history'.[13] If this is true, then some at least of the biblical writers would seem to have been aware of it, and we might draw on their treatment. They were aware, that is, that there are many ethical matters that are not within the scope of laws and regulations yet are essential parts of the moral life, and they dealt with these not by drawing up lists of principles but by describing their occurrence within specific human lives. The story of David handles human anger, lust, ambition, and disloyalty without ever commenting explicitly on these things but by telling its tale in such a way that the reader is obliged to look them in the face and to recognise his or her affinity with the characters in whom they are exemplified. Thus the story has a high moral purpose, but one that is not easily captured in any ethical system other than that proposed by virtue ethics—or so one might argue.

2. Second, there is the question of how we use or should use the Bible, irrespective of what it may originally have meant. Even if there is little or no virtue ethics *in* the Bible, may not the Bible be used constructively by those who are trying to achieve what virtue ethics puts forward as the great aim of human life: the achievement of stable and good moral character? Christian experience certainly suggests that this may be so. If we may stand the more usual way of thinking about the Bible and morality on its head: whereas people usually think that the Bible is a moral authority because all of it has the force of divine law—and then have to interpret even the narratives as if they were laws—it might be possible to treat all or most of it rather as if it were narrative and to apply it to the work of moral edification in much the way I have just been suggesting that some at least of the narratives were intended to be applied. That is, we may treat all of what we find in the Bible as contributing to a kind of profile of the good life by imagining possible lives or lifestyles in which its precepts are instantiated. This in a way is how the Bible has often functioned in many traditions of meditation, and how, for example, the Psalms tend to work in traditions where they are regularly recited and prayed. The biblical text

works in some way on what we might call the subconscious mind, helping to shape and train it. We should be concerned in this for just *how* the mind is shaped, for there is a variety of material in the Bible, indeed even in the Psalms, and one could end up misshapen, I should think, by attending to the wrong parts of the material. We all know that one can be encouraged in various sorts of malevolence by concentrating on certain parts of the Old Testament to the exclusion of others, and many people tend to think that that is a natural consequence of what they see as the general nastiness of the Old Testament. I do not need in this context to argue that implacable vengeance is not the only teaching in the Old Testament, as people so often suppose; but it is there, and uncontrolled meditation on it could easily help to form a very unchristian character. So there are hazards. Nevertheless one might certainly press the Bible into the service of a virtue ethic, even if one believed that it did not itself contain one. We do this kind of thing with the Bible all the time, and it is capacious enough to allow us to do so.

I am reluctant, in coming to a close, to draw up a balance sheet and to decide whether the Bible does or does not support a virtue ethic. As we have seen, much depends on what we mean by 'the Bible': Are we talking about what the individual parts of the text originally intended, or about some legitimate use to which the finished text can be put, or what? Questions about biblical interpretation cannot be kept out of a discussion such as this. But it is certainly worth asking about 'virtue in the Bible', and interesting possibilities are opened up by doing so.[14]

PART TWO

Explorations
in the Prophets

6

Amos's Oracles against the Nations

A Study of Amos 1:3–2:5

INTRODUCTION

Why does the book of Amos begin with a series of oracles against Israel's neighbours, and only then turn to denounce the prophet's own people? Is it a remnant of an older way of prophecy, the way of Balaam and of the four hundred prophets of Ahab, reinforcing a narrow nationalism with a word of power? Is it the expression of a radically new insight, the discovery, made for the first time in the eighth century, that not just Israel but all nations, whatever their prestige and vaunted might, stood under the judgement of Yahweh? Or is it a literary device, designed to throw the urbane and comfortable sins of Israel into high relief by seeing them against the background of the apparently grosser outrages perpetrated by barbarian nations, whom the prophet's complacent hearers would be only too ready to condemn, not noticing until too late that in condemning them they were condemning themselves? All of these explanations are possible, none is self-evidently right, and combinations of them are conceivable.

Another question which might be asked, however, adds considerably to the difficulty of choosing between them. Why does Amos think that these other nations *are* accountable for their atrocities—wherein does their particular atrociousness lie? Is it that Yahweh, Israel's lawgiver and judge, has laid down laws which even foreign nations must obey—that extension of Yahweh's moral sphere of influence with which the eighth-century prophets used commonly to be credited? Is Amos drawing some kind of analogy between Israel's known obligation to its God and one supposed to be incumbent on foreigners, perhaps especially on those foreigners who belong to the immediate world of Palestinian politics, who had formed the components of David's empire? Or should we see the prophet's evident sense of moral outrage as indicating a belief in moral principles held to be obvious to all right-minded people, or even as evidence that actual conventions about the conduct of war and international relations existed in the Palestine of Amos's day, to which he might tacitly appeal? Here, then, is a second range of questions which have attracted rather less attention than the first but which are equally important to an understanding of Amos's thought, and unless both sets of questions are tackled together, we are unlikely to make much progress in forming a coherent interpretation of the prophet and his book.

The purpose of this study is to examine the oracles against the nations in the first two chapters of Amos, in an attempt to discover exactly what point the prophet was making when he condemned Israel's neighbours for atrocities in war, and did so in this particular literary form. It will be suggested that he was appealing to a kind of conventional or customary law about international conduct which he at least believed to be self-evidently right and which he thought he could count on his audience's familiarity with and acquiescence in. We shall further maintain that this has important consequences for understanding Amos's whole approach to ethics, since at a crucial place in his message he sees moral conduct as a matter of conformity to a human convention held to be obviously universal, rather than to the overt or explicit demands of God: in other words, ethics in Amos is not simply a question of theonomy, as it is quite widely thought to be. We shall also be concerned with other instances of conventional morality, inside and outside Israel, and with other problems about Amos, his book, and his prophetic role, which our interpretation of chapters 1–2 raises.

I

Rather than beginning with a lengthy survey of the state of the question, I propose in this section to outline the interpretation of Amos's oracles against the nations which it will be the task of the rest of this study to justify. I shall set it out as a continuous argument, and then indicate the points at which it seems specially to stand in need of justification. In the sections that follow, each of these will be taken up and discussed against the background of recent work.

Apart from the oracles of Balaam, Amos 1:3–2:5 constitutes the earliest example in the Old Testament of a genre that was to become a regular feature of prophetic books, the cycle of oracles against foreign nations. These oracles, with the probable exception of those on Judah, Edom, and Tyre, are the work of the prophet Amos himself, and are probably among his own earliest oracles. Unlike many prophetic oracles, they are neither old material adapted by the prophet for a new purpose, nor short, individual sayings collected by an editor, but are a free composition which formed from the beginning a continuous whole. The purpose of the oracles on the nations is to lead up to the oracle on Israel in 2:6ff.; though it is no longer clear where this ends, it was intended by the prophet as the climax to the whole cycle, and the overall effect is to produce surprise and horror in the intended audience. This is achieved by a rhetorical trick similar to that found in Nathan's parable (2 Sam. 12), Isaiah's Song of the Vineyard (Isa. 5), and Amos's own visions in Amos 7. The prophet begins by condemning the surrounding nations for atrocities committed during military campaigns, and by mentioning well-known incidents he ensures that his hearers will experience a sense of moral outrage—which indeed he fully shares himself: the condemnations are meant with full seriousness and might well have been felt by his audience to be a proper expression of his prophetic vocation. Having won the people's sympathy and agreement, he rounds on them by proclaiming judgement on Israel, too.

This technique has two obvious advantages. First, it ensures that the prophet's word of doom will be heard, since he has gained his audience's attention by flattering their feelings of superiority and their natural xenophobia. Second, it makes it much harder for them to exculpate themselves or dismiss the prophet's message as mere raving, since they have implicitly conceded that sin and judgement are rightly linked by their approval of what has gone before. (For our purposes it matters little whether we think of the audience as literally present—say, at a festal gathering, as some suggest—or as present only to the prophet's imagination, and the oracles as a literary composition.)

For Amos to have supposed that this technique would be successful, he must have held the following beliefs about his intended audience's mentality:

1. That they thought manifest evil-doing both deserved and would receive divine punishment.
2. That they regarded the nations condemned as moral agents, that is, as answerable for their actions, particularly in the conduct of war.
3. That they thought Israel had a specially privileged position which indemnified her against divine judgement.
4. That they did not expect prophets to proclaim judgement on Israel.
5. That they did not regard the kind of sins of which Amos accuses Israel as at all comparable in gravity with atrocities in war.
6. That it was more obvious to them that the nations had moral obligations towards each other than that Israelites had moral obligations among themselves.

It cannot be shown that any of these assumptions was in fact correct, but it can be shown that unless Amos thought they were, his tactics in constructing chapters 1 and 2 were unintelligent. For if he did not believe nos. 1 or 2, he could not expect people to react with approval to his condemnation of the nations; if he did not believe nos. 3 or 4, he could hardly expect to surprise them with the oracle against Israel; if he did not believe no. 5, then the Israel oracle could not be expected to produce any *more* surprise than the others; while unless he believed no. 6, his chosen literary form would be a piece of sheer bathos. For so far from the Israel oracle coming as a surprise, it would be the only part of the cycle that would occasion none. Any successful didactic technique must begin from the better known and move on to the less well known; and if the moral obligation owed by the nations is a novelty, whereas that owed by Israel is common ground, then the whole cycle is very incompetently put together, building down to a spectacular anticlimax.

It might be thought that we should add a seventh assumption: that the people expected prophets to denounce foreign nations. Otherwise would they not have been surprised at Amos's foreign oracles, and thus spoiled for the extra surprise of the Israel oracle? But this is an unnecessary supposition. Certainly, it cannot have been thought strange that anyone should denounce foreigners, but need the people have thought of this as a specially prophetic activity? One might guess that anyone was welcome to speak out against the crimes of aliens. We may not validly deduce that it was regarded as part of a prophet's role to do so, though, of course, this might be true, in fact, and demonstrable on other grounds.

If this analysis is correct, then certain conclusions may be drawn about the moral norms appealed to in the oracles against the nations, and also about the theological importance of Amos. These are as follows:

1. Amos did not think that he was being original in claiming that foreign nations were subject to certain moral obligations, at least in their international relations, nor in claiming that God would punish infringements of them. In this he was merely echoing what he took to be popular belief and sentiment. Consequently no interpretation of the prophet can be correct which regards him as an innovator in this respect.

2. Since Amos thus appeals to a supposed consensus so far as the conduct of war by the nations is concerned, it is unlikely that we should be able to discover any underlying rationale for such moral norms. In particular, it is improbable that they were seen by the prophet's audience as deeply theological, or as deriving from divine laws; rather they seem best classified as customary law or convention, or even a kind of commonsense morality. After all, they need reflect no more than the feeling that there ought to be a convention banning certain kinds of conduct, even where no convention exists. It would be interesting to compare these with the norms of conduct Amos supposes to be binding within Israel. Prima facie, there is no reason to suppose that the prophet had any overall 'theory' of ethical obligation, such as that it derived

from the covenant relationship, from the universal rule of God, or from the order of nature. The existence of merely conventional morality in the Old Testament has not been much explored, so we may hope to break a little fresh ground. Further, since the area of conduct involved is that of international relations, especially in warfare, it will be interesting to explore the question of whether any conventions did, in fact, exist on this subject, either inside Israel or elsewhere in the ancient Near East. Here we hope to provide a convenient summary of some material not previously collected together.

3. Although we have been careful throughout to say that Amos *supposed* his hearers to hold certain beliefs rather than that they did, in fact, hold them, it would be odd if he were badly mistaken in his assumptions. What someone takes for granted in arguing with opponents, and never feels it necessary to prove, is generally the best evidence for the popular beliefs of his day precisely because it is not being insisted upon.[1] It is therefore probable that the first six points outlined above do fairly represent the beliefs of a good many eighth-century Israelites, though we should, of course, reckon with the possibility that Amos deliberately exaggerates their obtuseness, just as St. Paul would widely be held to exaggerate the heterodoxy of teachers against whom he warns his converts. We can therefore form some idea of popular notions about morality, prophecy, and divine judgement, and also about the relationship of Yahweh and Israel. And in the light of this it will make sense to raise the perennial question about the distinctiveness of classical prophecy, attempting to pinpoint the 'new thing' in the preaching of Amos. Our conclusion must be that Amos is not original in proclaiming that sin calls down divine judgement, nor in seeing that Israel had moral obligations to Yahweh, but chiefly in two things: (a) in regarding social morality as a decisive area of conduct, just as important for the continuance of Yahweh's favour as the avoidance of much crasser and more 'obvious' crimes; and (b) in arguing with the people so as to show that their conduct is unreasonable and their complacency foolish and shortsighted. It is presupposed by the use of the 'surprise' technique and also by the insistence on giving reasons for Yahweh's judgement that the people are at least in principle open to rational persuasion, even if in practice they have succeeded in blinding their own eyes and are now too far gone to recover—the problem which both Isaiah and Ezekiel were later to face and discuss. This emphasis on rationality in Amos, indeed, aligns him very clearly with Isaiah, and our discussion is related to recent attempts to trace 'wisdom influence' on his book—though we shall not try to define the point in precisely that way.

In the sections that follow we shall discuss in detail what may be regarded as the 'sensitive' areas of this line of interpretation.

Since our argument is that the thought of Amos himself may be detected behind the oracles in chapters 1 and 2, we shall devote a section to examining the provenance of these oracles, considering a number of recent arguments which try to show that the prophet or his editor is simply taking over an older collection, possibly cultic in origin.

In section 3 we turn to examine the oracles for authenticity, attempting to decide on literary and historical grounds whether any of them need to be regarded as later additions to Amos. These two sections together may be seen as making a case for at least a core of the oracles against the nations as the work of the prophet himself, and as an attempt to make their simple exegesis clear.

This leads us, in section 4, to ask whether the historical circumstances of the atrocities they condemn can be established, and we conclude that, although it is fair to think that all of the events will have been readily identifiable to the prophet's audience, there is not enough evidence for us to identify them positively. This in turn rules out interpretations of the oracles which absolutely require that they refer either to very remote or very recent events.

Section 5 looks in more detail at the case for seeing an effect of climax in the juxtaposition of oracles against foreign nations and against Israel, suggesting that this is both inherently probable and consonant with what we know of the prophet's method from other parts of his book.

Finally, in section 6 we try to show that it is better to see the underlying ethical approach in these oracles as an appeal to (at least supposedly) international norms of conduct than to tie them down to any covenant- or Israel-centred ethic.

An appendix surveys a little of the evidence for the existence of such international conventions on war and other matters in Israel and among her neighbours. It is intended to show that the kind of interpretation we have proposed is not historically impossible and to illustrate it with some interesting parallels, but it is not supposed to be in any way probative.

II

Do the first two chapters of Amos represent a new departure in Israelite prophecy, or are they part of a long-established tradition? There seems to be something like a consensus in recent writings on the prophets that Amos is here drawing on a tradition already very old by his time, and perhaps even on old oracles against the nations which he simply selected because they suited his purpose. Thus R. E. Clements, in his study *Prophecy and Tradition*, writes,

> In the earliest literary collection of such prophecies in Amos 1:3–2:6 there are strong indications that the form of such oracles, the style of their presentation, and perhaps also the type of motive adduced for such threats, were already well-established features of prophetic preaching.[1]

The main reasons for such a judgement were summarised in N. K. Gottwald's detailed study *All the Kingdoms of the Earth*[2] and developed by J. H. Hayes in an article four years later,[3] though both build on a great deal of previous discussion. The arguments may be reduced to three main types, all in fact closely connected.

1. Hayes suggests that prophetic oracles against the nations have their roots in 'the tradition of Holy War' and are closely related to taunts and challenges to battle.[4] But whereas a taunt is essentially directed against an individual and is specially appropriate in cases of single combat,[5] the prophetic oracle is primarily directed against the whole hostile nation. The earliest example of this form in the Old Testament is probably Num. 21:27–30, the taunt song against Heshbon, which Gottwald suggests may go back to a pre-Israelite poem, perhaps from the Amorite period.[6] Cases of the actual use of the second-person form in time of war are not common in the Old Testament, but it passes into the prophetic tradition and appears in classic form in Isaiah 10 and 14, and Ezekiel 27 and 28. But the commonest form of prophecy relating to war is reached when the direct second-person address to the enemy[7] is abandoned in favour of an assurance given to the prophet's own nation or its ruler, referring to the enemy in the third person and denouncing him. This form reaches its first literary expression in Israel in the oracles of Balaam, which recent studies have suggested go back at least to the period of the United Monarchy and are probably based on premonarchic poems.[8] But that it was one function of a prophet to deliver such oracles is plain, according to Hayes, from 1 Sam. 15:2–3, 1 Kgs. 20:26–30, and 2 Kgs. 13:17b—and we might add 1 Kings 22. Several commentators have suggested that Isaiah's oracles in 7:3–9 can be understood against this background as an 'oracle of assurance to the king in time of battle' (*Kriegsansprache*);[9] and their common use of such forms has been one of the factors inclining Old Testament scholars to see affinities between Israelite prophets and the ecstatics of the Mari letters.[10]

But even supposing all this to be right, its relevance to Amos's oracles against the nations must surely be judged very slender. The theory of dependence on such a prophetic tradition can be dismissed on quite general grounds: we can appeal to Fohrer's standard objection[11] that the context in which a form originates tells us very little about its use in any given case, especially when that use is manifestly literary. We might also argue that Israel was not at war with any of the nations in question, and even in theory could scarcely have been at war with all of them at once.[12] Yet against this idea it might still be held that Amos was taking an old tradition and transforming it for his own purposes. But we can surely go further and maintain that the 'tradition of Holy War' (supposing such a 'tradition' to have existed) has played no part at all in shaping these oracles. Not only is Israel not at war with the nations mentioned;

their attitude to Israel is in several cases not the point at issue anyway, as is made specially clear in the oracle against Moab (2:1).[13] Amos is neither encouraging his people to fight in assurance of victory nor encouraging them to remain passive in expectation of Yahweh's deliverance. He is not, indeed, encouraging them at all, but in view of the oracle on Israel, our point is that he is not even pretending to encourage them. We shall have later to examine the actual incidents referred to and shall suggest that at least some of them may have taken place during comparatively recent attacks on Israel by the nations concerned; but it is not plausible to suppose that Amos, prophesying under Jeroboam II, saw Israel threatened and hemmed in on all sides.[14] Common sense tends rather against the derivation of these oracles from the background of 'Holy War'.

We may add as a rider an interesting observation made by Clements on prophetic oracles against the nations in general. He points out that the feature of Israel's enemies most commonly condemned by the prophets is their pride or hubris towards Yahweh; thus in Isa. 14:12ff.; 16:6; 23:6–12; Jer. 48:28–33; Ezek. 28:1ff.; 31:1ff.; 32:1ff.; 32:12ff.[15] Now, in most of these cases the most likely reason for such a charge would seem to be the wish to suggest that the nation in question has failed to subordinate itself to Yahweh by accepting the privileged position of Israel, and instead has set itself up as God, thinking to put down Yahweh's chosen people. A case could reasonably (I think not compellingly) be made for seeing this particular charge as a lineal descendant of the taunt before battle: compare David's exchanges with Goliath in 1 Sam. 17:43–47. But Amos's oracles make no mention of hubris; they concentrate on moral outrages committed by one nation against another. Thus the similarity between Amos 1–2 and other prophetic oracles against the nations is not very great, and Hayes's interesting suggestion cannot readily be made to cover the case of Amos.

So much can be said even on the supposition that Hayes's general thesis is correct. But Clements[16] adduces powerful arguments that suggest that it is not. As he points out, it is hardly surprising that oracles on the downfall of foreign nations should use military expressions and be similar to propaganda against an enemy; no form-critical explanation is necessary. We may also note a further weakness in Hayes's case. This is that the execration or taunt in the second person is formally quite distinct from the *Kriegsansprache* speaking of the enemy in the third person, and the development of the two should be considered separately. Now, where the taunt does appear in prophetic oracles against the nations, it is most often in the form of a taunt *song*, which is generally held to owe more to the funeral lament than to anything connected with the conduct of war. And the third-person references in the Prophets are only occasionally (as in Isaiah 7) cast in the *Kriegsansprache* form anyway; in most cases they have no relation to any decision on the part of the Israelite king about whether or not to fight, and in many cases are directed towards nations with which Israel is, in any case, not at war. Hayes's theory gains its plausibility from lumping all 'oracles on the nations' together, and mixing form-critical considerations with observations about content. It does not really illuminate the complex picture presented by classical prophecy.

2. Hayes's second point (really a closely related one, in view of the cultic associations of 'Holy War') is that another *Sitz im Leben* for oracles against foreign nations may be found in cultic ceremonies of lamentation, as attested by the existence of communal laments in the Psalter and elsewhere. He cites Psalms 20, 21, and 60; Lam. 4:21–22; and 2 Kgs. 18:13–19:37. The transition from lamentation about military defeat (or petition for aid) to thanksgiving for either promised or actual deliverance has long been acknowledged as a common feature of communal laments,[17] and form critics have proposed various explanations: most commonly, that a cult prophet intervened between the two halves to give an oracle of assurance, perhaps by denouncing in Yahweh's name the enemies at whose hands the people were suffering.[18] Indeed this could very well be one *Sitz im Leben* for the *Kriegsansprache* just discussed. In Psalm 20 the prophet's words are not recorded,[19] but Psalm 60 may perhaps provide what we are looking for in verses 6–8.[20] This is of particular interest for us since the nations it names—Moab, Edom, and Philistia—also occur in Amos 1 and 2, and it looks very much as though such a psalm could be the model for Amos's oracles.

The idea that Amos modelled his oracles on some kind of prophetic liturgy of denunciation designed to bring victory to the armies of Israel has, in fact, a respectable history in the study of the prophet. Its most persuasive advocate was Würthwein, in his 'Amosstudien'.[21] According to him, Amos was originally a conventional cult prophet, who foretold *Heil* for Israel in accordance with his traditional role. It is to this period of his life that the two visions in 7:1–3 and 7:4–6 belong; only later did Amos become convinced that Yahweh's intentions were now hostile towards Israel, and he then added 7:7–9. Similarly, in 1:2–2:3, the *Heilsnabi* uses the traditional form of doom on his people's enemies, thus implying prosperity for Israel. It was only at a later date that he came to see that Israel, by its transgression of the covenant with Yahweh, was in even worse case than its enemies, and added 2:6–16.

A number of objections arise on points of detail. Against Würthwein, few commentators would now accept the designation of Amos as a converted *Heilsnabi*, so that the most we might salvage from his theory would be that Amos used the form of oracles on the nations as if he were such a prophet for dramatic effect. But it is not altogether obvious that it was a peculiarly prophetic function to pronounce such oracles in any case. Begrich's article already cited (note 20) suggests the priest as a likelier candidate, and, of course, it is hard to identify the intended speaker in Psalm 60:6–8, and still more in Psalm 20 where even his words have dropped out! In the case of individual laments and petitions, almost our only evidence is 1 Samuel 1 and 2, where it is the priest who delivers the assurance of God's favour; in 2 Kgs. 18:13–19:37, Hayes's example, the prophet Isaiah is consulted but does not speak during a cultic ceremony, and here in any case the oracle in 19:21–28 seems to many most likely to be postexilic.[22] More serious, it seems to me, is an objection which again depends on the content of the oracles and which therefore necessarily anticipates some later discussion: that Amos 1 and 2 is not concerned as is Psalm 60 with the possibility of Israel avenging itself, by God's help, on the nations who have oppressed it, but with the fact that God will himself find means to avenge atrocities not necessarily directed against Israel. Once again, therefore, Amos is not even parodying a stock form of oracle; these oracles are not related except very superficially to prophetic or priestly utterances during lamentations in times of national crisis.

3. The third line of approach supported by Hayes and Gottwald also sees prophecies against the nations within a cultic setting but attempts to broaden the area of interest considerably and to think in terms of a feature common to many cultic celebrations, not just to services of national lamentation. Würthwein's subsequent article on the prophetic *Gerichtsrede* also worked along these lines.[23] Basic to this interpretation is the belief that a prophet's role was understood to be that of bringing salvation to his people not just by denouncing Israel's current enemies[24] but by a general and systematic execration of 'foreigners'. This execration was closely linked with the notion of Yahweh's covenant with Israel and probably took place during a covenant festival—very likely that much-overworked feast, Tabernacles. Although cult prophecy does not now arouse the enthusiasm it once did, and many commentators regard any direct connection of the eighth-century prophets with the cult as unlikely, despite Reventlow's continued reconstructions,[25] it is still quite widely held that the prophetic oracles on the nations are a use of this genre, not a new creation by Amos and his successors; and so the theory must be examined so far as it relates to Amos 1 and 2.

Its most popular form derives from Bentzen's attempt to link Amos 1 and 2 with the pattern of Egyptian execration texts.[26] This idea is still highly influential and is accepted by both Hayes and Gottwald. Bentzen, it should be noted, maintains not that Amos was familiar with any execration texts but that the pattern of his oracles entitles us to argue to a similar form and hence a similar *Sitz im Leben* in the Israelite cult. The execration texts, he says, call down curses on the enemies of Pharaoh in a fixed order, viz. southern nations—northern nations—western nations—individual Egyptians. The order in Amos is northeast (Aram)—southwest (Philistia)—northwest (Phoenicia)—

southeast (Edom, Ammon, Moab)—Judah, Israel. Certainly there is a resemblance of form here sufficient to make one think of a common pattern—though it would be upset if, as can reasonably be argued, some of these oracles should be deleted.[27] But as M. Weiss has argued,[28] this 'common pattern' does not prove very much, for (a) *all* Egyptian documents follow the order south-north-west, not just the execration texts,[29] and (b) the order in Amos, if one ignores the fact that intermediate points of the compass are involved, is *not* south-north but north-south, or perhaps east-west-north. He further shows that one cannot bolster up the 'common pattern' by drawing on other prophetic oracles, as Fohrer does,[30] since no agreed geographical order can be extracted from them. Compare the following:

Ezek. 25–26	Ammon, Moab, Edom, Philistia, Tyre
Jer. 27:3	Edom, Moab, Ammon, Tyre, Sidon
Zeph. 2	Philistia, Moab, Ammon, Ethiopia, Assyria

Weiss thinks that the reason for the Egyptian order is an orientation to the south (the source of the Nile) as the cardinal point.[31] One cannot be certain in what order, if any, people in Amos's day in Israel boxed the compass, but Weiss argues, I think persuasively, that at any rate the east-west axis was primary rather than the north-south: this may be supported by noting that the west is called *āḥôr*, and the south *yāmîn*, suggesting a person facing east, and is confirmed by the order in Psalms 75:6 and 107:3.

If this interpretation is correct, then Amos differs from the execration texts in using an order different from that generally prevailing in his own culture. The simplest solution seems to be that the order is more or less arbitrary, or that other considerations than geography have dictated it.

One of the consequences of Bentzen's view, if accepted, is to eliminate any element of surprise in the Israel oracle.[32] The inclusion of Israel in the oracles is not to be seen as a surprise sprung by the prophet, who has lulled the people into expecting only good things for themselves when all the nations around them have been condemned; rather, it is the natural conclusion of a series of execrations, and it is surprising only in that, unlike its Egyptian models, it attacks the entire people instead of just the overt criminals among them and threatens doom to them all. Wolff's commentary[33] seems to me, however, to dispose of this argument once and for all, going further than Weiss and, in fact, sharply challenging the whole cultic basis for these oracles. He argues that, even setting aside the geographical question, the execration texts are very remote from Amos 1 and 2. Thus:

1. The Egyptian texts are in general mere lists of names and exhibit nothing comparable to the structure of Amos 1 and 2.

2. It is not really plausible that all the crimes concerned are against Israel, as those in the execration texts are against Egypt.
3. The comprehensive threat to the whole Israelite nation is not just a touch of originality but one that undermines the whole basis of the comparison. In no case does an Egyptian curse turn against the Egyptian people as such.
4. The Egyptian texts are magic formulae, designed to ensure the destruction of the nation's enemies: Amos's oracles are delivered in the name of Yahweh and betray no attempts to influence him against the nations. They are predictions, not curses.

In addition, Wolff notes that there is no evidence at all that ritual cursing of the kind envisaged formed part of the New Year festival, as Bentzen thinks, still less that it had to do with a special 'covenant festival'—Reventlow's view.[34]

But Wolff's arguments do not just demolish the evidence for thinking that Amos actually uttered these oracles at a cultic ceremony akin to the execration ceremonies of second-millennium Egypt; they remove any reason for thinking they are even a literary use of such a form. In short, the execration texts throw no light at all on Amos 1 and 2, and they in no way support the argument that the prophet has drawn on an already existing tradition.

There are two other, more specific arguments, which claim to show that Amos was drawing on older traditions here.

(a) Gottwald suggests[35] that 'the historical allusions . . . seem to refer to a period as much as fifty to seventy-five years before the prophet'. Insofar as this is an argument against these oracles' being a free creation by Amos, it will be dealt with below;[36] but Gottwald himself is far from confident about this: 'The historical argument is not decisive in itself, for it is always possible that Amos selected instances of national wrongdoing without respect to their modernity. The fact that they were committed years ago would not diminish his conviction that such wrong must be requited. It is when the historical argument is joined to the literary character of the oracles that the probability of a pre-Amosean prototype for the foreign oracles becomes very strong'.[37] So this is at best a supplementary argument, and we hope to have suggested that there is nothing for it to supplement.

(b) Gottwald further suggests that the use of the words 'for three transgressions of . . . and for four' is anomalous, as in each case only one crime is mentioned (except in the Israel oracle). Of course, this form usually suggests multiplicity rather than exact enumeration (compare NEB: 'for crime after crime of . . .'), but it remains true that in other Old Testament examples—see especially Prov. 30:18–19, 21–23, 24–28, 29–31; Sir. 26:5—the cases are in fact enumerated, and the fourth case often constitutes a 'punchline' (compare Sir. 25:7–11). It is difficult, however, to see that this apparent lack of 'fit' proves that Amos is here selecting from already existing collections concerned with the crimes of the nations, as Gottwald claims.[38] Clements simply speaks of 'an element of traditional formalising',[39] which is certainly safer. Two countercomments might be made. First, as Wolff suggests, it may be that Amos is simply giving the fourth, clinching example in each case—the last straw; there are several instances in the Old Testament where only the final (x + 1) example is an actual crime—compare Sir. 23:16–21; 26:28.[40] And second, if this is, in fact, a traditional form, all the indications are that x and x + 1 sayings are to be located in wisdom, whether by this we understand oral folk tradition or bureaucratic textbooks, and not in prophetic circles. This is a didactic device, not an oracular form.[41] Here then is a strong argument for Amos as an *innovator* within the prophetic succession rather than a recipient of tradition.[42]

Our arguments in this chapter have all tended to underline Clements's conclusion:

> That any one sphere of Israel's life, the royal court, the cultus or the military organisation of the state with its inheritance of holy war ideology, formed the exclusive setting of the category of the oracles against foreign powers cannot be regarded as established. Rather we must regard these prophecies as a distinctive genre of their own which drew from many aspects of Israel's life.[43]

But we may add that Amos 1:3–2:5 is the earliest extant example of the genre. Of course, we cannot prove that the prophet had no predecessors, but there is no reason to suppose that he had. If he was indeed using an earlier form, the conclusion nearest to hand is that he was adopting a popular proverbial form of speech, the numerical saying, and transforming it into prophecy by prefixing 'Thus saith the Lord'. If such forms had previously been used to condemn the sins of nations, that would help to suggest that its use by the prophet would ensure rapport with his audience; but I see no compelling evidence that this is so. It is the content of the oracles against the nations, rather than their form, that wins the audience's approval. There is no need for any complicated form-critical hypothesis as to the oracle's *Sitz im Leben*; as Wolff comments, 'People never minded hearing their enemies being condemned'.[44]

III

Our next task must be to identify more clearly what Amos is saying in these oracles. First, we will set out a translation of the text, with brief textual notes; then give a simple exegesis; and finally proceed to a discussion of the oracles' authenticity.

Translation

Against the Aramaeans

> Thus says the LORD: 'For three transgressions of Damascus and for   1:3
> four, I will not reverse my decree; (a) because they have threshed
> Gilead (b) with threshing-sledges of iron. So I will send a fire upon the   4
> house of Hazael, and it shall devour the strongholds of Ben-hadad. I
> will break the bar of Damascus, and cut off him that sits on the throne   5
> (c) from Biq'ath-awen and him that holds the sceptre from Beth-eden;
> and the people of Syria shall go into exile to Kir', says the LORD.

Against the Philistines

> Thus says the LORD: 'For three transgressions of Gaza and for four, I   1:6
> will not reverse my decree; because they carried into exile a whole peo-
> ple to deliver them up to Edom. So I will send a fire upon the wall of   7
> Gaza, which will devour her strongholds. I will cut off him that sits
> on the throne from Ashdod, and him that holds the sceptre from   8
> Ashkelon; I will turn my hand against Ekron; and the remnant of the
> Philistines shall perish', says the LORD (d).

Against Tyre

> Thus says the LORD: 'For three transgressions of Tyre and for four, I   1:9
> will not reverse my decree; because they delivered up a whole people
> to Edom (e), and did not remember the covenant of brotherhood. I
> will send a fire upon the walls of Tyre, and it shall devour her strong-   10
> holds'.

Against Edom

> Thus says the LORD: 'For three transgressions of Edom and for four,   1:11
> I will not reverse my decree; because he pursued his brother with the
> sword, and cast away his obligations towards him, and his anger tore
> perpetually, and he kept (f) his wrath for ever. So I will send a fire upon   12
> Teman, and it shall devour the strongholds of Bozrah'.

Against the Ammonites

> Thus says the LORD: 'For three transgressions of the Ammonites and   1:13
> for four, I will not reverse my decree; because they have ripped up
> women with child in Gilead that they might enlarge the border. So I
> will kindle a fire in the wall of Rabbah, and it shall devour her strong-   14
> holds, with shouting in the day of battle, with a tempest in the day of
> the whirlwind; their kings shall go into exile, he and his princes
> together', says the LORD.

Against the Moabites

> Thus says the LORD: 'For three transgressions of Moab and for four,   2:1
> I will not reverse my decree; because he burnt to lime the bones of the
> king of Edom. So I will send a fire upon Moab, and it shall devour the   2
> strongholds of Kerioth, and Moab shall die amid uproar, amid shout-
> ing and the sound of the trumpet; I will cut off the ruler from its midst,   3
> and slay all its princes with him', says the LORD.

Against Judah

> Thus says the LORD: 'For three transgressions of Judah and for four,   2:4
> I will not reverse my decree; because they have rejected the law of
> LORD, and have not kept his statutes, but their idols have led them
> astray, after which their fathers walked. But I will send fire upon Judah,   5
> and it shall devour the strongholds of Jerusalem'.

Notes on the Translation

(a) The highly elliptical phrase *lō> ăšîbennô* presents some problems of exegesis. We cannot do better than follow Wolff's account of the various interpretations it has received:

1. 'I will not make the Assyrians return from attacking them'—thus H. W.
   Hogg.[1] This has little plausibility.
2. 'I will not let the deported population of Damascus return'—thus the Jewish commentators, Rashi, Ibn Ezra, Kimhi. This will work in the first oracle but cannot be made to apply in the oracles where there is no mention
   of exile.
3. 'I will not return a favourable answer'—this is the view of Néher,[2] who sees
   Amos as a cult prophet whom the nations come to consult for an oracle
   from Yahweh. This stands or falls with the whole question of the plausibility of seeing Amos as a cult prophet, which we have already discussed.
4. 'I will not make them return to me'—thus Morgenstern.[3] This is clearly a
   possible sense, but first, the meaning of the oracle is obscured: while this
   phrase speaks of Yahweh's abandoning the nations to their sin, in the sequel
   he intervenes to punish by fire. Second, the nations are generally spoken
   of either in the plural (*ʿal dûšām*) or in the feminine singular (*ʿal
   ʾarmĕnôtehâ*), rarely in the masculine singular (1:11; 2:1).
5. 'I will not withdraw the punishment'—thus RV, NEB ('I will grant them no
   reprieve'), and many commentators from Wellhausen to Cripps. There is
   a good deal to be said in favour of this exegesis. Whether the punishment
   is seen as following inexorably on the crime or as imposed by Yahweh, or
   both, does not matter: Yahweh refuses to 'recall' it. This is the most obvious sense of the passage, unless it is given a little more accurately by the
   following interpretation.
6. 'I will not rescind my decree'—thus Wolff, Weiser,[4] and the wordy
   Jerusalem Bible rendering 'I have made my decree and will not relent' 7:2f.

and 5f., and 8:2, suggests that Amos had once seen some possibility of Yahweh's altering his decision to punish Israel but had become convinced that the time for such change of heart was past. Similarly here with the nations: Yahweh has decreed their destruction and will not alter his decree. Compare Num. 23:20b, in the Balaam oracles, where *lōʾ ǎšîbenno* is connected with 19a 'God . . . will not repent (*nḥm*)'.

(b) The Septuagint has *tas en gastri echousas en Galaad*, but compare 1:13, though K. Budde[5] defends the LXX against the MT.

(c) The singular *yôšēb* in parallel with *tômēk šebeṭ* suggests this sense, against Septuagint *tois katoichountas* (thus Wolff in his commentary, compare RV Margin and JB).

(d) Omitting *ʾădōnay* with the LXX.

(e) *ʾědôm* is again sometimes emended to *ʾărām* on grounds of geographical probability (Maag[6] and Robinson[7]); the false pointing is explained as due to influence from 1:6. This makes good sense but must remain doubtful; in any case much depends on the dating and authenticity of the oracle.[8]

(f) *šěmārâ* is odd. Wolff suggests pointing *šāměrâ*, 'his anger kept watch', that is, 'did not rest'; but most commentators follow Olshausen in reading *šāmar lāneṣaḥ* (compare BHS).

Exegesis

Aram

The crime of 'threshing' Gilead is variously taken as a metaphor for harsh treatment in war (Nowack,[9] Weiser[10]), or as a literal description of torture meted out to prisoners of war (thus the Targum, which reads 'the inhabitants of Gilead'); Harper[11] gives details of the kinds of threshing instrument which might have been used to inflict it. Edghill[12] and Wolff suggest it is a metaphor, which nonetheless corresponds pretty closely to the kind of treatment captives could expect. Tiglath-pileser I once uses the same imagery: 'the land Bit-Amukkani I threshed as with a threshing instrument; all its people and its possessions I brought to Assyria';[13] compare also in a vassal treaty of Esarhaddon: 'May Shamash with an iron plough (cut up) your cities (and your districts)'.[14] But the explicit 'threshing sledges of iron' seems to suggest a quite literal interpretation.

Biqʿath-awen and Beth-eden present difficulties. It has been common to identify the latter as the Aramaean state of Bit-Adini, which since 856 B.C. had been an Assyrian province ruled latterly by the brilliant governor Šamši-ilu (773–746).[15] This identification is generally accepted at 2 Kgs. 19:12 and Ezek. 27:23, and is supported in this verse by Wolff. The LXX *ex andrōn charran* evidently thought the same. But this interpretation has been challenged by M. Haran,[16] who points out that the comparatively distant Bit-Adini could be implicated in the crimes of Aram-Damascus only if Amos were lumping all the Aramaeans together indiscriminately; this would be specially inept in view of Bit-Adini's status as an Assyrian province, having nothing to do with the king in Damascus or with the line of Hazael and Ben-hadad. No one 'held the sceptre' in Til-Barsip. Gottwald's proposal[17] that Bit-Adini may have allied with Damascus in Amos's day would seem to be impossible. Haran considers rather that we should see the names as deliberate corruptions by the prophet of hated features of Aram-Damascus. ʿāwen is used for just such a purpose in Hosea 4:15 (Beth-aven for Bethel), and the reference here is probably to the plain between Lebanon and Anti-Lebanon (el-beqaʿ, the biqʿat-hallĕbānôn of Josh. 11:17). Certainly this gives a much more limited denunciation of Aram-Damascus, rather than of the entire Aramaean area. Of course, none of this argument will hold if the prophet is here taking over an older oracle.

Philistia

There is some doubt about the exact nature of the crime here referred to. The root sgr in Deut. 23:15 and Obadiah 14 means 'hand over (a fugitive to his rightful sovereign)', and the Aramaic cognate skr is so used in the Sefire treaties to refer to extradition.[18] Néher supposes the verb to bear the same sense here. But it is difficult to see how any sense can be made of the oracle on this interpretation of it; it must surely be meant to refer to the common practice of turning captured enemies into slaves.[19] There is no indication in the text which nation was handed over to the Edomites; and, as so often in the Old Testament, it has sometimes been conjectured that we should read 'Aram' for 'Edom': on both these points, see the discussion that follows.

Tyre

Again there is no way of telling what gālût šĕlēmâ refers to: certainly it does not demonstrably mean that Tyre sold Israelites to Edom. Nowack and Edghill pointed out that it could well refer to oppression by Tyre of other Phoenician cities; in the seventh century Tyre assisted Assyria in suppressing rebellion in the surrounding country, and her own destruction was due to a largely Phoenician army. Such interpretations explain the phrase bĕrît ʾaḥîm as a reference to the racial ties between Tyre and those she oppressed. On the other hand, more recent studies have made it clear that ʾāḥ can be a technical term for 'treaty partner', regardless of actual blood relationship: compare 1 Kgs. 20:32 and ANET 199f., 201f. (the treaty between Rameses II and Hattusilis III) and the extensive evidence cited by Fishbane.[20] This makes it clear that Nowack's explanation, though attractive, is not necessitated by the text, whose exact reference remains obscure. Tyre has broken a treaty with another state by selling its inhabitants to Edom (or possibly Aram); which state, we do not know.[21]

Edom

The sense of *wĕšiḥēt raḥămayw* is obscure: the Septuagint renders *kai elumēnato mētran epi gēs* (compare Vulgate), construing *raḥămayw* directly from *reḥem; Pesiqta Rabbati* 48a says that Esau ripped his mother's womb when he was born, indicating a similar exegesis. The easiest interpretation is from *rḥmym*; thus NEB 'stifling their natural affections'. Fishbane cites frequent uses of *raʾamu* in treaty contexts: thus in the Amarna Letters the combination *raʾáʾ-mu-ta ù aḫu-ut-ta*, 'friendship and brotherhood', is frequent; and compare Elephantine Papyrus 408, where *raḥmān* can be construed as 'treaty recognition'.[22] Probably, therefore, as in the preceding oracle, the breaking of a treaty is meant, and this is confirmed by the use of *ʾāḥ* (see above). Once again it is not quite certain who Edom's 'brother' is meant to be, but the frequent occurrence of the theme of Israel's brotherhood with Edom in the Old Testament suggests that, quite apart from the treaty background, it is Israel that is intended.

Ammon

This oracle requires little comment here. The crime denounced is mentioned a number of times in the Old Testament—for example, 2 Kgs. 15:16,[23] and see below, p. 124.

Moab

Weiser says that the bones were soaked in lime to burn them: the Targum makes the gruesome suggestion that they were used for making lime to whitewash the Moabite king's house. Generally commentators take *lĕśîd* as an indication of the complete destruction of the bones—compare Vulgate *usque ad cinerem*. In any case the crime consisted of defiling the corpse, whether this is felt as wicked because of the disrespect it implies towards a fallen enemy or because of the idea that the unburied dead do not rest. This cannot be regarded as in any sense a crime against Israel; Würthwein's suggestion[24] that Edom's special relationship with Israel ('brotherhood') makes any crime against them automatically a crime against Israel rests rather on his theory of a cultic provenance for the oracles against the nations than on any indications in the text. It is, of course, possible that the Masoretic pointing here represents a misunderstanding of an original *molk ʾdm*; this is suggested by Torczyner.[25] The reference might then be, as suggested by J. R. Bartlett,[26] to the action of Mesha, 2 Kgs. 3:27, but this is by no means certain: see discussion that follows.

Judah

This oracle presents no textual or exegetical problems; but as we shall argue there is a very high likelihood that it is not authentic.

Authenticity

It is extremely hard to establish any objective criteria for deciding on the authenticity of particular prophetic oracles. Nevertheless it may be worth trying to distinguish between arguments based on syntactic and poetic structure and historical content, on the one hand, and those which avowedly rest on some particular theory of construction and *Sitz im Leben*, on the other. On purely historical grounds only one oracle is really suspect, that against Edom. Its most obvious setting is in the exilic situation, and on these grounds Nowack, Marti,[27] Fosbroke,[28] Weiser, Wolff, and Mays[29] all argue that it is not by Amos. As we shall see, there is a possibility that the aggression by Edom is to be located in the rebellion mentioned in 2 Kgs. 8:20, or that it does not refer to hostility against Israel at all but against some other ally of Edom; but on the whole the argument for an exilic date has much to commend it. In any case literary arguments can be brought to tip the scales. No doubt Amos may have varied his style of address, but still the impression left by this oracle and the preceding one, against Tyre, is distinctly different from that made by other oracles in 1:2–2:3. Wolff[30] notes three differences in the Tyre and Edom oracles, viz.:

1. The infinitive clause with ʿ*al* is expanded with one or more finite verbs.
2. The threat of punishment is shorter: it repeats only the elements common to all the oracles, and does not particularize.
3. The final ʾ*āmar yhwh* is missing.

In addition, the crime in the Tyre oracle is the same as that in the preceding one on Philistia; and though for lack of evidence we may not accept Wolff's suggestion that *higlâ gālût* is avoided because, in the exilic period, it had become a technical term for exile to Babylon, so that the Philistines could only 'deliver up' fugitives from the greater deportation, yet *hasgĕrâ gālût šĕlēmâ* does read awkwardly, and gives rise to the suspicion that it is an abbreviation of the charge in the preceding oracles. A further small point made by Wolff is worth noting: the phrase *zākar bĕrît* is not otherwise attested before the priestly writer (e.g., Gen. 9:15f.; Exod. 2:24; Lev. 26:42).

Commentators are by no means agreed in deleting these oracles,[31] though the trend seems to be in that direction. On the whole we may decide to agree with Weiser and Wolff and deny them to Amos on literary and historical grounds.

The Judah oracle is much more generally dismissed as inauthentic, whether for its style, strongly reminiscent of the Deuteronomic historian, or for its insipid content (I am inclined to think the latter is the more convincing argument). It is hard to believe that Amos could not have found some more definite sin with which to charge Judah, and, in any case, the tone of general disapprobation for disobedience to law is quite out of keeping with the indictment of the other nations for war crimes (foreign nations) and social injustice (Israel).[32] In addition, much the same literary considerations apply here as for the Tyre and Edom oracles.

The only other of the oracles whose authenticity has been seriously questioned is 1:6–8, against the Philistines. Here the argument is a mixture of literary/historical considerations and rather more tendentious theory. Marti,[33] following Duhm,[34] argued that the historical circumstances are not those of Amos's day, since Gath is not mentioned. It was not destroyed until 711 (by Sargon) and the oracle must consequently be later than this. Furthermore, the verses composing the Philistine oracle 'lack the originality of the prophet Amos';[35] they are based on Joel 3:4–8. But the most important factor is the geographical progression of the oracles and the structure of the whole passage. If the oracles on Philistia, Tyre, and Edom are omitted, the cycle follows a natural geographical progression—Aram, Ammon, Moab, Israel; and the three ten-line strophes of the Israel oracle are paralleled by three ten-line strophes on the nations.

It is doubtful whether anyone now pays any attention to Marti's hypotheses, since such wholesale deletion of prophetic oracles on a priori grounds went out of favour. Its strongest point is the absence of Gath, but there might be any number of reasons for Amos to pass that over in silence. Amos himself, in 6:2, suggests that Gath had already been damaged enough to serve as a typical example of helplessness. This could refer to its capture by Uzziah, reported in 2 Chron. 26:6. Marti further argues that it is reasonable for an Old Testament writer to worry about geographical progression, and we may agree that there can be no grounds for denying the possibility; only we should look to see if he has, in fact, done so. Similarly Marti's strophic arrangement is very effective and satisfying, but there is no reason to think that it was also Amos's.

But the geographical hypothesis needs to be mentioned if only because it is a two-edged sword, for in Bentzen's hands it became the means of defending the authenticity of the whole section.[36] We have already suggested that Bentzen's arguments are far from compelling and that the order in which the nations are named is probably more or less arbitrary, or that other considerations than geography have been taken into account. Both edges of this particular sword are blunt, and we make no progress by using it.

So we conclude that the Judah oracle is certainly, the Edom oracle almost certainly, and the Tyre oracle very probably, not by Amos; the other oracles are authentic words of the prophet.

IV

In discussing possible derivations for these oracles against the nations, we argued that they are not in any simple sense directed against 'Israel's enemies'; all the nations named had indeed been at war with Israel at some time, but they were not all currently opposing Israel by force. At best we could speak of 'Israel's traditional enemies'. On the other hand, it is clear that all the nations in question had at some time perpetrated atrocities, whether against Israel or against their other neighbours, a fact which Amos could count on his hearers' being familiar with and scandalized at. We now have to ask, when did these atrocities take place and in what context?[1]

The traditional view has been that Amos is here referring to events from the far distant past, probably from the previous century, and that the period of the 'Aramaean wars', in the regions of Ahab, Ahaziah, Joram, and Jehu of Israel, especially the latter part of this period (say the 850s onwards), would fit best.[2] Clements argues for a still earlier date: 'Some obscurity regarding the precise historical context of these crimes remains, but the indications are that they had all taken place long before the time of Amos, probably more than a century before . . . they represented traditional examples of inhuman conduct'.[3] By 'more than a century' Clements implies that they took place during the breakup of the 'Solomonic empire' in the early ninth century.[4] Wolff, however, has argued that it is more likely that Amos would appeal to contemporary or near-contemporary events, and that a place can be found for most of these atrocities during the reign of Jeroboam II.[5]

It is probably unwise to argue this case on a priori grounds. In any case, we have no way of knowing that all the events referred to took place in the same period; they could, for example, be the most recent memorable atrocity in each case. It will be better, therefore, to examine each oracle in its own right. We will not attempt a general sketch of the period; Wolff provides an excellent one, and for a detailed survey see Herrmann's *History of Israel*.[6] As Herrmann himself points out, however, the period from the revolt of Jehu to the accession of Jeroboam II is unfortunately a very obscure one, and it will be surprising if we can come to any firm conclusions.

On Aram[7]

The Aramaeans are accused of 'threshing Gilead'. The Aramaean wars with the Israelite kings present great problems to the historian, partly because the Old Testament accounts of them seem to have suffered dislocation through the editors' desire to associate them with events in the careers of Elijah and Elisha, partly because the memory of numerous similar campaigns seems to have become vague and muddled. 'We gain the impression that a variety of reminiscences were current of the considerable political activities of the Aramaeans of Damascus and the battles which extended all over Transjordania, in which troops from both Israel and Judah were involved'.[8] Nevertheless Old Testament scholars have generally thought of three main periods of Aramaean expansion, in which attacks on Gilead to the south would have been likely.

1. The first has its roots as far back as the reign of Solomon and was in part responsible for the breakup of the Davidic-Solomonic 'empire'. This is Clements's 'more than a century before' Amos. According to 1 Kgs. 11:23–26, Solomon had to face attack from Rezon ben Eliada, who seceded from Aram-Zobah and asserted his rule over the kingdom of Aram-Damascus;[9] possibly Solomon lost most of eastern Syria.[10] By the reigns of Asa and Baasha, the Aramaeans were sufficiently strong to intervene on behalf of Judah in a border dispute (1 Kgs. 15:18–22). The Old Testament does not mention any attacks on Gileadite territory in this period, but the possibility cannot be dismissed out of hand.

2. The second period is during the reign of Ahab, when, according to 1 Kings 20 and 22, Israel fought the Aramaeans at Aphek, east of Lake Gennesaret, and at Ramoth-gilead. Here one has the impression that both sides are overstretched and prepared to make concessions, provided that prestige is not lost, but the truces are uneasy (1 Kgs. 20:34). Aramaean expansion is curtailed by the threat of the rising Assyrian power under Shalmaneser III, which makes itself felt in Palestinian affairs for the first time at the battle of Qarqar (853) at the end of Ahab's reign, linking Aram and Israel in an ad hoc coalition.[11] This coalition lasted until at least 845.[12] Recent studies have made it doubtful whether this period can be considered very seriously as the background to Amos's oracles, since it is not clear that the Old Testament is right to attribute Transjordanian campaigns to the reign of Ahab at all. J. M. Miller,[13] noticing the vagueness of attribution to 'the king of Israel' in 1 Kings 20 and 22, argues that these chapters preserve all that was remembered of the three victories against the Aramaeans predicted by Elisha in 2 Kgs. 13:19, which occurred in the reigns of either Jehoahaz or Jehoash. This misplacing is readily explicable on the hypothesis of a southern collector for these traditions who did not know which 'king of Israel' was intended, but who noted that he was allied to 'the king of Judah' and too hastily assumed that this latter must be Jehoshaphat (cf. 1 Kgs. 22:2–4; the same applies to the Moabite campaign of 2 Kgs. 3). The difficulties which this theory removes are many. There is no longer any need to postulate a multiplicity of Ben-hadads; nor is any complicated explanation needed of why Ahab's Aramaean opponent is called Ben-hadad in 1 Kings while

his ally at Qarqar, who must be the same man, is called by the Assyrians Adad-idri (= Hebrew Hadadezer).[14] Instead we have a simple succession: Hadadezer, Hazael, Ben-hadad.[15] Furthermore, the Israelite-Aramaean alliance need no longer be regarded as an ad hoc affair but as a settled policy, and this also fits in much better with the Assyrian evidence that Qarqar was not Shalmaneser III's only encounter with this confederacy of Syrian and Palestinian king-doms[16]—that it formed, in fact, a recognizable political entity. As to the general likelihood of Transjordanian campaigns under Ahab, it may be noted that 2 Kgs. 10:32–33 seems to imply that the whole of Gilead was safely in Israelite hands until the rise of Hazael; and 1 Kgs. 21:27–29 may be taken as indicating that the Deuteronomic historian supposed Ahab to have died in his bed—the story of his repentance being recorded precisely to explain this surprising fact.[17] Of course, we cannot say with certainty that Ahab did not fight the Aramaeans, but the difficulties in supposing him to have done so are considerable.

3. The third period of Aramaean expansion began with the accession of the usurper Hazael,[18] who abandoned the alliance with Israel and once more launched an attack on Gilead (2 Kgs. 8:28f.). After reverses against the Assyrians in 841 and 838, he again attacked Transjordania (2 Kgs. 10:32f.) and even invaded Israel up to the borders of Judah (2 Kgs. 12:17f.). This period of Aramaean ascendancy is said to have lasted through the reigns of Joram, Jehu, and Jehoahaz, ending around 802 with the conquests of Adad-nirari III.[19] It is to this period that most scholars attribute the atrocity against Gilead in Amos 1:3.

In fact, the picture is again complicated. At the very beginning of this period we have 2 Kgs. 8:28, which records how Ahab's son Joram formed an alliance with Ahaziah ben Jehoram of Judah to fight Hazael, and the immediate sequel to this is the rise of Jehu, so that it must be dated 843/2, presumably during a lull in Shalmaneser's campaigns and not long before his victory recorded on the Black Obelisk. Miller thinks that this battle at Ramoth-gilead is one of the two conflated in 1 Kings 22. It is in Jehu's reign that Transjordania was gradually lost to Israel, according to 2 Kgs. 10:32–33; but Herrmann points out that there are no actual accounts of Aramaean attacks on Israelite towns from this period,[20] and it may be that a considerable break in hostilities followed the isolated campaign of Joram. It is a question of just how long Aramaean domination lasted in the area. Second Kings 13:5 may be taken as an indication that Jehoahaz himself began to throw off the Aramaean yoke, whereas according to 13:19 and 13:25 it was his son Jehoash who first began to beat them in battle.

Miller argues that the first suggestion is the correct one and that it was, in fact, Jehoahaz who won the three victories predicted by Elisha, the prophet dying during his reign, somewhere before 799/8. I doubt if the text is, in fact, so contradictory as he supposes. In view of 2 Kgs. 13:7, it seems rather unlikely that Jehoahaz should have been able to *defeat* the Aramaeans; and 13:4–5 suggests not that he regained any lost possession, say in Transjordania, but only that under him Israel 'escaped from the hand of the Aramaeans'. This is perhaps most readily understood as meaning that Aramaean armies ceased actually to *invade* Israel, and it would still be reasonable to associate the recovery of Israelite independence with the reign of Jehoash.[21] It is possible that we have more information about Israel's 'deliverance' under Jehoahaz in a garbled form elsewhere in Kings. Miller himself argues, as we have seen, that 1 Kgs. 20:1–21 ought to be placed in the reign of Jehoahaz (Ben-hadad having succeeded Hazael during Jehu's reign). A siege of Samaria by the Aramaeans is quite conceivable in this time of Israelite weakness: note the smallness of 'Ahab's' army in 20:27 (cf. 2 Kgs. 13:7). According to 2 Kgs. 12:17, Aramaean troops overran Palestine as far as Gaza and took tribute from Jehoahaz's contemporary Joash of Judah.

But a further complication is surely introduced by the narrative of 2 Kgs. 6:24–7:20.[22] This looks like another version of the siege in 1 Kgs. 20:1–21, slanted towards Elisha and attributing the deliverance to a 'rumour' in the manner of 2 Kgs. 19:7. If this is, in fact, a variant version of Jehoahaz's deliverance from Aram we should probably conclude with Miller that Elisha is the 'saviour' of 2 Kgs. 13:5, but there is little difficulty in thinking that the rumour of attack by 'kings of Hatti and Musri' is a garbled reference to Adad-nirari's attack on Damascus. First Kings 20 continues in verses 22–43 with a battle of Israel against Aram at Aphek in northern Transjordania, which puts a decisive end to the period of Aramaean oppression and opens up the way for a subsequent battle at Ramoth-gilead (1 Kgs. 22).

Aphek can easily be attributed either to Jehoahaz or to Jehoash (see below). First Kings 22 presents more problems. Miller argues that it conflates two battles in Gilead: first the battle in which Joram of Israel and Ahaziah of Judah joined forces (see above)—and this battle results in defeat; second, a battle led by Jehoahaz with help from Joash. We can no longer tell what was the outcome of this battle, but it seems more than likely (against Miller) that it too resulted in defeat for Israel. Miller points out that the prophet Micaiah is placed in the custody of 'Amon, the governor of the city, and Joash, the king's son' (1 Kgs. 22:26), and argues that this Joash may well be the J(eh)oash who succeeded Jehoahaz—no recondite exegesis of *ben hammelek* is needed.[23]

But if this is so, Micaiah's gloomy prophecy must be associated with the Jehoahaz-Joash alliance rather than with Joram-Ahaziah, and it is reasonable to think that the story was recorded because the prophecy was fulfilled and Israel routed. Plainly there is now small chance of untangling this chapter, but it does seem unlikely that it contains a record of an Israelite *victory* at Ramoth-gilead. It looks as though Jehoahaz's victory at Aphek, if such there was, was only a temporary *setback* for Ben-hadad, as the prophet of 1 Kgs. 20:42 seems to suggest. Indeed, it would be simpler to attribute it to Jehoash; there is no insuperable objection to this on literary grounds, since the link in 1 Kings 20 between verses 1–21 and 22–43 is clearly loose. We might then be able to trace an abortive campaign against the Aramaeans in Gilead; a subsequent weakening of Aramaean power in the last days of Jehoahaz's reign, with the siege of Samaria thwarted by domestic trouble, probably the attack of Adad-nirari; and a qualified victory for Jehoash at Aphek about the turn of the century, recovering Israel's independence as predicted by Elisha in 2 Kgs. 13:17. This, I think, is as coherent as Miller's hypothesis and does not entail any rearrangement of 2 Kings 13. Jehoash then followed up his victory at Aphek with two other campaigns and recovered 'the cities which (Ben-hadad) had taken from his father Jehoahaz in war'—possibly including some in Transjordania, if it was indeed under Jehoahaz that these had been lost.

The effect of the reconstruction so far has been to bring the whole of the Aramaean wars down to a later period than has usually been assigned to them, beginning perhaps not until quite late in Jehu's reign (with the exception of Jehoram's battle at Ramoth-gilead) and reaching their height under Jehoahaz and Jehoash. There is no doubt that there is plenty of scope for placing Amos's reference to an Aramaean invasion of Gilead in the days of Jehoahaz. However, a third possibility has since been suggested and is developed by M. Haran:[24] he suggests that it was only under Jeroboam II that Israel began to regain its holdings in Transjordania, for it was he who according to 2 Kgs. 14:25 'restored the border of Israel from Lebo-hamath[25] as far as the Sea of Arabah'. The burden of Haran's argument is that the 'Indian summer' theory of Jeroboam's reign is not tenable in the light of Assyrian expansion during this period and that it was not until almost the end of his life that Jeroboam was free to pursue his plans for expansion. He suggests that some attacks on Transjordania may have been possible during the reign of Assur-dan III (771/2–754/5), though even he invaded Syria, but that no real Israelite conquest of Damascus and Hamath can be envisaged before the time of his successor Assur-nirari V (753/4–745/6), who left Syria-Palestine entirely unmolested for a brief period before Tiglath-pileser III succeeded him. This would mean that Jeroboam's celebrated 'empire' lasted no more than seven or eight years; it would also mean that the Aramaeans could have retained control or freedom of movement—hence freedom to plunder and pillage—in Gilead and the rest of Transjordania until as late as the 750s.

It is not clear, however, that even Haran's estimate of the political situation in the first half of the eighth century does justice to its complexities, for there is the additional factor of Urartu to be reckoned with. The partial recovery of Israel's fortunes under Jehoash is readily explained by the ascendancy of Adad-nirari III and his stranglehold on the Aramaean states; and similarly for later achievements, such as the recovery of Transjordanian territory, a powerful

Assyria would have been a help rather than a hindrance to Israel. It was in periods of Assyrian quiescence that the Aramaeans were able to assert their power by striking south into Gilead, in periods of Assyrian ascendancy that Israel might strike back and expect to win. Assyrian control over Aram-Damascus lasted until Adad-nirari's death in 782, but by 773 Urartu under Sardur III seems to have reduced Assyria under Shalmaneser IV to a position where it is possible that the Aramaeans were able to attack her themselves.[26]

As Haran rightly observes, the ensuing period under Assur-dan III and Assur-nirari V was not one during which Jeroboam is likely to have made much headway in Transjordania, but this is because Aramaean power was then once again unleashed rather than because the Assyrians themselves posed any threat as he seems to suggest.[27] From 773 until the rise of Tiglath-pileser III, Aram was once more free to involve itself in affairs east of the Jordan, and Israel could not count on any stronger power to bind it. If Jeroboam did 'capture' Damascus, as 2 Kgs. 14:28 claims, Israel had lost all hold on it again by the time Tiglath-pileser came to conquer it, and it seems probable that the biblical account of Jeroboam's 'empire' is somewhat exaggerated. The truth would rather seem to be that neither Israel nor Aram held the ascendancy in these years of Assyrian decline under the shadow of Urartu, but that there was sporadic fighting between them; thus we should reckon with a second period of Aramaean aggression, separated by only a few years from the end of the first in the days of Jehoash.

The advantage of this scheme from the point of view of interpreting Amos is clear. In 6:13–14 he refers to Israelite victories in Transjordania which must be recent if his comments are to have any point: the people pride themselves on the conquest of Lo-debar and Qarnaim,[28] cities apparently reclaimed from the Aramaeans during Jeroboam's attempts to secure the other side of the Jordan. It would be quite in keeping with this if he were countering Aramaean aggression in the same area, repelling an Aramaean advance into Gilead. Of recent commentators, Wolff favours this dating for the events referred to in Amos 1:3, and there is no difficulty about accepting it as a possibility.[29]

We may conclude, then, that Amos 1:3 may refer either to nearly contemporary events or to Aramaean expansion in the days of Jehu or Jehoahaz some forty to fifty years earlier, or possibly to much earlier events in the breakup of Solomon's empire. We must now examine the other historical allusions, and for this the historical outline as so far drawn will prove useful.

On Philistia

Our information about Aram-Damascus in the ninth to eighth centuries is copious but confused, but when we turn to the other nations condemned by Amos, evidence is scanty. The Philistines are accused, apparently, of handing

over prisoners of war either to Edom or to Aram.[30] Of contacts between the
Philistines and Edom we know nothing. If the reading 'Aram' is preferred,
there is a possible occasion for such trading during the reign of Hazael.
According to 2 Kgs. 12:17–18, as we have seen, Hazael went on raids as far as
Gath during the reign of Joash of Judah and was only prevented from attacking Jerusalem too when Joash bought him off; this extension of Aramaean
power fits in well with what we can reconstruct of the reigns of Jehoahaz and
Joash from elsewhere. It is possible that the Philistines paid Hazael a tribute
of slaves at this time. Nothing in the texts suggests that these slaves were
Israelite or Judaean prisoners, but if they were they could possibly have been
captured at the time of Philistine raids on Judah during Jehoram's reign,
reported in 2 Chron. 21:16–17, some time during the 840s, or in subsequent
raids unknown to us. If, however, the reference is to friendly trade[31] between
the Philistines and Aram, we can do nothing to date it.

On Tyre

The historical reference in this oracle, which we have judged probably inauthentic, is totally obscure. Most oracles against Tyre seem to postdate the
accession of Nebuchadnezzar II (604)—see Wolff, ad loc.

On Edom

Again we have presented literary reasons for thinking this oracle secondary,
and if these are accepted then it will probably fall into the large category of
anti-Edomite oracles composed during the exilic age and reflecting the
Edomite involvement in the sack of Jerusalem recorded in Obadiah 11. However, if the literary problems are ignored, a case can be made out for an earlier
reference. Kaufmann[32] suggests that Edom's breach with Judah in the reign of
Jehoram (2 Kgs. 8:20) is in Amos's mind here, in which case the date might be
close to that of the Philistine atrocity. Haran thinks rather in terms of
Amaziah's Edomite war (2 Kgs. 14:7; cf. 2 Chron. 25:11–12) and of atrocities
evidently committed by Edomites while engaged in it. This seems a little
unlikely, since the Old Testament accounts consistently present it as a war of
aggression by Judah. Memories of numerous unrecorded border raids could
be at the back of this oracle, and in that case no specific period can be suggested, but I still prefer to explain the oracle as exilic.

On Ammon

Here we are back with material whose authenticity there is no reason to dispute. But once again the incident referred to, apparently so specific, has as its

background the neverending border disputes between Gilead and Ammon. The most that can be said is that Ammonite incursions into Gilead are most likely to have occurred in periods when Transjordania was not engaging the attention of empire builders, and this might be thought to tend against a dating in the days of Hazael, as argued by Gottwald. Hazael himself practised this particular atrocity (compare 2 Kgs. 8:12), and so did the Israelite king Menahem in Isaiah's day (2 Kgs. 15:16). Gottwald makes the interesting suggestion that warfare in Transjordan tended to run more readily to such brutality and that its inhabitants were regarded by the more sophisticated states in Palestine and Syria as mere barbarians. As we saw above, the period immediately before Amos, when Urartu held Assyria in check and freed the Aramaeans once more, was probably a time when many petty states could harass unprotected areas across the Jordan, so we might well follow Wolff in placing this atrocity here. But again, many datings are possible.

On Moab

If *mlk-ʾdm* is understood as 'a human sacrifice', then there is no certain way of dating the reference. It might be a quite general criticism of Moabite religious practice, though the other crimes mentioned in these oracles are apparently more specific, and all are concerned with international relations. The only recorded instance of such a sacrifice is in 2 Kgs. 3:27, during the Moabite campaign of the Israel-Judah-Edom coalition. Since this or its aftermath has also been suggested as the context for the 'burning of the king of Edom's bones'—which, following MT, is more commonly thought to be the crime condemned here—we must look at it in more detail. Taking 2 Kings 3 as it stands, it is Mesha, the only Moabite king whose name is recorded in the Old Testament, that sacrificed his son in order to turn back the coalition's advance. As with the accounts of the Omride period already discussed, however, there is some reason to suspect that the narrative was originally anonymous.[33] Five arguments are set out by K. H. Bernhardt[34] to suggest a later date than the reigns of Jehoshaphat and Mesha:

1. It is very unlikely that the coalition would have attacked Moab from the south had any other route been open to them, for the chances of a successful onslaught via the steep ascent of the rift of the Arabah were very slight, and (as 3:21 confirms) surprise was impossible. This suggests a time when the routes into Moab from the north were held by some foreign power, that is, after the gradual loss of Transjordanian holdings in the reign of Jehu at the earliest.[35]

2. Since an attack from the south entailed a much heavier burden and greater danger for Judah than for Israel, the king of Judah must either have been a vassal of Israel or have had a paramount interest himself in keeping the Moabites under control. Neither of these alternatives is readily compatible

with the confident reign of Jehoshaphat; Judaean internal weakness, combined with such a loss of control on Transjordania as to involve the risk of border raids, is much more easily fitted into the reign of Joash (836/5–797/6)—compare 2 Kgs. 12:17—or of his son Amaziah.

3. According to 1 Kgs. 22:47ff., Jehoshaphat had turned Edom into a province under a Judaean governor, so there will have been no 'king of Edom' until the Edomite rebellion under his son Jehoram (850/49–843/2). This does not of itself necessitate a much later date than the narrator suggests, but it does tend to favour the original anonymity of the king of Judah in the account, and hence to open the door for different datings. Furthermore, the king of Edom must have felt threatened as seriously as the king of Judah, which supports point no. 2.

4. Judah and Edom can hardly have wished to capture Moab in order to subjugate it to Israel; everything in the narrative, especially the desperate character of the campaign, suggests that self-defence rather than expansion was the motive, and the scorched-earth policy advocated by Elisha (2 Kgs. 3:18–19) supports the view that the object is the annihilation rather than the annexation of Moab.[36] This again tends to argue for a date later than the reigns of Jehoshaphat and Joram. Second Kings 13:20f. reports that Moabite bands were invading Israelite territory in the period when Elisha *died*. Even if we take the view that Elisha was buried in Gilead,[37] this would suggest that they were a severe hazard, while on Bernhardt's own suggestion that Elisha was buried at Jericho, the place where his master Elijah had left him (cf. 2 Kgs. 2), they would clearly have been dangerous enough to warrant an expedition even as hazardous as that of 2 Kings 3.

We may be able to gain further support from 2 Chronicles 20, where Judah, too, under Jehoshaphat, has to face attacks from Moabites and Ammonites. It is noteworthy that the campaign of 2 Kings 3 is absent from the Chronicler's work, and it is tempting to see this narrative as a substitute for it, a view with the advantage of omitting any suggestion of an alliance between the pious Jehoshaphat and the apostate northern kingdom. Second Chronicles 20:10 and 22 maintain that the 'men of Mount Seir' joined the Moabite-Ammonite coalition against Judah, but in verse 23 the coalition falls apart and the 'men of Mount Seir' are destroyed by their allies. It is not far-fetched to think that the Chronicler might thus have scrambled 2 Kings 3, veiling the true reason for Moabite destruction of Edom, her alliance with Judah, which again would have reflected on Jehoshaphat's religious purity.[38] This campaign could well be the one in which Moabites burned the king of Edom's bones, as suggested above. The whole complex of 2 Kings 3 and 2 Chronicles 20 would therefore fit well into the period around the death of Elisha, which could have been as late as the beginning of the reign of Jehoash (799/8–784/3) if the foregoing reconstruction of the Aramaean wars is accepted.

5. Finally, Bernhardt argues that Joram could not have attacked Moab since throughout his reign he was fully engaged either in fighting in the Aramaean coalition against the Assyrians, like his father Ahab, or in rebelling against Aram and trying to recapture territory in Gilead (2 Kgs. 8:28f. and 9:14). This does not seem fully convincing, since the Gileadite campaign of 2 Kgs. 8:28f. is clearly Joram's last, and there might be a gap of a year or two between his leaving the Aramaean coalition and his attempt to regain Ramoth-gilead, a gap into which the Moabite campaign could be fitted. But Bernhardt clearly has a point. The reigns of Jehu and Jehoahaz see both Hebrew kingdoms too weak for such an undertaking; it is only after the victories over Aram, which we have suggested were won by Jehoahaz at the earliest and more probably by Jehoash, that Israel and Judah are again in a position even to attempt excursions into Transjordania.

The earliest likely date for the Moabite war, therefore, is the reign of Jehoash of Israel (acceded 799/8), with either Joash of Judah (died 797/6) or his son Amaziah[39] as the Judaean king concerned. The *terminus ad quem* is Amaziah's attack on Edom (2 Kgs. 14:7) and his foolish challenge to Israel (2 Kgs. 14:8f.), when Jehoash was still king in Israel (d. 784/3). So the Moabite campaign can probably be dated between 799 and 783; if Amos is referring to the king of Moab's sacrifice of his son *or* to an atrocity committed during reprisals against Edom, this would be the most likely period. We must now add, of course, that he may have some quite different incident in mind; if so, we do not know when it occurred.

Conclusion

Our conclusions in this section are chiefly negative. There is no hope of dating the events Amos refers to with anything approaching certainty. So long as we are looking for a single period to which to ascribe them all, we can at best say that a fairly recent date is likelier than an early one; but once this presupposition is given up, there is little to force our hand. The very obscurity of the crimes might argue recent occurrences; topical references are often harder to identify than traditional examples. But only a priori suppositions about the nature of these oracles can yield a firm dating; the dating cannot, then, itself be used as the basis for any interpretation. As will be seen, our own explanation of the oracles is compatible with any dating.

V

Most commentators agree[1] that these oracles build up to a climax in the oracle against Israel, and that the prophet's intention is to startle his hearers by suddenly turning on them after lulling them into a false sense of their own security by denouncing their neighbours. But since it is essential to our interpretation of Amos's teaching that this should be so, this section will examine the case for it briefly.

There are two points to be made in favour of the 'climax' view.

1. As Weiser argued at length in his classic study, it simply makes eminently good sense of this peculiar combination of attacks on foreign nations and on the prophet's own people. It is difficult to think that he would have juxtaposed the two sorts of denunciation without having any special purpose in doing so, for the denunciation of foreigners almost inevitably has a soothing effect on those at home,[2] and it is hard to imagine that Amos was not aware that the Israel oracle would rudely reverse this.

2. It is consonant with what we know of Amos's method from elsewhere in the book.

(a) In 3:2 we have, in the opinion of most commentators, a saying either actually used by the people[3] or alleged by Amos to be a fair summary of their attitude: 'Only us has Yahweh known of all the families of the earth—therefore he will forgive us all our iniquities'. The prophet cites it as though he is about to endorse it, and then he gives it a twist and rejects it: 'You alone have I known of all the families of the earth—therefore I will punish you for all your iniquities'. Not only the technique but the point made is the same as in chapters 1 and 2: apparent privilege in fact entails responsibility; Israel is even worse than the admittedly ungodly nations whom she presumes to despise.

(b) In 7:1–9 we have what again is surely a deliberately composed sequence of three visions. In the first two, Amos intercedes against the threatened destruction of Israel and prevails, only to hear God's word of irrevocable doom in the third. Now, of course, several interpretations are possible. One could argue, with Würthwein,[4] that for a certain period Amos was a *Heilsnabi* and honestly thought that Israel could be saved, but later (in the third vision) came to see that there was no hope left. This might be supported by pointing out that the literary form of the three visions is not identical. But it is surely an attractive hypothesis that Amos, in recounting his inaugural visions, shows how he was disabused by any hopes he had for the people's safety by being allowed to pray for them successfully twice, and hearing them finally condemned only after he himself had been convinced that they had been given every chance.[5] At all events, the pattern of hope held out temptingly, only to be more cruelly withdrawn, is certainly present as the text now stands.

(c) The much-discussed passage at 9:7b embodies the same approach. Wolff is no doubt right in taking 'Did I not bring up Israel from the land of Egypt?' as a further *Zitat*.[6] Amos repeats the people's confession of faith with approval and then instantly neutralizes it—'*and* the Philistines from Caphtor, *and* the

Syrians from Kir'. 'When everyone is somebody, then no one's anybody.' Again the rug is pulled out from under the audience's feet.

It is interesting that this technique does not occur in Amos's contemporary Hosea, though it arguably is used by Isaiah, in the Song of the Vineyard (Isa. 5:1–7), where the prophet's hearers are made to condemn themselves unwittingly in verses 3–4 and only identified as the subjects of the parable in verse 7.[7] The classic Old Testament example is, of course, Nathan's parable (2 Sam. 12). Its use by Amos is simply one more example of his literary skill and intellectual expertise, which may be added to the other instances which are adduced to prove his affinities with the so-called 'wisdom tradition'.[8] We are not at all concerned to support this conclusion, but simply to agree that Amos does emerge as an intellectual, whose ability to use literary tricks is not surprising.

But various objections can be raised to this interpretation of these chapters:

(i) Würthwein takes much the same line over chapters 1 and 2 as over chapter 7: that they represent a revision by the mature Amos of his earlier work. Integral to this understanding of the prophet is a belief that he began life as a 'cultic' prophet, and that the function of such prophets was to foretell victory for Israel and defeat for her enemies—a view we have already examined. The oracles against the nations, then, are really an indirect prediction of deliverance for Israel by means of a denunciation of her enemies, and when the prophet delivered them, he believed in them as such—he was simply doing his job as a cult prophet. Later he came to see that Israel, too, was doomed, but in adding the Israel oracle he was not constructing a coherent literary whole but simply cancelling his earlier view.

Würthwein's interpretation assumes that Amos began life as a professional cult prophet, a view that is not so popular as it was.[9] But even on its own terms it does not square comfortably with the text. As we have tried to show, the oracles against the nations cannot easily be taken as a denunciation of Israel's enemies, if by that is meant nations with whom she was now at war, nor are their crimes all anti-Israelite. At best we can speak of oracles against Israel's *traditional* enemies; there is no implication that the oracles are an effective means of securing Israel's victory over them.[10] Nor is there any reason to suppose that Amos later renounced his belief that the nations deserved and would receive punishment for their sins. This means that only an alleged unspoken implication—the victory of Israel—is reversed by the addition of the Israel oracle; and if we do not find the implication there anyway, then Würthwein's case falls to the ground.[11]

(ii) Another 'cultic' interpretation of Amos which also rules out any element of surprise in the Israel oracle is Bentzen's theory already discussed.[12] So far from arguing for a complete break after the oracle against the nations, he supposes that the execration of both foreign nations and Israelites was a normal procedure during the autumn festival, and that neither sort of oracle could be expected to occasion any particular surprise. It may be noted that even Kapelrud, who accepts Bentzen's reconstruction in the main, is concerned to dissociate himself from this conclusion, suggesting that denunciation of Israel as a whole for its sins goes far beyond anything that could have formed part of a regular ritual pattern.[13] As we have seen, Wolff regards this as a fundamental weakness in Bentzen's whole case, which destroys the similarity to Egyptian execration texts on which the theory rests.

So we may reasonably conclude that the 'climax' interpretation of these chapters is as likely as any, and that none of the alternatives can easily be made good.

VI

A number of commentators have discussed the basis for Amos's condemnation of atrocities in these chapters, and their suggested answers can be conveniently classified under four headings.

1. *Nationalism and covenant*: The nations are denounced for opposing Israel, Yahweh's chosen covenant people.
2. *Logical extension*: The moral obligations which Israel is *known* to owe to Yahweh are supposed by extension to apply also to the nations.
3. *Universal law*: All nations, Israel included, are subject to divine law which derives from Yahweh's dominion over all mankind.
4. *International customary law*: The nations are condemned for infringing customs of war accepted or believed to be accepted by all civilised nations.

It is the fourth of these lines of interpretation that we wish to develop and clarify; but first it will be proper to discuss the other three.

Nationalism and Covenant

We have already dealt with the main lines of 'nationalistic' interpretations in sections 2 and 4. Its main proponents are those who think in terms of a cultic *Sitz im Leben* for Amos's oracles and who maintain that the prophet's function is to denounce the enemies of Israel and so ensure her victory over them when they assail her. So far as the cultic setting is concerned, our comments on Würthwein[1] will suffice. But the nationalistic interpretation is continued by Haran, who regards the only alternative as 'ethical monotheism', which he thinks an unacceptable understanding of Amos:

> It is . . . difficult to agree with the opinion prevailing in commentaries on Amos to the effect that a new theological concept finds expression

here: God is supposedly regarded as the national sovereign of Israel alone, yet has already come to make moral demands (thus far moral, not cultic) upon other nations as well. Accordingly, Amos is elevated to the role of progenitor of moral monotheism as against the mono- latry or national henotheism typical of his contemporaries. . . . In actual fact, the demands are national rather than moral in nature and the major part of this prophecy is designed according to the older nationalistic pattern.[2]

But our survey of the historical circumstances has made it clear that, with the possible exception of Aram, if we follow Wolff in seeing 1:3–5 as a reference to recent atrocities, the threat to Israel from the nations mentioned was largely past in Amos's day, so we can at best speak of traditional enemies. The oracle on the Philistines need not be concerned with a crime against Israel, and that on Moab almost certainly is not: there is not much cogency in Würthwein's attempt to justify the inclusion of the burning of the king of Edom's bones among anti-Israelite crimes on the dual grounds that (a) Edom was a 'brother' to Israel[3] and (b) 'hier handelt es um ein Verbrechen von besonderer Unge- heuerlichkeit' ('this concerns a crime of particular gruesomeness')—this is just special pleading. The nationalist interpretation does not seem to do justice to Amos's thought.

Weiser also thinks that the source of the moral norms to which Amos is appealing is to be found in nationalist sentiments: 'Der Boden, auf dem der Prophet sich dabei bewegt, liegt nicht über dem Niveau der nationalen Volks- religion' ('The ground on which the prophet is moving here does not lie above the level of the national popular religion').[4] He uses this point, however, in order to argue that Amos's originality cannot be located in a discovery that the nations, like Israel, stand under God's moral authority, which is what we shall also be concerned to argue—not to suggest that Amos endorsed the crude nationalist feelings of his day. The difficulty about Weiser's view, nonetheless, is that it assumes the condemnation of atrocities in war formed part of a folk mythology about the character of Israel's enemies whereas the fact that the identity of the victim of atrocities appears to be irrelevant seems to suggest that condemnation of atrocities belongs in a broader, more generally humanitarian tradition. Weiser is likely to be right in stressing that the moral convictions underlying Amos 1:3–2:5 were common to the prophet and his audience, but he was prob- ably mistaken in thinking that they derive from a narrow nationalism.

Logical Extension

But if we reject the line of interpretation that would see opposition to Israel as the essence of the nations' sin, we may still hold that Israel is somehow seen as the focus of moral obligation. For a prophet acquainted, as Amos clearly is, with the convention that Israel owes a special obligation to Yahweh as his chosen people, it might seem to follow that any moral principles binding outside Israel will be so by extension from those known within the covenant relationship. It is not that Israel and the nations share a common covenantal relationship with God; rather, Amos asserts that the ethical obligation incumbent upon Israel is to be seen as binding also on the nations: a startling innovation, so far at least as the popular mind of his day was concerned. Like the cultic view already discussed, this is basically Israel-centred in its emphasis. It has the advantage of safeguarding the centrality of God's dealings with Israel, and more particularly of the covenant relationship in the Old Testament, which is an understandable preoccupation of some scholars. Certainly any interpretation which appears to ignore the importance of the covenant has to make headway against much substantial evidence and theorizing. Thus Fensham writes,

> The important trend of thought was that maledictions against a disobedient people shall overtake them, because they have breached the covenant. Calamities predicted against foreign nations must have developed out of these maledictions.[5]

Clements[6] comes to substantially the same conclusions about the prophetic denunciation of Israel's enemies: they always derive from the covenant ethic by extension. The nations are assumed to be under ethical obligations because Israel—through the covenant—is known to be under them: compare 1 Kgs. 17:18 for an example of this process. Mays[7] is otherwise ready to recognise noncovenantal ethics in Amos, but he still feels that the covenant relationship is primary and the obligation on the nations a secondary extension:

> Amos specifies the basis of Israel's responsibility to Yahweh in 3:2, the election of Israel ... Amos sees Yahweh as the sovereign of history who moves nations in their national careers and can remove them to their earlier spheres (1:5). By analogy with Yahweh's relation to Israel, that sovereignty in the nations' history furnishes the foundation for their responsibility to him.

But it seems to me that, if we accept the 'climax' view of the structure of these chapters, whereby the condemnation of Israel comes as a surprise, we shall have to allow for a less Israel-centred view of ethics than is compatible with such a theory of extension. Amos's hearers are not surprised that foreign nations should be condemned for their atrocities; what startles them is that Israel should be included under the same condemnation. Weiser presents this point with the utmost clarity: the oracles against the nations, he maintains, 'sagen nichts, was den Hörern innerlich fremd ist, sondern enthalten Elemente des Volksglaubens und der Volkshoffnung' ('say nothing that is essentially alien to the hearers, but contain elements of popular belief and popular hope').[8] This strongly suggests that the process of extension works in exactly the opposite direction. That war crimes such as foreigners commit are displeasing to Yahweh and will be punished is a commonplace, obvious to all the prophet's audience; much less obvious is the guilt of Israel, for its election by Yahweh has been taken to excuse it from any stringent moral claims upon it and to preclude any possibility of divine vengeance. Israel is not subject to the restrictions that bring the rest of mankind before God's judgement seat. Amos's preaching, then, is designed to bring home that Israel must be judged on the same terms (even if by different laws) as her neighbours, and with equal impartiality. Unless something like that is the correct interpretation of Amos's oracles, the possibility of surprise in the Israel oracle is excluded; indeed, it would be the only oracle that would occasion none.[9] The moral obligations owed by foreign nations must be not less but more evident than those imposed on Israel if these chapters are to serve their purpose. And so we must reject any interpretation that sees such universal morality as deriving from, rather than as presupposed by, the special moral response demanded of the covenant people.[10]

Universal Law

If the validity of moral rules governing the conduct of the nations is, in fact, presupposed by Amos, then it will follow that he is invoking ethical principles common, or supposed by him to be common, to all humankind. Generally the commentators who have thought along these lines have analysed the basis for such an assumption in terms of a universal divine law: something parallel or analogous to the law of Yahweh known in Israel, though not (as we have seen) actually derived from it or identified with it. It is often supposed to stem from the authority of God as the controller of human history,[11] and it is sometimes actually called 'international law'—in the sense not of an internationally agreed code but of the divine, revealed law obligatory for all humankind, whether or not they accept it.[12] Lindblom states the principle clearly: '[The nations] are condemned because of their wickedness and cruelty as such, because of the fact that they have offended against the holy will of Yahweh, which is valid for all peoples'.[13] According to him, this derives from Amos's virtual 'ethical monotheism': Yahweh as the God of the whole universe makes demands on all humankind, not just on the chosen people.[14]

Now, this certainly makes better sense than the interpretation in terms of logical extension from the covenant law, but it still seems to me basically unsatisfactory. If we say that the humanitarian principles the nations are condemned for flouting are part of the divine law, we still run the risk of suggesting that they are condemned for breaking an edict they were unaware of.

What reason was there to think that God's will had been revealed to them? In other words, we shall seem to accuse Amos of irrationality if we hold that he appealed to a supposed divine law, and even if we like to say that he was *not* rational (if that means 'sweetly reasonable'), this interpretation has the serious flaw that it seems to contradict what, according to our arguments so far, Amos was actually trying to do. He is precisely not saying that the nations will perish because they have—all unwittingly, for all he knows—broken the decree of Yahweh; he is saying that they deserve punishment for contravening moral principles which even they should have recognised. The parallel with Israel makes this clear, for the essence of his attack on them is that they, too, should have known better.

There seems no escape from the conclusion that Amos thought the foreign nations were infringing humanitarian principles whose force they themselves appreciated; and if that is so, we can call these principles 'God's law' only in an attenuated sense. Either 'God' will have to be understood to mean not 'Yahweh' but 'whatever ultimate principle or force the nation in question recognizes', 'their own ultimate religious sanction'; and this is perhaps the interpretation that would be accepted by those who stress the prophet's indebtedness to the international 'wisdom' tradition. Or we shall have to understand 'God's law' to mean a law which God enforces rather than one which God enacts. In that case, the 'law' is not theological in its roots but only in its application. This is the interpretation we shall be defending, under the next heading.

International Customary Law

In the oracles against the nations, we suggest, God steps in to punish the nations because they are guilty of various atrocities, infringements of supposedly universal moral norms. But the question of the source of these norms is not discussed. They are thought of as part of the common moral sense of all right-minded people; that God shares this moral sense is taken for granted, since he is the very epitome of right-mindedness. But there is no real suggestion that the rightness of the moral norms actually derives from God. Thus the principles at stake in these oracles are essentially part of a conventional morality, which God is assumed to back up with fiery sanctions, rather than actual laws supposed to be issued by God for all the nations of the world to observe. This helps, I would suggest, to make clear the essential rationality of Amos's approach. Israel's neighbours are not denounced for sins which they could not have been expected to recognize as such (e.g., idolatry) but for offences against common humanity; not for disobedience to God but for failing to follow the dictates of their own moral sense.

Not many of the older scholars regarded Amos 1 and 2 in precisely this light. Humbert came near to it in speaking of 'un Dieu garant d'une morale universelle' ('a God who is the guarantor of a universal morality'), and of 'lois élémentaires de la morale humaine' ('elementary laws of human morality').[15] More recently, however, hints have been thrown out in this direction. Gehman discusses what he calls 'natural law' in the Old Testament and includes some examples of conventional morality,[16] seeing Amos's oracles as one of the clearest cases: '[T]hese nations outside Israel had violated the common or basic laws concerning the sacredness of human personality. . . . It was accordingly recognised and taken for granted that there are certain basic laws and customs which apply to all humanity and that the breaking of them is a transgression against God'.[17]

I have for convenience dubbed this 'international customary law', but an important distinction must be drawn. These conventions are called customary because they are clearly not the subject of explicit legislation, and 'international' because they are concerned with conduct between independent nations in time of war. It has been maintained that they represent a code of conduct actually observed or at least endorsed by the peoples mentioned; thus Max Weber speaks in this connection of 'a form of international religious law which was presupposed as valid among Palestine peoples',[18] and G. H. Jones maintains that 'it is suggested that there was an accepted norm of international behaviour in the ancient Near East, and that some actions would be regarded as atrocious against the background of this common ethos'.[19] Now, the existence of such a 'common ethos' is plainly possible, and in the appendix to this chapter we examine some of the evidence for it; but the argument does not require it. Amos clearly implies that the nations ought ideally to recognise the moral norms which they are transgressing, but it does not follow that they in fact did so. Even if it could be shown that such conventions did not exist outside Israel, Amos's condemnation would not thereby be rendered unreasonable, for the nations' failure even to recognise conventions of 'civilized' conduct might itself be part of the sin condemned. All that follows is that Amos held certain norms of international conduct to be both valid and *obviously* valid, and that he thought his Israelite audience was likely to agree with him. Our point is that he is appealing not to revealed law but to conventional or customary law. It is possible, however, (though we may think it unlikely) that the 'customs' to which he appealed would not have been accepted outside Israel, or even that not everyone in Israel would have seen the force of them. People do not always recognize the obvious. Consequently, we may well be cautious of assuming that Amos is appealing to a 'common ethos'; at most it is an ethos which he thought ought to be common.

VII

In this section we revert to the six theses we set out in the outline argument and attempt to form some idea of popular notions of morality, divine judgement, and the role of the prophet; then we examine the question of Amos's distinctiveness and originality.

Popular Belief

Our discussion of conventions of international conduct has already produced examples of popular belief about actual moral norms in this area, and there is nothing to add here. We have assumed throughout that Amos expected his hearers to share his outrage at such atrocities as he mentions, and that having thus awakened their moral sense he could turn it against them by leading them to self-condemnation. But, as we tried to suggest in our initial argument, a number of other conclusions may be drawn about the attitude of Amos's audience if we assume that he read their mood correctly.

First and most obviously, they must have believed that sin called down divine punishment. This may seem so trite as not to be worth saying, but it is useful in ruling out certain popular presentations of the prophets as almost the inventors of ethics. Probably no serious scholar now holds this: the awareness that in this as in so much else the prophets depend on a long and widely accepted tradition is one of the very solid gains in modern Old Testament study. But sometimes the moral insensitivity of the people at large in Amos's day is still alleged in a rather extreme form, as though all sense of connection between God and morality and all capacity for moral outrage had drained away from the sink of corruption that Israel under Jeroboam II had become. In this context it may still be worth stressing that Amos is not preaching in a total vacuum but assuming that his hearers have some awareness of moral principles and some conviction that God punishes sin with physical disaster; thus he has some foundation on which to build.

Second, Amos's hearers must be supposed to have regarded the nations as moral agents answerable for their conduct. Again, this is obvious, and it may be doubted whether any culture could be found where members of other nations were regarded as morally unaccountable. But it is perhaps not always seen that this fact renders some interpretations of the work of the prophets rather suspect. We have discussed a number of interpretations of the oracles against the nations in which Amos is seen as extending the scope of moral obligation from Israel to the nations, the most recent being that of Mays: 'By analogy with Yahweh's relation to Israel, that sovereignty in the nations' history furnishes the foundation for their responsibility to him'[1]—and we have argued that the conviction of the nations' moral obligations must on the contrary long antedate Amos. This is not necessarily to say that such obligations were seen as owed to Yahweh in any simple sense; of their supposed basis, if any, we know nothing. But the oracles against the nations must imply that Yahweh was seen as the avenger of acts that infringed the norms of conduct demanded of non-Israelites, and if we may press the Moab oracle, this would appear to be so even when the crime in question was not directed against Israel. It seems fair to conclude that the scope both of moral accountability and of Yahweh's power to avenge sin and hence to determine the fortunes of nations was popularly held to extend well beyond Israel by Amos's day—which rules out any attempt to find the prophet's originality in any tendency to ethical universalism or to an extension of Yahweh's power and authority. Weiser makes this point:

> Tatsächlich liegen die Dinge . . . so, dass die Hörer mit dem, was über die Feinde gesagt wird, einverstanden sind; dann ist aber auch die sittliche Motivierung der Strafe ein Gedanke, der bei ihnen vorausgesetzt werden muss ('Actually it must be the case . . . that the hearers are in agreement with what is said about the enemies; but then the ethical motivation of the punishment must also be a thought which can be taken as presupposed by them').[2]

Again, I do not wish to suggest that such a view is particularly widespread amongst recent students of Amos, but simply to stress that in any attempt to reconstruct what 'Israel' believed before the rise of the prophets we must be careful not to go on tacitly assuming it. It is not clear that Amos is here developing further an insight only partially grasped by his contemporaries; he seems simply to be meeting them on their own ground.

Third, the audience must suppose that Israel had a specially privileged position and hence was indemnified against punishment. This is universally agreed. In 3:2, Amos seems to accept the premise but deny the conclusion; in 9:7, to deny both.

Fourth, Amos's hearers clearly did not expect prophets to proclaim judgement on Israel. This is also generally agreed.

Fifth, if the surprise technique is to succeed, we must assume not that the people were unaware of the largely social obligations whose transgressions Amos condemned, but that they saw these as in no way comparable with the international conventions infringed by the nations. In other words, the average Israelite reacted much as we probably should to the suggestion that giving short measure in the market was as bad as (worse than?) disembowelling pregnant women. It takes some swallowing. There is therefore meant to be nothing in the least original in Amos's examples in 1:2–2:3, nothing that people would not have recognized at once with horror; the surprise is wholly in placing social justice on par with such offences, transferring as it were the horror to commonplace, everyday misdemeanours which people may have regretted but would mostly shrug off as the kind of thing that just happens in an imperfect world.

Sixth, and related to this, it seems in some sense to have been less *obvious* that Israelites had mutual obligations as individuals than that nations ought to observe the conventions of war. This is again rather what one might expect. Once we leave behind the idea that Israelites were heavily imbued with a sense of covenant stipulations as primary to their moral awareness, and to allow more place for custom, convention and common sense, it will not be surprising to find what Amos seems to have found: that people's moral sensitivity was more easily alerted by manifest atrocities abroad than by transgressions of the social order at home, in a nation prosperous and successful in both trade and war.

To sum up, the popular sentiments which we must suppose to have been widespread in Israel if Amos's message was to find its mark are these: All the nations of the world are bound by certain moral laws and are accountable for their conduct; and Yahweh, the god who chose Israel as his special people, exercises a vigilant control over the way they act, punishing transgressions by causing wars and so destroying sinful nations. Hence the fortunes of all nations are in Yahweh's control, and this control is exercised according to ethical criteria. Israel because of its special election is not subject to the divine judgement, and in any case its own sins, such as they are, are never of the same order as those of foreign nations, since Israel does not flout international customs. Its national life has all the marks of divine favour, and such disorders as society may manifest are quite trifling and easily forgiven. This reconstruction corresponds in part with traditional sketches of popular belief in eighth-century Israel and in part with traditional presentations of the message of Amos. Of course, it cannot be proved that it is more than a caricature, but we believe that it does clearly emerge from what Amos tells us, explicitly or by implication.

The Originality of Amos

We must not, of course, make the mistake of assuming that Amos's own message can be reconstructed simply by negating the outline just presented of the people's beliefs. Our whole purpose has been to define those areas where he accepts without question the popular beliefs of his day, those where he explicitly contradicts them, and those where he presents new ideas. We have suggested that the notion of international conventions of conduct of which Yahweh acts as a guarantor falls into the first category while Amos's idea that

Israel's election does not indemnify it against punishment for sin is an example of the second. It now remains to look for points at which Amos is actually adopting an original position. Two possible examples suggest themselves:

First, Amos is original in asserting that social injustices and transgressions of the moral code in Israelite society (perhaps equated with 'the law') have the same moral status as transgressions of the much more self-evident laws of international conduct and the practice of war. So far from international customary law somehow being assimilated into Israel's covenant law, Amos seems to think that he adds something to the moral intensity of the (revealed) social norms that hold within Israel by placing them on a par with international custom. E. W. Heaton writes that the discourse in the first two chapters of Amos 'discloses the prophet's fundamental conviction that the moral obligation of which all men are aware (and which in later centuries was called natural law) is identical with the personal will of Israel's God.'[3] On the contrary, it looks as though Amos is saying that the personal will of Israel's God, as it is known in the moral rules which should govern its social life, is as binding and as important as if it were part of the moral obligation of which 'all men' are aware. The novelty would then consist in maintaining, against popular opinion, that social morality (understood as impartiality in justice and care for the rights of the helpless) is not a mere piece of arbitrary divine legislation, nor merely a human convention, but almost part of the order of nature—self-evident to any right-thinking person.

Second, a further novelty was apparently Amos's conviction that Israel was not indemnified against punishment but was all the more accountable in view of its election. The argument is not that, since Yahweh has revealed his will to Israel alone, scrupulous Israelites ought to be keeping it and are therefore culpable if they transgress it, but rather, since the rightness of the obligations laid on Israel ought to be as obvious as if they were agreed on by everyone in the world, how much worse their guilt is when they also have the advantage of a special personal contact with God to endorse them! Amos thus totally reverses the popular idea of election. It becomes simply a factor aggravating still further the deep guilt of Israel and, in the end, is apparently to be altogether abrogated by Yahweh.

APPENDIX: INTERNATIONAL LAW
IN THE ANCIENT NEAR EAST

The purpose of this appendix is to set out a selection of comparative material from the ancient Near East on international conventions, especially those concerned with warfare. The subject deserves a full-length study in its own right, but for our purposes the need is simply to show that the conventions we have supposed Amos to be appealing to are not unattested in the ancient world. In other words, this is meant to serve as a 'feasibility study', not in any way as a 'proof' that our interpretation of Amos is correct.

Throughout the present study I have spoken of 'international law', and this might be thought unwise, since it is a closely defined concept which lawyers are generally wary of applying outside the context of modern international relations, with properly regulated and enforceable treaties and conventions. Incidentally, the same applies to the idea of war crimes, which we have freely referred to; it is arguable that such a category of crime has not been recognised until this century, and, of course, its exact legal status was one of the major problems attending the Nuremberg trials. International law properly so called may be defined as 'eine rechtliche Ordnung mehrerer selbständig nebeneinander stehender, sich gegenseitig als gleich berechtigt anerkennender und durch einen regelmässigen Austausch kultureller und wirtschaftlicher Art verbundener Staaten' ('a legally regulated order of a number of independent nations which exist side by side, recognize each other as having equal rights, and are bound together by a regular cultural and commercial exchange').[1] Older writers on international law, so far as I am able to judge, saw nothing approximating this in antiquity before some very rudimentary beginnings in Classical Greece and Rome.[2] More recently, however, with the publication of an increasing number of treatises from the ancient Near East, this judgement has had to be modified, at least by orientalists. Professional international lawyers have also altered their assessment of the origins of international law, though so far as the standard textbooks are concerned, this seems to have meant only the rather grudging addition of a few pages on preclassical antiquity rather than any more full-blown treatment. Thus we have little professional help available in studying the field. The only extensive study of international law in the ancient Near East that I can find which is really relevant to our concern is that of Preiser, quoted above, so I shall draw heavily on him.

We must not, however, limit ourselves entirely to 'international law' in the strict sense defined above—agreed codes of international conduct, confirmed by treaty. We shall also need to look at accepted international conventions of diplomacy and war, and also at those kinds of conduct in international affairs to which nations regard themselves and others as constrained, regardless of whether anyone but themselves in fact accepted them. In this way we may hope to cover the field of possible parallels to Amos 1:3–2:3. We may divide the subject into three classifications.

1. International law proper—treaties, etc.
2. Agreed international conventions not legally ratified
3. Unilaterally accepted norms of international conduct

International Law Proper

Preiser has studied the evidence for the existence of international law properly, so called in the ancient Near East, and has come to the conclusion that our only evidence for it is to be found in roughly the period from the beginning of the fifteenth to the end of the thirteenth centuries. Before this, the only suggestion of anything like international law is to be found in the protracted boundary dispute between the city-states of Lagash and Umma at the start of the third millennium, in the course of which the King of Kish at one point acted as mediator, setting up a boundary stone and binding both parties to accept the border thus defined.[3] But the details of this transaction are unclear, and there is some reason to think that the King of Kish was in the position of overlord to the rulers of Lagash and Umma, so that no question of strictly international relations arises.[4]

The clearest examples of international law in the usual sense will naturally appear in the so-called parity treaties between major powers, where there is no question of vassalage. The most famous of these, and the only one extant among the Hittite treaties, is between Rameses II and Hattusilis III.[5] Apart from being, as would be expected, a pact of mutual nonaggression, it includes a promise of military aid in the event of rebellion by the vassals of either party, a mutual obligation to ensure the succession, and an extradition treaty. It is not altogether clear whether this is meant to apply just to political prisoners who have escaped, or rather to all who leave one country for the other without permission from their own king. Mettgenberg[6] argues that the treaty is designed to make emigration in itself a crime, probably because of its possible harmful effect on the labour forces of both states involved. Interesting from our point of view is the provision that various specified punishments, in particular mutilation, may not be carried out on a man so extradited, or on his family;[7] these rules are reminiscent of our principle of refusing extradition to a state whose standards of justice or methods of punishment are not acceptable to us.

The only other parity treaty that demands consideration is that between Niqmepa, king of Mukish and Alalakh, and Ir-IM, king of Tunip, preserved on the second of the Alalakh tablets. This treaty provides for the extradition of marauders for judgement by their own king:

(55)　If someone in my territory shall have entered into your territory for banditry (?)

(56)　you shall surely not keep them as though they were of your land, you shall surely

(57)　not detain them within your territory but must return them to my territory.

(58)　You must round them up and return them to my territory.[8]

But unlike the Rameses-Hattusilis treaty, it explicitly provides that escaped prisoners may be granted asylum if they succeeded in fleeing from one state to the other:

(20) If a prisoner of my country escapes to your country then he verily free [sic].

(21) and if the prisoner has been freed you may neither seize (him) nor (return him to me).[9]

In the event of a citizen who is not a prisoner fleeing for asylum, his king must be informed;[10] but the tablet is damaged, and it is not possible to say whether further steps were taken.

Whether one can speak of international law in vassal treaties, it is harder to say. In modern terms one could not, but the line between parity and vassal treaties in the Near East is not so hard and fast. As Korošec's analysis shows, a parity treaty is formally no more than a mutual vassal treaty, and 'vassalage' is a very fluid idea, ranging from complete subjugation to merely nominal inferiority.[11] In the absence of any theoretically formulated concept of international law the borderline between this and 'state' law will hardly be closely definable, and some legal provisions are bound to fall on both sides of it.[12] For our purposes it does not much matter exactly how far we allow vassal treaties to contain international law; certainly some of them have provisions which closely approach it. The treaty between Šuppiluliumaš and Mattiwaza of Mitanni[13] is formally a vassal treaty, but the Hittite king lays emphasis, in the preamble which explains why his vassal should be willing to obey him, on the fact that while the Hittites have made war on many neighbouring peoples, they have never infringed on the sovereignty of Mitanni by removing so much as 'a reed or a twig'. The obligation to extradition again applies, though naturally enough it is unilateral.[14] Mattiwaza must extradite any fugitives from Hatti, while Šuppiluliumaš may grant asylum to Mitannian fugitives at his discretion.

The Sefire treaties also contain provisions similar to those of the Rameses-Hattusilis treaty described above;[15] thus in Sefire III[16] Mati'el is to hand over all who plot against Bar-Ga'yah, the overlord, as well as fugitives from justice; he has a duty to help maintain the succession, and his own is in turn guaranteed; he must allow Bar-Ga'yah's ambassadors to pass unhindered and refrain from participating in any plots against his household and, if necessary, avenge his assassination; and both partners must respect each other's territorial rights, though the vassal's rights are of course ultimately subordinate to his overlord's. Apparently this treaty also envisages mutual extradition pacts between Bar-Ga'yah and the (? sovereign) states around him—thus:

And as for the (k)ings of (my vicin)ity, if a fugitive of mine flees to one of them, and a fugitive of theirs flees and comes to me, if he has restored mine, I shall return (his; and) you yourself shall (no)t try to hinder me.[17]

Agreed International Conventions Not Legally Ratified

If so much 'international law' can be gleaned from legally ratified treaties, there is a much larger area of international agreement on matters not specifically codified but necessary if peaceful relations are to be preserved between states. One such matter that has already arisen, in Sefire III, is the question of ambassadors. Wherever Egyptian influence prevailed in the second millennium, the obligation to respect the person of the ambassador might be taken for granted. Thus Amarna letter no. 30[18] preserves a passport for an ambassador passing through Palestine. Letters 7 and 8 demand vengeance for attacks on properly accredited ambassadors: in letter 8, Amenophis IV is asked by Burraburiash to punish the inhabitants of Canaan (Kinahhi), where his ambassadors have been set upon and either killed or subjected to various atrocities (one man's feet have been cut off; another has been stood on his head). Disrespect of any kind for an ambassador is felt as an insult; thus in letter 3 a Babylonian prince complains that the pharaoh (Amenophis III) has kept his ambassadors waiting for six years without granting them an audience and without making sufficient provision for their needs. Again, Tushratta writes angrily to Amenophis IV because his envoys have not been allowed to return home; he threatens that he will himself retain the Egyptian ambassadors as hostages until his own are restored to him.

It seems probable that the conventions of diplomatic missions of the Amarna age are the final flowering of a continuous tradition going back to the turn of the second millennium. The evidence of the Mari letters, as discussed by Munn-Rankin,[19] suggests that such conventions were already commonplace in Mesopotamia by the eighteenth century, though in a less highly developed form. There is less immunity for ambassadors than in the Egyptian texts; thus Zimrilim's envoy is obliged to stay at Hammurabi's court until given permission to leave, even though he has been recalled;[20] and officials—though not private individuals—may detain envoys before they reach the court if their visit at that time is judged to be inopportune.[21] On the other hand, diplomatic missions were probably exempt from customs dues,[22] and there were elaborate codes dictating the safe conduct of ambassadors returning home, who had to be accompanied by a native of the country to which they had been accredited, not just to the border but all the way back to their own court.[23] Sending back ambassadors without such an escort is a calculated affront.[24] From a later age, there is independent evidence of the respect in which ambassadors were held in the ancient Near East in 2 Sam. 10:4, where the Ammonites' contempt for David's legation leads to war.

There is good reason to think that conventions of diplomacy extended beyond such basic provisions to include a careful regulation of the niceties of official procedure. This has been the subject of a study by J. Pirenne,[25] and there is also evidence from Mari.[26] Among the complaints about finer points of protocol in the Amarna letters is one from Šuppiluliumaš, who writes to Amenophis IV to upbraid him for reversing the accepted order of names in the greeting at the head of a letter, placing his own name before that of the addressee.[27] One cannot tell whether this was a deliberately contrived snub or simply a careless mistake by an official, but it is clearly a matter that could strain international relations. Failure to observe the accustomed protocol always requires an explanation. Thus the king of Alasia apologises abjectly for his failure to send a delegation to an Egyptian festival—he did not know it was to be celebrated.[28] None of these conventions, we may suppose, was a matter for formal, legal agreement; rather they were simply accepted norms of international diplomatic courtesy.

But there is also evidence of widespread agreement that certain acts of a more serious kind were unacceptable and deserving of censure and/or punishment. In some cases one can hardly imagine a civilised society that would not regard them so: for example, the assassination of rulers,[29] the plundering of innocent towns,[30] and wholesale massacre.[31] There are other offences which peoples of the ancient Near East thought of as extremely grave, hedging them about with dire curses, and which the modern world regards with rather less severity: such as the infringement of boundary-rights[32]—though this may include the infringement of national sovereignty—and disturbing the dead. This second crime is a commonplace. There are numerous examples in the texts collected by Donner and Röllig:

> Sarkophag, welchen (?)TB‘L, Sohn des ʾḤRM, König von Byblos, für ʾḤRM, seinen Vater, anfertigte, als er ihn in der Ewigkeit wiederlegte. *Wenn aber*(?) ein König unter den Königen oder ein Statthalter unter den Statthaltern oder der Befehlshaber eines Lagers gegen Byblos heraufgezogen ist und diesen Sarkophag aufdeckt, dann soll der Stab seiner Herrschaft entblättert werden, soll sein Königsthron umgestürzt werden und der Friede soll weichen von Byblos. (Sarcophagus which (?)TB‘L son of ʾḤRM, king of Byblos, made for his father ʾḤRM when he laid him down for eternity. *But if*(?) any king among kings or any ruler among rulers or the commander of any area rises up against Byblos and uncovers this sarcophagus, then the staff of his lordship shall be defoliated, his royal throne overturned, and peace shall depart from Byblos.) (c. 1000 B.C.)[33]

This sort of attitude one may suppose to lie behind Amos 2:1–3. In the same category belongs cannibalism: how heinous a crime it was held to be may be seen from its use as an ultimate curse in Esarhaddon's vassal treaties; thus

As the dismembered flesh of her young is put into the mouth of the ewe, just so may they make you eat the flesh of your women, your brothers, your sons and your daughters.[34]

Before we pass on to consider unilaterally held views on international conduct, we may mention a couple of other issues which appear to be taken as matters of universal agreement, though one cannot be quite sure. A recurring complaint in the Amarna letters is that the Egyptian official's children have been handed over to the enemy, possibly as hostages, or else as slaves, by way of tribute—thus, for example,

Dahin sind unsere Söhne (und unsere) Töchter neb(s)t uns selbst, indem sie gegeben worden sind in Iaraimuta für die Ret(tu)ng unseres Lebens. (Our sons [and our] daughters have departed wi[th] ourselves, having been given in Iaraimuta for the salvati[on] of our lives.)[35]

Rib-addi's point may be simply to show the extremity of need to which the Egyptian community has been reduced, and so to summon Pharaoh's aid; but it is at least possible that he is protesting about what is felt to be a cruel and illicit way of concluding a truce. We would then be reminded of 1 Sam. 11:2, where the Ammonites offer peace to the men of Jabesh-gilead on the condition that every man's right eye is put out: a condition felt to be so harsh as to contravene the laws of civilized conduct, and consequently to be answered by an immediate declaration of war. It is, we note, the Ammonites who are again seen practicing atrocities against Gilead in Amos 1:13–15, where they are accused of ripping open pregnant women. Here we seem definitely to be moving into the sphere of war crimes felt to be such only by particular nations: our third subdivision.

Unilaterally Accepted Norms of International Conduct

The atrocity just mentioned is also referred to with abhorrence in 2 Kgs. 8:12 and 15:16, and Hosea 13:16, but outside Israel it seems to be rather a normal and accepted practice. Tiglath-pileser I (c.1100) is praised because 'he hacked to pieces the women with child, and pierced the bodies of the weak',[36] and in the *Iliad* Agamemnon persuades Menelaus to harden his heart against the Trojans with these words:[37]

. . . tōn mē tis hupekphugoi aipun olethron
cheiras th' hēmeteras, mēd' hon tina gasteri mētēr
kouron eonta pheroi, mēd' hos phugoi, all' hama pantes
Iliou exapoloiat' akēdestoi kai aphantoi.

This is not to say, of course, that such an outrage was not felt to be very terrible—indeed it obviously serves as a paradigm of the worst destruction possible—but only that it was apparently an accepted feature of ancient warfare, and not forbidden by any 'rules of war', at least in the two instances we have cited. Evidently it was not accepted in Israel, though the law nowhere forbids it; it may also have been rejected by some other nations.

This brings us to a consideration of the rules of war, and here we shall do well not to assume any international agreement. So far as I know there is no evidence to suggest that any formal methods of declaring or waging war were literally agreed among the nations of the ancient Near East, and though no doubt there were some conventions governing the smaller details of battles, we have no reason to think of complicated rules of chivalry such as existed in medieval warfare; still less of anything approximating to the Geneva Convention. What does appear, however, is that each nation had its own ideas of what practices it might legitimately indulge in itself and what it might regard as legitimate in an enemy.

As we have seen, the treatment of pregnant women during an invasion was viewed differently by the Israelites and the Assyrians.[38] Prisoners of war also present a problem which each nation solves in its own way. Second Kings 6:22 suggests that Israel had some definite rules regarding the treatment to be meted out to such prisoners, though what the rules are is uncertain because of exegetical difficulties. Following the MT, one must probably conclude that 'captured by sword and bow' is a technical term, distinguishing those taken in battle from those who surrender voluntarily, in which case Elisha is appealing to a rule that prisoners of war who surrender are not to be executed and arguing that a fortiori those taken by force should be allowed to live.[39] But this argument is an oddity—it would be more convincing if reversed—and in any case these prisoners have been taken by trickery, not in any sense 'by sword and bow'. Perhaps, therefore, we should read $l\bar{o}$' with the LXX[40] and take Elisha to mean that prisoners who have not been taken in a fair fight ought not to be executed since they have not had a chance to defend themselves.[41] This suggests that it was otherwise regular to kill prisoners of war out of hand, which would accord with the religious practice of the ban. There is evidence, however, that, in practice, mercy might be shown to conquered enemies—cf. 1 Kgs. 20:3ff., where indeed verse 31 suggests that Israel was known (perhaps in contrast to Assyria) for her humane record in this respect. For other evidence for the rule of war in Israel see Deut. 20:10–20; cf. Josh. 10:24 and Isa. 51:23 for customs of asserting conquest.

Among the Hittites, too, there is definite evidence of the existence of a code regulating the conduct of war.[42] Hittite rulers, it appears, were no more willing than modern leaders to acknowledge self-aggrandisement and territorial expansion as motives for undertaking war; aggression was theoretically illicit (the contrast with Assyria is striking). Any nation that was to be attacked must therefore be 'convicted' by a judicial process, conducted through diplomatic channels, of some offence against Hatti, and war might then ensue as a divine sentence of execution. The rules for the treatment of prisoners and captured cities are reminiscent of those we have supposed to lie behind 2 Kgs. 6:22. A town that holds out against a siege must be plundered and burnt down, though the inhabitants must be removed alive and resettled; but in the case of surrender, the conquering general is empowered to allow inhabitants to remain after the town has been plundered, annexing them to the Hittite empire and imposing a vassal treaty. In neither case, apparently, might a wholesale massacre of the population be ordered. In the context of ancient Near Eastern warfare, such rules, like the Hittite laws, suggest that humanitarian considerations weighed more heavily with the Hittites than with most of their neighbours.[43] At all events, the Hittite rules of war are a clear example of a unilateral code of international conduct; probably they did not expect other states to observe them, and if they did, they must have been sadly disappointed.

Conclusion

We have now examined some of the evidence for conventions referring to international relations in peace and war, and we have found, I believe, enough material to justify our conclusion that Amos refers to some such conventions rather than, say, to divine covenant law when condemning the nations for their sin. Perhaps in the light of our threefold classification of the material from ancient Near Eastern sources (though the dividing lines remain somewhat uncertain and fluid), we might briefly attempt a more exact definition of these conventions. We argued that there is not enough evidence to justify the view that Amos is appealing to actual international agreements rather than to principles of conduct which he believes all nations *ought* to accept—though he may be. We have also seen that some of the material from non-Israelite sources is similarly ambiguous although there are clearly some rules, especially those relating to the conduct of war, where the nations acknowledged different norms even though each individual state supposed that its own norms had or ought to have a universal validity. In the case of Ammon, we have explicit evidence to suggest that the Ammonites did not recognise any such moral obligations in war as Amos clearly believed they should. In terms of our three classifications, then, we may remain uncertain about whether to assign Amos 1:3–2:3 to the second or third class, but with some inclination towards the latter.

It appears, however, that the Tyre and Edom oracles, whose authenticity we have already seen other grounds for doubting, really belong to the first classification, for as the studies of Priest and Fishbane have demonstrated, what is here envisaged is the breaking of a treaty rather than an infringement of the rules designed to prevent atrocities. Tyre and Edom have failed to remember obligations to which they are contractually committed—obligations of respect for national sovereignty and nonaggression; the other nations have committed war crimes which have nothing to do with the political or diplomatic relationship in which they stand towards their victims. One cannot claim that Amos could not have mixed the two kinds of accusation in one set of oracles—the division is made mainly for our own convenience though it does recognise a genuine logical difference—yet perhaps we may allow the distinction to count towards the cumulative argument for excising 1:9–12. With this passage removed, the oracles against the nations present a more coherent picture.

One final note: the connection of the international conventions we have discussed with God or the gods appears in general to be very slight, at least so far as explicit references are concerned. Usually the appeal is simply to the accepted way of doing things (this particularly in issues relating to diplomatic practice) or to some kind of moral sense of what is fitting. Only in treaties regulating international affairs is there special reference to the gods, who act as witnesses to the signing of the treaty and who will, it is hoped, intervene to punish the partner who breaks his promise to keep its terms. They are the guarantors of treaty obligation, not its source. We have already said that the relationship of Yahweh to the sins of the nations in Amos appears to be that of avenger of guilt rather than explicitly the source of the moral norms they have infringed: not lawgiver so much as judge. From such ancient Near Eastern evidence as we have been able to survey, this is just what we should expect.

Additional Note: The Hittite rules of war

Most of the evidence for rules of war among the Hittites is to be found in the Annals of Muršiliš.[44] A typical formal declaration of war is as follows:

> Zu Uḫḫa-LÚ-is aber sandte ich meinen Boten und schrieb ihm: 'Meine Untertanen, die zu dir kamen, als ich sie von dir zurückforderte, hast du sie mir nicht zurückgegeben. Und du hast mich ein Kind gescholten, und mich missachtet. Nun auf denn! Wir werden miteinander kämpfen! Und der Wettergott, mein Herr, soll unseren Rechtsstreit entscheiden' (To Uḫḫa-LÚ-is I sent my envoy, and wrote to him, 'You have not returned to me my subjects who came to you when I demanded them back from you. And you called me a child, and dishonoured me. So then, let us fight each other! And the weather-god, my lord, shall decide the outcome of our battle.')[45]

The burning of a town that resists, and the deportation of at least part of the population,[46] is several times recorded.[47] The mercy of the Hittite kings, however, is also frequently attested. They report instances of it with obvious pride, in sharp contrast to the gloating reports of massacre and sophisticated torture familiar from Assyrian sources. Thus Muršiliš relates how he sent an ultimatum to rebellious vassals threatening total devastation, but

> . . . wie die Leute von Kammamma und die Leu(te von . . . solches) hörten, erschraken (sie und) töteten (den Pazzanas und den Nunnutas). Die Leute von Kammamma aber und die L(eute von . . .) wurden mir (zum zweiten Male wieder) untertan (. . . when the people of Kammamma and the peo(ple of . . . heard) such a thing, they were terrified (and they) killed (Pazzanas and Nunnutas). But the people of Kammamma and the p(eople of . . .) became subject to me (for the second time).)[48]

A little further on Muršiliš tells how the inhabitants of a besieged city, worn down by hunger and thirst, came and pleaded with him, and how he transported some of the population but, as a reward for their submission, killed none of them;[49] while in another place he reports an act of mercy which any Assyrian king would have derided:

> . . . Aber sowie über mich (Manapa-Dattaš hö(rte): 'Der König des Hatti-Landes kommt', (fürchte)te er sich, und er (kam) mir infolgedessen nicht entgegen (und) sandte mir seine Mutter, Greise under Greisinnen (entgegen), und sie kamen (und) (fielen) mir zu Füssen. Und weil mir die Frauen zu Füssen fielen, willfahrte ich (den Frauen) zuliebe und zog darauf (nicht) nach dem Šehafluss(-land) (But when (Manapa-Dattaš hear)d it said of me, 'The king of the Hatti-land is coming', he (was afraid), and consequently he did not (come) against me (and) he sent me his mother and old men and women, and they came (and) (fell) at my feet. And because the women fell at my feet, I acceded to (the women's) requests and consequently (did not) travel to the (land) of the river Šeha).[50]

Finally we may note Muršiliš's boast that, in taking the land of Hurna, he was careful not to disturb the sanctuary of the storm god but allowed all its officials and votaries to continue as before; and the whole land was left in peace, under a light tribute.[51]

Commentaries on Amos since 1980

Andersen, F. I., and D. N. Freedman. *Amos*. AB 24a. New York: Doubleday, 1989.
Auld, A. G. *Amos*. OTG. Sheffield: JSOT Press, 1986.
Gowan, D. E. 'The Book of Amos'. In *NIB* 7. Nashville: Abingdon, 1996, 337–431.
Jeremias, J. *The Book of Amos*. OTL. Louisville, Ky.: Westminster John Knox, 1998.
King, P. J. *Amos, Hosea, Micah: An Archaeological Commentary*. Philadelphia: Fortress, 1986.
Paul, S. M. *The Prophet Amos*. Hermeneia. Minneapolis: Fortress, 1991.
Soggin, J. A. *The Prophet Amos: A Translation and Commentary*. London: SCM, 1987.
Stuart, D. *Amos*. In *Hosea-Jonah*. WBC 31. Waco: Word Books, 1987, 274–400.

Sweeney, M. A. *The Twelve Prophets*. Vol. 1. Berit Olam. Collegeville, Md.: Liturgical Press, 2000, 191–276.

Works on Amos's Oracles against the Nations since 1980

Čeresko, A. R. 'Janus Parallelism in Amos's Oracles against the Nations (Amos 1:3–2:16)'. *JBL* 113 (1994): 485–90.

Dietrich, W. 'JHWH, Israel und die Völker beim Propheten Amos'. *TZ* 48 (1992): 315–28.

Fritz, V. 'Die Fremdvölkersprüche des Amos'. *VT* 37 (1987): 26–38.

Geyer, J. B. 'Mythology and Culture in the Oracles against the Nations'. *VT* 36 (1986): 129–45.

Gosse, B. 'Le receuil d'oracles contre les nations du livre d'Amos et l'histoire deutéronomique'. *VT* 38 (1988): 22–40.

Jeremias, J. 'Völkersprüche und Visionsberichte im Amosbuch'. In *Hosea und Amos: Studien zu den Anfängen des Dodekapropheton*. FAT 13. Tübingen: 1996, 157–171.

———. 'Zur Entstehung der Völkersprüche im Amosbuch'. In *Hosea und Amos*, 172–82.

Melugin, R. F. 'Amos in Recent Research'. *Currents in Research: Biblical Studies* 6 (1998): 65–101.

Paul, S. M. 'A Literary Reinvestigation of the Oracles against the Nations of Amos'. In *De la Tôrah au Messie: Études d'exégèse et d'herméneutique bibliques offertes à Henri Cazelles*. Ed. J. Doré, P. Grelot, and M. Carrez. Paris: 1981, 189–204.

Pfeifer, G. 'Die Fremdvölkersprüche des Amos—spätere Vaticinia ex Eventu?'. *VT* 38 (1988): 230–33.

———. 'Jahwe als Schöpfer der Welt und Herr ihrer Mächte in der Verkündigung des Propheten Amos'. *VT* 41 (1991): 475–81.

Rottzoll, U. *Studien zur Redaktion und Komposition des Amosbuches*. BZAW 243. Berlin: 1996.

Works on the Bible and Human Rights

Bederman, D. J. *International Law in Antiquity*. Cambridge Studies in International and Comparative Law. Cambridge: 2001, esp. chap. 3, 'Religion and the Sources of a Law of Nations in Antiquity'.

Liwak, R. 'Menschenwürde und Menschenrechte: Anmerkungen zu alttestamentlichen Perspektiven'. In *Altes Testament: Forschung und Wirkung (FS. H. Graf Reventlow)*. Ed. P. Mommer and W. Thiel. Frankfurt a.M.: 1994, 139–58.

Otto, E. 'Human Rights: The Influence of the Hebrew Bible'. *JNSL* 25 (1999): 1–20.

Soares-Prabhu, G. M. 'The Bible as Magna Charta of Movements for Liberation and Human Rights'. In *The Bible as Cultural Heritage*. Ed. W. A. M. Beuken and S. Freyne. London: 1995, 85–96.

7

Ethics in Isaiah of Jerusalem

This paper is intended as a modest contribution to the history of ideas. It attempts to show that the natural-law tradition which has played a prominent role in Western moral philosophy and theology has roots not only (as is universally acknowledged) in the classical world but also in the Hebrew tradition as that is preserved in the Old Testament.[1] I shall try to show that the prophet Isaiah, working in Jerusalem in the eighth century B.C., already had a developed understanding of the basis of morality—one which has more affinities with Western theories of natural law than has usually been thought and less in common with the notion of moral imperatives as 'revealed' or positive law, given by God as the terms of a 'covenant' or contract with the people of Israel, than is supposed by many Old Testament specialists.[2]

It cannot be said that the subject I intend to deal with is central to Isaiah's concerns, and it is not my purpose to suggest that it ought to be included in any statement of his 'message'. First, he is plainly more interested in the particular moral offences that he finds to condemn in his contemporaries than in abstract questions of moral philosophy, even though, as I shall hope to show, these particular denunciations reveal a cast of mind that assumes something like natural law as its starting point. He is certainly not trying to convince his hearers that morality is a matter of natural law but that their actions are evil and will bring down the wrath of God. My concern is therefore with something taken for granted rather than with something that is being positively asserted or put forward for acceptance, and this of course makes the inquiry speculative. Indeed, it would be open to a critic to suggest that the questions I shall be asking simply do not admit of any answers since there is not the evidence on which to decide them. But, second, Isaiah has many other concerns besides morality in any case: in particular, an intense interest in what the immediate (perhaps also the remote) future holds for his nation. This interest has rightly been of concern to most commentators even since the rise of critical Old Testament scholarship rescued the moral teaching of the prophets from the obscurity into which it had been thrown by the traditional Christian con- centration on their role in predicting (as was thought) the coming of Christ. Despite this shift in emphasis, it is neither surprising nor regrettable that inter- est in the predictive side of Isaiah's teaching continues unabated and that most commentators have little to say on the question of the basis of the prophet's moral teaching. Nevertheless, I hope that the topic, though far from being the most important one in the study of Isaiah, is an interesting one in itself, and that it appears sufficiently important in the general context of Old Testament studies as well as for the history of ethics to justify a short study.

A study of Isaiah's ethical system is at least spared one of the greatest incon- veniences of Isaiah scholarship: on the whole the authenticity of the passages in Isaiah 1–39 which deal with questions of morality is not disputed. The fol- lowing list, which contains all the passages I shall be dealing with, should make this clear: a glance at any standard commentary will show that few of them are highly controversial from a literary-critical point of view, though in some cases there is no agreement about the period of the prophet's ministry to which they belong. The passages in question are 1:2–3, 10–17, 21–23, 29–30; 2:6–22; 3:1–12, 13–15, 16; 4:1; 5:8–23; 7:3–9; 8:5–8, 19; 9:8–21; 10:1–4, 5–19, 33–34; 17:7–11; 18:1–6; 19:11–15; 20:1–6; 22:8b–14, 15–19; 28:1–2; 29:11–12, 15–16, 20–21; 30:1–7, 15–17; 31:1–3, 6–7; 32:9–14.

I

Before setting out my own understanding of Isaiah's approach to ethics, which I shall present as a continuous whole without detailed discussions of the many exegetical cruces on whose resolution it depends, let me briefly indicate the comparative novelty of the questions I am trying to ask. Broadly speaking, studies of prophetic ethics have concentrated on two types of question. First, there have been studies of the actual moral conduct deprecated or enjoined by the prophets and attempts to set it in its social and historical context.[3] Thanks to studies of this kind, we now know far more than we did about the political and social climate of eighth-century Israel and Judah, about the standards of public and administrative life, and about the lot of those oppressed members of Israelite society whom the prophets championed. Second, there has in recent years been a great interest in the *sources* of prophetic morality. We have seen a slow but steady backpedalling from older views that seemed to make the prophets almost the discoverers of morality, and instead they have increasingly appeared primarily (at least until very recently) as links in a chain of tradition, handing on standards of morality long accepted as authoritative within the circles in which they themselves moved, and seeking to recall the people at large, who had lost touch with the roots of their own traditional culture, to a renewed allegiance to these uncompromising moral values. There has been conspicuously less agreement on where the sources of prophetic morality should correctly be located. Some see the prophets as appealing to values drawn from the legal and covenantal traditions,[4] with perhaps some mediation through the cult;[5] others regard the traditions of 'wisdom', in either its international or 'folk' versions, as a more likely source.[6] It seems to me that a good case can be made on both sides.

So far as Isaiah is concerned, if we leave aside 'extrinsic' arguments, such as that he was a scribe and therefore prima facie more likely to be familiar with wisdom than the 'covenant morality', and concentrate on the internal evidence of his moral teaching, we can easily find material to suggest that he appealed to the law in something like the form it has in the Book of the Covenant (Exod. 21–23): for example, his condemnations of murder (1:21), theft (1:21), oppression of widows and orphans (1:17b, 21–23; 3:14), bribery and corruption in the courts (1:23; 3:9a; 5:23; 10:1–2), perhaps also dispossession of the poor, in the interests of enclosure (5:8–10).[7] On the other hand, there is no shortage of features that seem to confirm the prophet's indebtedness to the wisdom schools. Negatively, it may be argued that his condemnations of the pride of the Assyrians (10:5–15) cannot derive from any tradition of morality which is concerned purely with the moral imperatives binding on Israelites alone, such as the law, and hence must come from that interest in humanity as such which is generally held to characterize international wisdom.[8] Positively, it may be noted that both here and in other places Isaiah is concerned with actions or attitudes which either were not mentioned in the law (e.g., excessive luxury, 3:16; 4:1; drunkenness, 5:11–17, 22; 28:1–14) or could not be in the nature of the case (e.g., pride, 5:22; cynicism about moral values, 5:20; failure to trust in God, 22:8–14), but which do find an echo in many texts from the wisdom tradition. This case is argued by Whedbee[9] and seems to me quite persuasive. It is possible that an attempt to do justice to both sides of the prophet's moral teaching might help us avoid oversimplifying the means by which ethical norms and attitudes were transmitted in ancient Israel and, incidentally, provide us with a little more information about the social and institutional background of the independent prophets, which in spite of much study remains relatively ill-defined and shadowy.[10]

It is not, however, my purpose to pursue these lines of inquiry any further. My concern is not the content, nor the social setting, nor the source, of Isaiah's moral demands and strictures, but their basis: what he took or assumed to underlie the particular norms whose transgression he condemned, what he thought was so sinful about sins. It would certainly be presumptuous to claim that no one has asked this question before. Von Rad, in particular, often touches on it,[11] and there are many pages on the prophets in general in Hempel's classic work on Old Testament ethics[12] and in the 'ethics' section of Eichrodt's *Theology*,[13] and on the basis of Isaiah's ethics in particular in Wild-berger's commentary.[14] Nevertheless, I do not know of any systematic treatment of the matter; rather, it is generally broached piecemeal in connection with specific texts. Thus it seems best to state my own thesis in a straightforward way, at the risk of appearing somewhat assertive, rather than working patiently through each relevant text with a survey of the history of scholarly opinion and then systematizing the results. Let me begin with a statement of the data to be accounted for and then present one interpretation of them which seems to me to do them the most justice.

II

If one combs the prophetic books for information about the prophets' moral values, one soon notices that any simple list of sins condemned or courses of action commended blurs a number of significant distinctions. For example, one might say that Jeremiah condemns his contemporaries for oppression of the poor, failure to submit to the Babylonians, rejection of Yahweh's will, blindness to moral values, adultery, inability to read the signs of the times, and ill treatment of slaves. But this would plainly be an unsatisfactory classification of what Jeremiah has to say about the conduct of his hearers. One of these accusations, that of rejecting God's will, may be taken implicitly to include, or to function as a summary of, most of the others. Another—blindness to moral values—refers to attitudes of mind taken to cause or condition the specific sins being castigated; and failure to submit to the Babylonians is a particular error in political policy, taken by Jeremiah to flow from a general moral and religious decline in the nation, but not a sin such as could be included in a catalogue of ethical norms (say, the Decalogue) which was meant to be valid for life in society in many different periods. Obviously, the 'sins' in our list are incommensurable and resist arrangement in such a simple, linear form. Now, of all the prophets, Isaiah presents the most complex case of this mixing of levels and categories in his comments on the behaviour and attitudes of those he criticizes, and it is abundantly clear that no list-like statement of his ethical concerns will do them justice. It seems to me that one can distinguish at least three different categories in Isaiah's comments on morality, though there is inevitably material whose correct classification must remain uncertain.[15]

First, Isaiah condemns a number of specific crimes, sins, and culpable errors in those he attacks, who seem to be chiefly the rulers of Judah as a whole, though he once singles out a specific member of the administration, Shebna (22:15–19), and also has oracles against the Assyrians (10:5–15) and against the wise men of Pharaoh (19:11–14) which many commentators regard as authentic. There are about a dozen types of sinful activity that can be readily distinguished, as follows. In the sphere of social relations are (1) oppressive treatment of widows and orphans (1:17, 21–23; 3:14); (2) theft (1:21); (3) murder (1:21); (4) perversion of the course of justice, especially by the acceptance of bribes (1:23; 3:9; 5:23; 10:1–2; 29:21); (5) expropriation of land belonging to the poor (5:8–10); (6) drunkenness (5:11–17, 22; 28:1–14); and (7) excessive luxury and personal adornment, and the accumulation of wealth and status (3:16; 4:1; 9:9–12; 22:15–19; 32:9–14). In the political sphere are (8) making preparations for national defence (7:3–9; 22:8–14; 28:14–18); (9) entering into foreign alliances (8:5–8; 18:4–5; 20:1–6; 30:1–5; 31:1–3); and (10) boasting of military conquests (10:5–15, against the Assyrians). In the religious sphere are (11) idolatry or cultic apostasy (1:29–30; 2:6–22; 8:19; 17:4–11; 31:6–7); and (12) the use of the sacrificial cultus (1:11–15).[16] In addition, there are passages which speak of people who (13) mock God (5:18–19) or (14) are sceptical of his power to act and to direct the course of events (5:20–21; 22:12–14), which may perhaps refer to specific and overt refusals to take into account God's power, probably by pouring scorn on the message of the prophet himself (cf. also 28:9–10). But with these passages we are already moving into the next major category.

Second, then, are passages where Isaiah denounces attitudes and states of mind which are in themselves culpable but the chief evidence for which is precisely those specific sins which have just been listed. (1) The first of these, which can be seen in the mockery of God and of his prophet, is the pride or arrogance of 'those who are wise in their own eyes' (5:21) or who attribute their successes to their own power (10:5–15). (2) Closely related to this is delight in prestige and self-aggrandizement: the sin of Shebna, 'hewing himself out a tomb on high' (22:15–19), of the women of Jerusalem (3:16; 4:1), and of the inhabitants of Samaria 'who say in pride and arrogance of heart, "The bricks have fallen, but we will build with dressed stones"' (9:9–10). Some commentators hold, indeed, that pride of this kind is the fundamental sin in Isaiah. Thus Eichrodt writes, '[For Isaiah,] the central sin of man lay in the overweening pride with which he set himself up against God. . . . Luther's dictum 'omne peccatum est superbia', all sin is pride, exactly sums up Isaiah's conviction.'[17] And clearly this is at least part of the truth. (3) Third, Isaiah identifies a failure or unwillingness to trust God alone as lying at the root of much that is wrong with the religious and political life of Judah; thus classically in 31:3 (against the Egyptian alliance) and also in 8:19 (on those who consult mediums). (4) Fourth, he speaks of the contempt felt by the nation's rulers towards legitimate claims on them: contempt for the rights of the needy and those with no legal status, which were a commonplace of the moral tradition of the ancient Near East, and also contempt for the just claim of God to exact obedience as Israel's father and owner (1:2–3). (5) And, finally, in a number of places Isaiah speaks of folly or stupidity as the motive force behind human sin. This emerges clearly from the unfavourable comparison instituted in 1:3 between Israel and domestic animals; in Robert Lowth's words this verse is 'an amplification of the gross insensibility of the disobedient Jews, by comparing them with the most heavy and stupid of all animals, yet not so insensible as they'.[18] And it may also be seen in the oracle on the wise men of Pharaoh (19:11–14), who are fools because they cannot perceive God's plans; how much more those Israelites who stupidly rely on them!

So much for denunciations of the attitudes that lie behind particular sins, which represent a second stratum in Isaiah's moral universe. A third category may be described as attempts to encapsulate, either by explicit formulation or (more commonly) by metaphors and analogies, what is the essence of both sinful actions and wrong attitudes: passages which therefore give us some hints of what Isaiah saw as the basis or essence of morality or of sin. Such attempts are naturally of a high order of generality, and it is to them—to what might be called third-order moral statements—that we need to look in trying to find organizing principles for ethics in Isaiah. There are five passages that seem to me to belong in this category: 2:6–22; 3:1–12; 5:8–10; 5:20; and 29:15–16. Let us examine the first of them in some detail, and then make some more summary comments on the others.

I have already mentioned that Isa. 2:6–22 suggests to some commentators that human pride is being presented as the root of all sin: thus Eichrodt, in the passage already quoted, and Budde, in an article published in 1931:

> Pride and self-assertion, lack of humility before the exalted God, this is for Isaiah the cardinal sin of the creature, and it contains all other sin within itself. Hence his address begins with the highest thing to be found on earth, the forests which still crowned the mountains, and then passes to the mountains themselves, then to the proud works of man, and last to man himself.[19]

I have treated the pride which is undoubtedly the chief theme of these verses rather as an attitude producing sin than as what, in the last analysis, sin is. It seems to me that the extraordinary suggestion that God will 'punish' all the things in the natural world that are too high belongs to a rather subtle world of thought in which it is not merely asserted that pride is sinful, indeed the root of all other sins, but in which there is also some theory as to *why* it is sinful, *why* the created order should bow in humility before God. The reason is not simply that God occupies de facto the highest place in the world order but that he does so de jure. This universe forms an ordered whole in which each creature should know its place; and God's place, if we may speak so, is to be supreme. This world order is thus theological in the sense that God both has a place in it and also is the active force that keeps it in being, but it is not based on the idea of a potentially arbitrary divine lordship. I would suggest that the strictures on the mountains and trees in 13–15 are hard to account for by saying simply that pride is the root sin, if by that is meant self-assertion against God or the gods. Their haughtiness is rebuked (of course mainly metaphorically, but still it must be seen as in some remote sense 'sinful' for the analogy to work) because they step outside their proper place, that is, the place in which they most appropriately belong, by aspiring to scale the heavens.

If this admittedly nice distinction between humility and subordination, on the one hand, and acceptance of one's rightful place in the world, on the other, is accepted, it may be possible to fit in the references to the worship of idols in this passage (vv. 8, 20) without distorting the picture. With pride as the root sin, idolatry must be seen as some kind of self-assertion; and this is odd, since it seems on the face of it to involve precisely the opposite—reliance on things other than oneself even to the absurd extent (on the prophetic understanding of the use of images) of trusting in blocks of wood. If the chapter is simply a denunciation of human pride, the allusions to idols are out of place, and it is not surprising that they are sometimes excised or explained away by rather strained exegesis.[20] But if we take both pride and idolatry as examples of the effect of failing to observe order in the world, the passage forms a unified whole. We might sum up the logical structure of the whole oracle according to this interpretation as follows. When people ignore the universal moral order, they become foolish and lose both moral and practical insight. This produces two consequences in their ethical life. On the one hand, they come to overestimate their own importance, failing to keep to their appointed place in the world; and this pride leads to a delight in prestige and the accumulation of riches and status symbols. On the other hand, they fail to see where their trust and confidence should properly be placed and rely on sources of strength other than God—for example, on false foreign gods or on images of God, which they worship with blind idolatry.

With this example in mind, we may turn to examine the other passages more briefly. Isaiah 3:1–2 apparently sees both the social decay of eighth-century Judah and Yahweh's probable punishment of it as consisting in what we should call anarchy. Reversals of the proper order of society—rule by women and minors (v. 12) —is punished in the same coin (v. 4) by an enforced breakdown of all natural social relationships; the usurpation of power by the unworthy leads, paradoxically, to a time when men will refuse to accept power even when others try to force it on them. This is a 'poetic justice' text such as I have discussed elsewhere.[21] It seems to me to imply an ethical system which sets a high value on the received orders of society and sees the processes of history themselves, under God's hand, as operating according to similar orders and taking their vengeance on those who infringe them. Much the same may be said of 5:8–10, where those who build great houses by expropriating land— thus contravening the old-established orders of Israelite society—will find that the defeat of their country in war leaves their houses desolate; and those who join the fields of others into large farms will be left with so little yield that their efforts will have been wasted. (Compare 10:1–4 for a similar reversal.) Finally, 5:20 and 29:15–16 are more straightforward statements of principle. Verse 5:20 presents sin as a challenge to the natural and true order of things: 'Woe to those who call evil good and good evil, who put darkness for light and light for darkness, who put bitter for sweet and sweet for bitter!' And 29:15–16 presents us with a rhetorical question in which is made explicit what is sinful about the action of those who 'hide deep from the LORD their counsel, and whose deeds are in the dark', viz. that it involves treating the Creator as if he were a creature less perceptive even than oneself: 'Shall the potter be counted as the clay, that the thing made should say of its maker, "He did not make me"; or the thing formed say of him who formed it, "He has no understanding?"' The elliptical *hopkĕkem* at the beginning of this verse is translated with some freedom by the RSV 'You turn things upside down'; whether this is justified or not, some such interpretation of the whole oracle seems legitimate.

So much, then, for the different types of material that deals with ethical issues in Isaiah's oracles. It seems clear that any adequate analysis of this material must allow not only for the variety of actual moral norms involved but also for the distinction between first-, second-, and third-order assertions about morality, as I have tried to present them. Ethics in Isaiah cannot be adequately described by simply drawing up a list. This, no doubt, is one reason why the quest for the *sources* of his moral teaching has proved somewhat inconclusive: it has necessarily had to work with catalogues of sins condemned and has found it hard to allow for higher-order statements of moral principle or attitude. It may, of course, not be wholly safe to assume that Isaiah's ethical teaching does, in fact, form an ordered whole—it might be that his occasional suggestions about the basis of morality were merely stray thoughts which have no real bearing on the practical questions of actual sin and transgression with which he had to deal; but to accept this is something of a counsel of despair, and I should like at least to attempt a description of an ethical system that would display an inner coherence and account for all the data so far discussed. I do not claim that we can know Isaiah held it, but only that his extant oracles make more coherent sense if he did.

III

Isaiah, then, begins with a picture of the world in which God is the creator and preserver of all things and occupies by right the supreme position over all that he has made. The essence of morality is cooperation in maintaining the ordered structure which prevails, under God's guidance, in the natural constitution of things, and the keynote of the whole system is order, a proper submission to one's assigned place in the scheme of things and the avoidance of any action that would challenge the supremacy of God or seek to subvert the orders he has established. Such is the basic premise from which all Isaiah's thinking about ethical obligation begins.

Sin takes its rise, therefore, in disregard for the order and in a deliberate refusal to see the world in its true colours. The first and most obvious manifestation of this may be described as folly, ignorance, or perversity: a perversity which humans alone seem capable of, for while the natural and animal worlds seem to observe order by instinct, human beings, in this respect more degraded than their own domestic animals, go against the principles of their own nature. This moral blindness is culpable in itself because it refuses to God the respect that is God's due, and prefers the purposes of mere mortals to those of their creator; and it is also the root of other evil attitudes, which in their turn produce the specific sinful acts which distort human life. Folly produces a disregard for the orders in society which should mirror God's ordering of the universe, and anarchy ensues, an anarchy in which those with power no longer feel any respect for the claims of others—especially of those who themselves have no power or legal means to assert their claims—nor for those positive laws which God has given to ensure that right prevails.[22]

The practical effects of this dual failure in respect (for other people and for the law that protects them) are the crimes against social order which were listed above: theft, murder, bribery and corruption, oppression of orphans and widows, enclosure of land. Folly, since it means blindness to the proper orders of the world, also naturally produces pride and arrogance, a 'presumptuous neglection of degree', which affects everyone, Israelites and foreigners, high and low alike. One of its cruder manifestations is the boastfulness that goes with too much drink: drunkenness, indeed, is not only a typical mark of the fool but can also serve as a paradigm of the befuddled mind that lies at the root of so many other sins. But cynicism about moral values and mockery of God and God's prophets also flow from pride; so does that delight in prestige and status which are seen in the parvenu Shebna, with his elaborate tomb, and in the enjoyment of trivial self-adornment in the midst of a city threatened with famine and pillage that characterizes the women of Jerusalem. And at the other end of the scale, the boasting of the king of Assyria amounts to nothing more:

he, too, is a fool, deluded by his own success into thinking he can vie with God, instead of recognizing that he is no more than a tool in God's hand. Symbol of all these examples of overweening pride are the high mountains and tall cedars of Isaiah 2, which will be humbled on the day of Yahweh.

Folly also leads to a false estimate of where true security lies for humankind. In the true order of reality, its only hope of safety lies in giving God God's proper place; but human blindness and perversity seek protection in things that are not God. In the religious sphere, this produces idolatry, which for all its appearances of entailing submission to divine powers (even if false ones, as prophets like Elijah and Hosea had emphasized) is more correctly seen as a form of self-worship and reliance on the work of one's own hands. It also produces a false confidence in the paraphernalia of cultic worship, which, though apparently 'Yahwistic', is, in fact, equally self-centred, as Amos had already suggested. The word 'apostasy' would be a somewhat misleading one to describe either kind of cultic offence: the trouble with the sort of worship that is practised in a society blinded to reality is not that it involves disloyalty to God so much as that it simply ignores God, even while claiming to do God honour. It thus degenerates into a form of self-worship.

Very similar consequences follow in the political sphere. It is not that treaties with foreign powers entail religious syncretism but that they imply a reliance on what is ultimately unreliable (the Egyptians are humans, not God). A society which brings about its own downfall by its internal neglect of order and justice and its pursuit of self-interest, and then seeks to protect itself by inventing religious rites that happen to suit its own taste and relying for aid on other merely human states which are in a condition of mental and moral confusion just as bad as its own, is simply walking in its sleep and has lost its hold on reality. God can no longer get through to such a people, whose condition can best be summed up in two of Isaiah's most vivid images: the drunkard of chapter 28, staggering in his own vomit, to whom the more plainly one speaks, the more one's warnings will be dismissed as childish babblings; and the Kafkaesque sealed book of chapter 29, which the learned cannot read because it is sealed, and the unlearned cannot read because they cannot read at all. The intolerable sense of frustration that such perversity produces in the prophet will reach its climax in Jeremiah, who (it has been suggested) seems almost to welcome the exile, however harsh, as a return to reality after two long centuries of delirium.

If this analysis of Isaiah's ethical teaching is correct, we have in him an early example of that way of approaching ethics which begins with a hierarchically ordered universe whose moral pattern ought to be apparent to all whose reason is not hopelessly clouded, and one which derives all particular moral offences from the one great sin, a disregard for natural law. Of course, what we have in Isaiah is a theological form of natural law, as were most natural-law theories before the Enlightenment: one might perhaps speak equally well of a theory of 'general revelation'. It is the remote ancestor of one of the classic source texts for such theories, Rom. 1:19–25:

> For what can be known about God is plain to them, because God has shown it to them. Ever since the creation of the world his invisible nature, namely, his eternal power and deity, has been clearly perceived in the things that have been made. So they are without excuse; for although they knew God they did not honor him as God or give thanks to him, but they became futile in their thinking and their senseless minds were darkened. Claiming to be wise, they became fools . . . because they exchanged the truth about God for a lie and worshiped and served the creature rather than the Creator.

IV

There are no doubt many objections that could be made to the thesis presented here, but two at least are so obvious that it seems right to deal with them at once.

1. First, if morality was conceived in terms of what we might describe as 'natural law' by both Isaiah and, as I have hinted, a good many other people in ancient Israel, then it is reasonable to ask why this has apparently left no mark on the Hebrew language. It is widely held that a concept akin to natural law was current in Egypt, but there is a term—ma'at—which in at least some of its uses provided a way of making the concept explicit.[23] H. H. Schmid, who holds that a belief in natural orders of roughly the kind I have been describing was ubiquitous in the ancient world—to such an extent, indeed, that there would be nothing peculiar to Isaiah at all in the ethical approach here ascribed to him—argues that ṣedeq/ṣĕdāqâ and also mišpāṭ function in Hebrew as approximate equivalents for ma'at,[24] but it does not seem that this suggestion has commended itself very widely. At all events, if ṣĕdaqâ can be used in this sense, it can undoubtedly be used in narrower senses, too, and each alleged instance of a 'natural order' use would require detailed demonstration. Isaiah, in fact, uses the word rather little by comparison with Deutero-Isaiah, in whom it is very frequent, and it would be hazardous to rest the present case on it.[25]

A more satisfactory reply to the objection would perhaps be that a lack of terms for abstract ideas like 'order' is characteristic of biblical Hebrew in its extant texts in any case: a point which, of course, very large theological constructions have made in the past but one which needs to be examined carefully before it is regarded as an index of 'Hebrew mentality'. There are no noun forms readily translated 'order' in biblical Hebrew, nor are there terms for 'history', 'revelation', 'event', or 'ethics'. There are also no modal verbs corresponding to 'ought' or 'must'; thus it is hard to see how notions like 'assumption', 'theory', or 'presupposition' could be expressed with the resources of the language known to us. But if this sort of observation tells against the suggestion that Isaiah saw ethics in terms of natural law, it tells equally against a great many other interpretative models in Old Testament ethics and Old Testament theology.[26] In fact, however, the importance of observing the very characteristic lack of abstract terminology in Hebrew is not that it shows any given interpretation of the Israelite worldview to be impossible, but rather that it reminds us of a truth which applies to *all* our interpretations, not just of ancient Israel, but of any culture. This is the entirely general point that we cannot explain the presuppositions of another culture to ourselves without some translation into terms and categories which did not have exact linguistic equivalents in the culture in question. This point is easily overlooked when dealing with cultures nearer at hand and with those whose languages are closer to our own, but it is in reality just as important in such cases as it is when we are handling apparently rather remote societies such as that of ancient Israel. Thus, although it is perfectly true that Isaiah's vocabulary contained no terms corresponding to any of our normal categories for discussing ethics (or indeed theology), this does not in itself mean that we cannot decide which of these categories gives the most adequate impression of his assumptions. To argue against a particular interpretation of this kind on the grounds that it uses terms untranslatable into biblical Hebrew is, in fact, a subtle form of special pleading, since *all* our interpretations of the Old Testament are subject to the same drawback. It is to present a quite general problem in hermeneutics, in social anthropology, and in the history of ideas, as if it were a peculiar and specific objection to this one line of interpretation. This is not to deny that the preference for 'concrete' forms of expression and the lack of 'abstract' terms in Hebrew are interesting and important features. It is clear that they make the task of Old Testament theology a peculiarly difficult and precarious one, in which intuitions about the meaning of texts are often difficult to check or even to assess. Nevertheless, there is no cause for undue alarm; difficulty is not the same as impossibility.

2. There is, however, another possible problem arising from the characteristic mode in which Hebrew prophecy, in particular, is expressed which is less easily disposed of, and this leads to a fundamental objection to the case I have been arguing. One of the great achievements of modern critical study of the prophets has been to stress that their message was always addressed to a concrete historical situation and that they did not enunciate theological systems or lay down general principles. Rather, they spoke rhetorically and with an awareness of the effect their words would be likely to have on their immediate audience. Sometimes, indeed, this led to express ideas which would have been mutually incompatible if they had been intended as parts of a coherent

and timeless system. Furthermore, form-critical studies have insisted that one cannot understand the prophets' message by beginning from its content—as though that could be read off from their words without regard to the forms in which they are couched—but that one must begin from the *Gattungen* into which prophetic speech falls.[27] Form critics, like more recent structuralist critics, are convinced that meaning inheres as much in the form and genre of a communication as in the overt information being communicated. Now, both of these emphases in modern Old Testament scholarship may be thought to call into question the enterprise I have been engaged on in this paper. So far from Isaiah having expressed a belief in a *system* of natural law, it may be said, he did not even express a disapproval of *particular* sins and an adherence to *particular* moral norms in the way this paper has suggested; he was not condemning pride or drunkenness or political activism as such, drawing up as it were a moral code in which these things were proscribed, but speaking to the specific situation of eighth-century Judah. Furthermore, is it not methodologically unsound to extract information about ethics, as I have done, from many different kinds of oracle, ignoring the difference between a *Scheltwort* (e.g., 3:14), a woe oracle (e.g., 5:8), and a *Königsansprache* (e.g., 7:4–5)?

I believe that such an objection fails to understand the aim of the investigation undertaken here, but it helps to throw into relief what the issues actually are. The purpose, as mentioned briefly at the outset, is not to suggest that Isaiah was constructing a theoretical system of ethics or writing a work of moral philosophy but that he was unfortunately hindered in this by the conventions of prophetic style so that we have, as it were, to reconstruct his system for him. Isaiah was speaking highly specific words of rebuke, threat, and accusation to a particular group of people, and he was a successful prophet, not a systematic theologian *manqué*. What Isaiah was trying to tell his audience, his 'message' as it is usually described, has been studied in minute detail, and I have nothing to add to existing summaries of it. But any message makes sense only against a background of unspoken assumptions, and it is these that this paper has attempted to draw out and make explicit. In this respect my presentation differs from the work of H. H. Schmid, who (if I understand him correctly) believes that the Old Testament is in some sense 'about' natural law or cosmic order and that the existence of such orders is one of the truths it seeks to convey.[28] At least so far as Isaiah is concerned, this seems to me incorrect. The argument here is that Isaiah takes some such notion as given, just as (most commentators would agree) he takes as given the idea that God is concerned about sin, not indifferent to it. It is one of what a sociologist might call his 'domain assumptions'.[29]

To deal properly with the form-critical point would require a much fuller discussion than can be undertaken here. But it ought to be said that, while form criticism is a useful method for extracting certain kinds of information from Old Testament texts, it is not necessarily the only valid one, and on the whole it is difficult to see how one would move from a study of prophetic *Gattungen* to the type of question dealt with here. As I see it, the effect of approaching these questions in a form-critical way would probably tend not so much to invalidate the conclusions so far drawn about the assumptions underlying Isaiah's oracles as to call into question the idea that they are peculiarly *Isaiah's*. Thus one might say that the 'tit-for-tat' form of divine punishment, which may involve a 'natural law' view of ethics, and the rhetorical questions, such as 29:16, which seem to imply that sin is a reversal of natural orders, are conventional types of prophetic utterance. If they do indeed reflect a distinctive understanding of morality, this must have been widely diffused in the religious culture that gave birth to such traditional forms, rather than being the peculiar insight of a particular prophet, such as Isaiah. This, again, would tend to support Schmid's if anything *more* ambitious project of finding natural law everywhere in ancient Israel, rather than undermining the whole idea. Nevertheless, it would put a question mark over the claim of this paper to have penetrated one specific prophet's mind, since the conventional character of the utterances he uses would make it impossible to know whether he was conscious of their implications or not.

In the end, much will depend on one's general attitude towards form criticism and one's assessment of the balance between conventional form and original or personal content in the oracles of the classical prophets. It will be obvious that my discussion of Isaiah stands in an English tradition, not only in its very interest in natural law but also in its assumption that the balance comes down in favour of the individual writer and thinker even when due allowance has been made for the conventional speech forms in which his thoughts are expressed. But I believe that some of my conclusions could be defended even within a more rigorously and committedly form-critical environment. Since, as has been repeatedly stressed, the argument is about assumptions rather than assertions, it may, in the end, matter less than might appear on the surface whether one speaks of the presuppositions of Isaiah or the culturally given conventions within which he was working. At all events, the fact that support for natural law in the Old Testament has come from a German-speaking scholar like Schmid, who stands firmly within a form-critical tradition of Old Testament scholarship and is sensitive, as few of us in this country can be, to the theological pressures that make such a notion highly suspect as a possible part of the scriptural witness, encourages me to think that it is neither a sign of methodological weakness nor hopeless anachronism to see signs of it in the thought of Isaiah of Jerusalem.

Works relevant to Ethics in Isaiah since 1981

Blenkinsopp, J. *Isaiah 1–39*. AB. New York: Doubleday, 2001.

Childs, B. S. *Isaiah: A Commentary*. OTL. Louisville, Ky.: Westminster John Knox, 2001.

Houston, W. 'The Kingdom of God in Isaiah: Divine Power and Human Response'. In *The Kingdom of God and Human Society: Essays by Members of the Scripture, Theology and Society Group*. Ed. R. Barbour. Edinburgh: T. & T. Clark, 23–41.

Uffenheimer, B. 'Isaiah's and Micah's Approaches to Policy and History'. In *Politics and Theopolitics in the Bible and Postbiblical Literature*. Ed. H. Graf Reventlow, Y. Hoffman, and B. Uffenheimer. JSOTSup 171. Sheffield: Sheffield Academic Press, 1994, 176–88.

8

Ethics in the Isaianic Tradition

In the last twenty years, the book of Isaiah as a complete text has moved into the centre of attention, relegating its supposed components—Proto-, Deutero-, and Trito-Isaiah—to a subordinate position they have scarcely had since Duhm first showed how composite 'Isaiah' really was.[1] It has begun to look rather old-fashioned to give courses, or write books, on 'Deutero-Isaiah' or 'Isaiah of Jerusalem'; Isaiah, simply, is now the focus of interest, that is, Isaiah 1–66. Partly this reflects a concern for the 'final form' of biblical books, which may be the fruit either of 'canonical criticism' or of the current vogue for 'literary' readings of the Bible. But partly it represents a growing conviction among those concerned with the Prophetic books that the old fragmentation of these works did less than justice to the architectural skill with which they were assembled. One need not embrace any particular theory about final-form interpretation to be convinced that exegetical practice has been too alert to signs of possible division, too inattentive to indications of unity and coherence, in a book such as Isaiah.[2]

An interest in the 'final form' of Isaiah, or any other biblical book, may in theory be combined with any opinion about how, as a matter of historical fact, the book reached its present form. To take the extreme case, one might think that it resulted from a completely random collection of tiny fragments dating from many centuries and still hold, on theological or literary grounds, that the exegete's duty was to interpret the book precisely as it stands—just as one could think the book a perfect unity of purpose and design and yet interpret it atomistically (the latter option was common in 'precritical' scholarship). But in practice theories about the book's growth tend to be strongly correlated with theories about what will make an appropriate style of exegesis, and there is often a certain circularity about this. Exegetes who are convinced that the biblical books are composite are often ill-disposed towards final-form exegesis; interpreters who look first to the final form tend to regard hypotheses about complicated compositional developments as implausible and undesirable. Thus the fact that the wind is set in the direction of final-form approaches tends to mean that scholars are predisposed to seeing unity and coherence in Isaiah. However, this does not mean that there has been a wholesale rejection of the old idea of three major sections in the work: 1–39, 40–55, and 56–66. It means that we are predisposed to expect some degree of continuity among them and to think that a single 'school' may have been responsible for the whole development. This theory has reached its logical conclusion in H. G. M. Williamson's recent brilliant study,[3] in which he assembles a massive cumulative case for seeing Deutero-Isaiah not just as a continuator of the work of Isaiah of Jerusalem but actually as the editor who ordered most of 1–39 and inserted many oracles of his own into it, at the same time as he added a complete block of his own oracles (40–55) to the end of it. A final-form interpretation of Isaiah 1–55 is thus justified not just on modern theological or literary grounds but also because this block of material was designed to be read as a single whole by the editor/prophet we call Deutero-Isaiah. There is thus a historical reason for practising a final-form approach. I would guess that Williamson's arguments will be widely accepted and will form the basis for a holistic approach to Isaiah which is both 'historical-critical' and 'literary-theological'.

I

As a small contribution to this trend in studies of Isaiah, I offer here some suggestions about the ethical ideas to be found in Isaiah 1–66. Studies of possible evidence for unity in Isaiah have tended to concentrate on rather 'technical' matters such as vocabulary and construction, rather than theological themes. But there is surely room for some consideration of what the various strata in the book have to say about substantive issues. I have long been interested in ethics in the Old Testament, and in Isaiah particularly,[4] and it seems natural for me to ask how the 'inauthentic' sections of Isaiah deal with ethical questions that receive a distinctive treatment by Isaiah himself, so far as we can reconstruct him.

I take it as given that Isaiah did indeed have a distinctive approach to ethics. This emerges at three levels.

First, though Isaiah shared many of the concerns of the other eighth-century prophets, such as the imperative of 'social justice', he had his own preferred topics for condemnation. Oppression of the poor is seen as focused specifically on the expropriation of ancestral land (5:8–10) and on miscarriage of justice (1:23; 3:9; 5:23; 10:1–2; 29:21). At the same time, those committing such acts of oppression are condemned not merely for their injustice in itself but for the predisposition towards it which comes from their habitual drunkenness (5:11–17, 22; 28:1–14). Most of these themes do occur in other prophets, notably the other Judaean prophets of the period, Amos and Micah, but they are strongly concentrated in Isaiah and presented as a single and outrageous whole. Furthermore, such social misdemeanours are linked, uniquely, to the political attitudes of the leaders of Judaean society who are their perpetrators, and specifically to their attitudes towards other nations. The leaders are condemned for their willingness to forge alliances to avert the various military threats of the eighth century. In each time of military crisis Isaiah's advice may be called 'quietistic'—not in the strictly religious sense but in the practical realm of foreign policies. The answer to the question, 'What shall we do?' is in each case 'Nothing. Trust in Yahweh, avoid dealings with foreign powers, keep your heads down' (see 7:4–9; 22:8–11; 28:12; 30:15; 31:1).

The second level of ethical teaching in Isaiah, which is scarcely to be found in the other prophets at all, is his interest in the *attitudes* of his audience (and others). The most obvious example is Isaiah's concern with human pride (2:12–19; 3:1–5; 3:16–4:1; 22:15–19), under the influence of which people get above themselves and start to usurp the place of God or to create their own ideas of God—hence to commit idolatry (2:8: '[T]hey bow down to the work of their hands, to what their own fingers have made'). Indeed, it is a kind of pride that leads to all the attempts at self-defence condemned by Isaiah—trusting in what is 'flesh, and not God' (31:3). Pride makes people 'wise in their own eyes' (5:21) and leads them to despise God's ways (5:18–20). Remarkably, the theme of pride enables Isaiah to condemn the Judaeans and the Assyrians for the same sin, an unusual if not unique feature in the prophets: 10:5–19 regards the victorious Assyrian king in just the same light as the leaders of beleaguered Judah, an axe boasting against the one who wields it (10:15).

A second higher-level problem is folly. Like Proverbs, Isaiah treats folly (*nĕbālâ*) as a moral offence, not as a mitigation of guilt, and he sees specific sins as examples or products of this overarching moral category (e.g., 1:2–3). It is folly not to acknowledge Yahweh's supremacy, a folly committed equally, again, by the Assyrians and by the rulers of Judah.

A further example of a false attitude represents one of the ways in which Isaiah is likely to seem alien to many modern readers. In the political sphere, he was clearly strongly conservative, believing that the political ideal was the way things had been in the time of David, when everyone knew his (and especially her) place: when the people did not 'oppress one another' (3:5), when 'children' were not their 'oppressors', and 'women' did not 'rule over them'

(3:12). The official Shebna is condemned for constructing himself a rock-hewn tomb when he has no property or family in Jerusalem (22:16). Isaiah's vision of society is one of a stable, aristocratic state, in which the poor are protected by an attitude of noblesse oblige on the part of the ruling classes, and property-owning males are given their 'rightful' preeminence. Humility towards God goes hand in hand with respect for the long-established orders of society.

In chapter 7, 'Ethics in Isaiah of Jerusalem', I argued for a third ethical level in Isaiah, from which all the examples we have considered so far logically derive. This is the belief in a moral order built into the way the world is, something like what is often called 'natural law'—of course, using the term very loosely, since Isaiah is outside the Western ethical tradition in which it is at home. I would not want to press this point here, but simply note that the supremacy of Yahweh, which seems to be Isaiah's most cherished belief, is presented as being de jure, not just de facto, as if there is some principle in the world which justifies his position of supreme reverence and power. In other words, what holds Isaiah's ethics together is a theological conviction that the God to whom all Judah's traditions bear witness is entitled to the reverence God traditionally receives; every individual moral precept, and every higher-order principle such as social conservatism and the call for humility, seem to him to derive from the supremacy of God.

II

Thus we have a picture, I hope coherent, of the 'system' of ethics which operated in the teachings of Isaiah of Jerusalem. I have not mentioned questions of authenticity because, for the most part, the 'ethical' sections of Isaiah 1–39 have never been problematic, and almost all commentators treat them as authentic (there are exceptions, such as, of course, O. Kaiser[5]). The question now is whether similar themes are to be found in the nonauthentic sections of Isaiah, in such a way as to suggest that parts of it were written or edited by people who saw ethics in a similar way to the prophet Isaiah himself. If so, then the case for seeing the book as the result of purposeful editing, rather than as a random collection of prophetic material, will be that much more plausible.

To begin with the first level, specific moral failings and misdemeanours, there are references to the oppression of the poor in 59:1–8, in the course of which we find an apparent quotation from Isaiah (v. 3, cf. 1:15): '[Y]our hands are defiled with blood, and your fingers with iniquity'. In the previous chapter, there are references to oppression of workers (58:3) and a general condemnation of heartlessness towards the poor, including even people's own relatives (58:6–7). All this is perfectly in keeping with Isaiah but shows no sign of any specific connection with his thought; other Prophetic books contain much the same ideas. We do, however, find attacks on taking bribes in 29:21 and 33:15, though these again have no specially Isaianic features, and 33:15 is part of a general catalogue of sins which the righteous man avoids, whose closest links are to the 'entrance liturgies', Psalms 15 and 24. Drunkenness, so far as I can see, is not mentioned at all in the non-Isaianic parts of Isaiah. So far, therefore, we have little to link the teaching of the book with the characteristic and distinctive features of the teachings of Isaiah.

Things are different when we turn to Isaiah's political message, with its insistence on trust in God and the avoidance of all human expedients. This theme runs through the book of Isaiah in a way difficult to explain on the theory that it is a random collection. It is found in the 'Isaiah Apocalypse' (24–27): 'Thou dost keep him in perfect peace, whose mind is stayed on thee, because he trusts in thee. Trust in the LORD for ever, for the LORD GOD is an everlasting rock' (26:3). Here we already see the tendency to take Isaiah's concrete political advice and turn it into a general spiritual counsel of quietness and trust—something that Christian tradition has done to the (clearly political) Isaianic oracle in 30:15, '[I]n returning and rest you shall be saved'. The theme of quiet trust also occurs at 33:2, where the people are presented as 'waiting' for God every morning, and especially in time of trouble; and, as in Isaiah, human waiting corresponds to, and is an appropriate response to, the exaltedness of God (33:5–6), whose sovereign status assures the stability and peace of his people. This is a very 'Isaianic' nexus of ideas, and it is interesting to find it appearing in the 'anonymous' complex of chapters 32 and 33. The whole presentation of Zion as Yahweh's chosen city is full of Isaiah's vision of peace, quiet, and safety: 'Your eyes will see Jerusalem, a quiet habitation, an immovable tent . . . there the LORD in majesty will be for us a place of broad rivers and streams' (33:20–21).

More striking perhaps than any of this is the recurrence of the Isaianic theme of trust and quietness in the oracles of Deutero-Isaiah. Deutero-Isaiah picks up Isaiah's theme that there is no need for the nation to fear, and consequently that fearlessness is the quality Yahweh chiefly demands of them. In doing so he probably—again like Isaiah—makes use of the 'Holy War' tradition which we find in the exhortations to Israel's leaders not to fear (e.g., Josh. 1:8). It has been usual to argue that one particular expression of this, the so-called *Königsansprache*, the oracle of assurance to the king, lies at the root both of Isaiah's advice to Ahaz in 7:4 and of Deutero-Isaiah's encouragement to his community in 41:14; 43:1; and 54:4: 'Fear not. . . .'.[6] There is a great difference in the use of this form in the two prophets: Isaiah is demanding trust and confidence as a *precondition* of divine help, whereas Deutero-Isaiah is uttering words of reassurance, stressing that there is no *need* to fear. But these are,

I think, the only prophets who speak explicitly in terms of confidence as the essence of the relationship of Israel (Judah) to Yahweh, and it seems unlikely to be an accident that their messages are preserved in the same book. And it is worth noting that even in Deutero-Isaiah the message is not, blandly, that God is automatically on Israel's side, even if the relationship is less precarious than for Isaiah of Jerusalem. The oracles that reassure Israel are uttered in the awareness that Yahweh was, until very recently, far from being on Israel's side, and has still to prove his faithfulness if the people are to believe in it. Thus 43:1 follows an oracle about the disaster of the exilic age, when God 'poured upon him [Jacob] the heat of his anger and the might of battle' (42:25). Deutero-Isaiah and his predecessor are alike confronted with an audience that cannot believe the message they are being offered, and not wholly without reason in either case: in both periods deliverance looked highly unlikely.

When we move up the scale to Isaiah's higher-order ideas about ethics we find still more parallels in the secondary parts of the book. The theme of pride and humility seems almost to be the uniting theme of the whole work, occurring in almost every stratum. After it is first introduced, in 2:11–3:8—words regarded by most commentators as essentially authentic to Isaiah—it is applied to the women of Jerusalem in 3:16–4:1, a passage certainly including interpolations, if not wholly secondary. The 'pride' that constitutes rebellion against God in the political and cultic sphere is here seen in the form of a delight in personal adornment, apparently regarded as equally reprehensible. If the listing of cosmetics and clothes in 3:18–23 is later than Isaiah, as most believe, it is certainly in line with his thinking, combining the theme of pride with misogyny, very much in his vein. The self-satisfaction and pride of women similarly surface at 32:9–20, reckoned by most commentators to be non-Isaianic. Yet the theme hardly occurs in the other prophets, where women are accused of many things but seldom of pride (Amos 4:1–3 is a rare exception).

As we saw above, a distinctive feature of Isaiah's own thinking is the association of pride with idolatry. This is established through the argument that worshipping an idol is worshipping something one has made oneself, and worshipping something one has made oneself is worshipping oneself, and so those who worship gods other than Yahweh are guilty of sinful pride. (This is reminiscent of the apocryphal obituary: 'He was a self-made man, who worshipped his creator'). This argument recurs in Isaiah 40–55, especially in a prose passage generally regarded as secondary to Deutero-Isaiah, 44:9–20. In this passage the idolater is derided for worshipping half of a log whose other half he has just used to cook his dinner. But it is also implied in 41:5–7, which presents the making of idols as a matter of taking and manipulating physical objects, and then goes on to stress that Yahweh 'takes' Israel; and in the taunt against Babylonian idols in 46:1–3, where idols have to be carried by their worshippers whereas Yahweh himself 'carries' Israel. The consistent point is Yahweh's utter independence of his worshippers, by contrast with the idols' dependence on those who make them, and for whom therefore they are in effect an extension of the idolaters' own personalities, not alternative sources of power.

This perception of foreign gods is not particularly common in the Old Testament, where it is commoner to present such gods as dangerous rivals to Yahweh. The view that eventually established itself in Judaism, however, was that all other gods are to be seen as 'nothings' or 'idols', trivial beings whom it was mere idiocy to worship. This view can reasonably be called the 'Isaianic' view of the matter, deriving equally from Isaiah 1–39 and Isaiah 40–55. It is one of the topics on which there is most obviously some connection between at least two parts of the book of Isaiah. (Note also 17:8 for the accusation that idols are 'what their own fingers have made', quoted perhaps from chap. 2).

Allied to the interpretation of idolatry as self-serving is the suggestion that the official Yahwistic cultus is just as bad as the worship of foreign gods, because it, too, is the veneration of rites which have been devised by merely human thought. The classic presentation of this idea is in 1:10–15, regarded by most scholars as authentic to Isaiah of Jerusalem (it is also found in Amos 4:4–5), but it may also lie behind the obscure 43:22–24. An exactly similar argument appears in 58, where not feasting but fasting is the subject, yet exactly the same things are said as in Isaiah's own diatribe against sacrifice: fasting serves the people's own religious self-satisfaction and covers up their social misdemeanours. Justice, not fasting, is what Yahweh requires (vv. 6–7). It should be noted that this is superficially less plausible than the prophetic strictures against the sacrificial cult. For the cult involves at least some sacrifices in which the worshippers can eat the meat and enjoy a 'feast' in the everyday sense of the word, so that to see it as a form of self-indulgence makes perfectly good sense. Where fasting is concerned, the element of purely physical satisfaction is obviously absent, so 'Trito-Isaiah' must have a more cerebral kind of pleasure in mind: a feeling that in fasting the people have 'done their bit' to please Yahweh. It is not impossible that he had so far internalized the Isaianic idea that cultus is to be equated with self-indulgence that it seemed natural to him to apply the same model to the less plausible case of fasting. The idea passes on to Zechariah (7:1–7), but it seems to have originated in 'Isaianic' circles.

The ideal of humility as the essence of a proper response to Yahweh seems rooted in both Proto- and Deutero-Isaiah: the 'servant' passages in particular present a humble and unassertive figure as the ideal human being (42:1–3; 50:5–6; 53:1–3). Whatever assessment we make of the identity of the Servant, the theme of his/their/its humility is a constant. It makes good sense in the context of a book bearing the name of Isaiah, whose own harshest condemnations are reserved for human pride in whatever form. But we can go further and draw in Trito-Isaiah, too. In 57:15 we have a declaration of the divine nature which can serve as a perfect emblem of the doctrine of God's transcendence and immanence in the Judaeo-Christian tradition: 'Thus says the high and lofty One who inhabits eternity, whose name is Holy: "I dwell in the high and holy place, *and also with him who is of a contrite and humble spirit*"' (italics added). Humility is seen as the appropriate response to the majesty of God and will be rewarded with a gift of his presence. Isaiah of Jerusalem would surely have applauded.

Alongside pride, the other main sin of attitude we find in Isaiah is folly, and this too is a prevailing theme in the later sections of the book. Within the oracles against the nations (13–23), the anti-Egyptian oracle, in particular, is marked by the theme of human folly and the contrasting wisdom of God: 'The princes of Zoan are utterly foolish; the wise counselors of Pharaoh give stupid counsel' (19:11). By following the advice of Egypt, Judah implicates itself in Egypt's stupidity. These oracles may come from Isaiah himself and reflect the machinations of the years around 715. But many commentators regard them as secondary, and if they are, then it is noteworthy how 'Isaianic' they nonetheless succeed in being. The same is true of one of the narrative portions of the book, chapter 39, usually supposed to have a 'Deuteronomistic' provenance. Here Hezekiah's folly is illustrated by his willingness to let the Babylonian envoys see the contents of his treasuries: a folly which, as the book stands, we are probably meant to see as leading directly to the plight of the exiled Judaeans who are the audience for 40–55. From this point of view, the whole book might be seen as a treatise on human folly and divine wisdom, with 28:23–29, the parable of the farmer, as a pivotal statement about Yahweh's wise governance of the world, which is so at odds with the folly of human beings (28:7–10).

Finally, we may turn to the third and highest level of Isaiah's ethical teaching, that which concerns the ultimate divine justification for ethical imperatives. As we saw, folly and pride are sins because they are attempts to supplant God as the chief, indeed the only real, power in the universe—in Shakespearean terms, an offence against 'degree', the proper hierarchy in the world, where God is supreme and human powers are subject to God. It seems to me very clear that such an idea is just as dominant in Deutero-Isaiah as it had been in the teaching of Isaiah himself. Humans sin against God's supremacy in Isaiah by self-aggrandizement, arrogance, and refusal to trust God. In Deutero-Isaiah there is, of course, far less condemnation of the people's sin, which is thought of more as a past state from which they are about to be rescued. But it is still the case that the prophet's audience is seen as unwilling to trust in the good designs of Yahweh and as doubting his power to save. If anything could deprive them of their coming salvation (perhaps nothing at all can), it would be this attitude of doubt and vacillation. It is not an accident that Isaiah 40, inaugurating the prophet's message, deals with two themes: (1) Yahweh's power and supremacy and (2) the people's doubt and fear. The lengthy passage in praise of Yahweh's power (40:12–26) is, in context, not simply an 'all-purpose' paean of praise to the almighty God but a specific response to expressions of doubt such as 40:7 and 40:27. The God whose 'understanding is unsearchable' (40:28), and who 'gives power to the faint' (40:29) is the God in whom complete trust can be placed. He is the supreme ruler of the world, of whom it is an absurdity to suspect the kind of weakness that characterizes idols (40:18–20) or afflicts even the strongest of human beings (40:15, 30).

Thus the theological vision in 40–55 is close to that found in the authentically Isaianic sections of 1–39. If we treat Deutero-Isaiah as an exponent of 'ethical monotheism', we should acknowledge that his ideas are already present in embryo in Isaiah of Jerusalem. To put the matter in a way more acceptable to a modern 'final-form' critic, monotheism finds its clearest expression in the Old Testament in the Isaianic corpus. The whole book of Isaiah is imbued with it to a greater extent than other prophetic books, and this may be seen as more important than asking 'historical' questions about the ideas of this or that stratum within the book. The correspondences between the first and second sections of Isaiah on this issue are striking and dwarf the differences between them.

I would not want to go so far as to say that the book of Isaiah is a literary and theological unity: I do not find I can ignore what seem to me obvious dislocations and signs of complex growth. But what has been presented here, even if only some of it is correct, seems to me enough to dismiss any idea of the book as a purely adventitious grouping of unrelated oracles. Just as there is a 'Deuteronomic/Deuteronomistic' flavour to some books, which we can learn to recognize, so there is an 'Isaianic' flavour in this collection which transcends the probably multiple authorship of its various sections. The distinctively Isaianic approach to ethics involves tracing ethical obligation to its highest source, which lies in the supremacy of God, from whom all good and all power derives, and doing, saying, and thinking nothing which might derogate from that supremacy. No other part of the Old Testament quite captures this vision, but every part of the book of Isaiah does so.

9

Theological Ethics in Daniel

ETHICAL CONCERNS IN DANIEL

The book of Daniel is usually classified as apocalyptic literature, and this has consequences for what we expect to find in it so far as moral teaching is concerned. If apocalypticism is the literature of small, beleaguered groups looking for deliverance from oppression, then the ethics of apocalypticism can be expected to manifest the characteristic mind-set of such groups, with their desire to stress all that binds them together and makes them distinctive.[1] As with the Qumran community, one looks for strict rules of membership, a code of discipline to bind the group together, and an authoritarian structure that will ensure that individuals conform to the ethos of the group.

In fact, Daniel only partly conforms to these expectations. On the whole its ethical concerns are those that came to characterize 'mainstream' Judaism in later times.[2] The first chapter sets the tone for this, with its emphasis on Jewish food laws as the point on which Daniel and his three companions feel obliged to insist: 'Daniel resolved that he would not defile himself with the royal rations of food and wine' (1:8). He asks for permission to be limited to a vegetarian diet, and God vindicates him by ensuring that he and his companions enjoy more blooming health than the young men who eat the royal rations of rich food and wine. The concern for the food laws can also be seen in the book of Judith, which may be from much the same period as Daniel and similarly reflects the Maccabean situation. Here, it will be recalled, Judith is particularly scrupulous about matters of diet, and even when going to deliver her people by killing Holofernes she is careful not to eat his defiled food but takes with her her own supplies, odd as this seems for someone invited to a banquet:

Then he [Holofernes] commanded them to bring her in where his silver dinnerware was kept, and ordered them to set a table before her with some of his own delicacies, and with some of his own wine to drink. But Judith said, 'I cannot partake of them, or it will be an offence; but I will have enough with the things I brought with me'. (Judith 12:1–2)

When Holofernes expresses a fear that her supplies may run out, she retorts, with dramatic irony, that they will last her until 'the Lord carries out by my hand what he has determined' (12:4).

Observance of the food laws is a crucial symptom of a general ethical attitude that pervades the book of Daniel, that of intense loyalty to the God of Israel. This manifests itself in another practice which is not formally included in biblical law but was certainly by this period a feature of Jewish piety: prayer towards Jerusalem at certain times of the day. In Daniel 6, the 'presidents and satraps' have Darius enact a law forbidding the worship of any god but himself, and Daniel's immediate reaction to it is to continue to observe set prayer times:

Although Daniel knew that the document had been signed, he continued to go to his house, which had windows in its upper room open towards Jerusalem, and to get down on his knees three times a day to pray to his God and praise him, just as he had done previously. (Dan. 6:10)

Thus he registers his loyalty and devotion to his own God in spite of the danger of arrest which, of course, promptly follows. When Daniel is vindicated and freed from the lions' den, he attributes his deliverance to the fact that he has been found 'blameless'; presumably it is his constancy in prayer that results in this verdict on his conduct.

Of course, a similar theme appears in the story of the burning fiery furnace (Dan. 3). Here again the issue is whether Shadrach, Meschach, and Abednego are prepared to show disloyalty to their God, and despite the king's threats they absolutely refuse to do so. The ethics of exclusive obedience to the God of Israel is here stated in a peculiarly 'disinterested' form, and the three young men insist that they will be loyal to God even if he does not choose to deliver them (Dan. 3:18). Religious commitment here takes a strikingly self-abnegatory form—though it is naturally vindicated in the outcome of the story, so for the reader the 'moral' is that disinterestedness pays off! The insistence on the prerogatives of God, who is free to decide as he chooses, is of a piece with what is said by Daniel when he is asked to reveal the king's dream in chapter 2: '[T]his mystery has not been revealed to me because of any wisdom that I have more than any other living being' (2:30), but simply to enable God to be glorified when what he foretells comes about.

ETHICAL CONCERNS SHARED
WITH OTHER JEWISH LITERATURE

The themes discussed previously are common in Judaism of the Second Temple period and do not mark Daniel off as a distinctive kind of literature. They are shared, for example, with Tobit, where again passionate loyalty to Jewish religious customs is demanded even without the promise of reward, though vindication for the faithful Jew arrives, as we expect it to, in the end. It is not prayer that gets Tobit into trouble with the authorities but burying the dead (1:18; 2:7). Living as an observant Jew brings dangers in its wake, as many in the Maccabean age learned to their cost. But the moral standards that are implied in Tobit, as in Daniel, do not have the sect-like qualities that one instinctively associates with apocalypticism; instead they are part of what came to be typical of Judaism in all its varieties. We might say, perhaps, that Judaism in general had some of the classic characteristics of a sect within the world of Hellenistic belief and practice; but the stream of thought represented by Daniel, Judith, and Tobit is certainly not a sectarian variety of Judaism.

This impression is strongly confirmed by the great lament or confession in Dan. 9:4–19. There is nothing here that suggests any different set of ethical standards from those that apply to all Jews, and the prayer is, in fact, strikingly similar to those uttered by Ezra in Ezra 9:6–15 and Neh. 9:6–37. There is hardly any specification of how the people have sinned, but reference is made to the prophets' indictment of the nation, and the reader is presumably intended to understand that what Israel has done is what the prophets had inveighed against: primarily, perhaps, the commission of cultic sins against the unique status of YHWH, just as is commonly asserted in Deuteronomistic passages (for example, 2 Kgs. 17:7–18). They have committed 'treachery' (9:7) and have failed to obey YHWH's 'commandments and ordinances' (9:5). The calamity that has overtaken the people (that is, the exile, in which Daniel is putatively living) accords with what 'is written in the law of Moses' (9:13), which is assumed to be the authority to which conduct ought to be referred.

What is still more striking in Daniel is that there are assumed to be ethical norms binding also on non-Jews. Typically sects are bound internally by strong moral standards, but they have nothing to say about the external world, which is a *massa perditionis* and is going to the devil. It is not the role of any sectarian to issue moral directives to the world in general. Thus, notoriously, the New Testament has very little to say to the powers of the world. Christians are advised on how to behave towards the 'powers that be', as in Romans 13. But no advice is given to those powers, for they are, of course, not listening.

This is one of the reasons that it is so difficult to use the New Testament profitably in moral discussion about the rights and duties of the state, which lay outside the purview of the New Testament writers themselves, people of no political consequences as they were. But in Daniel, Jews are portrayed as in close contact with the state authorities, and Daniel himself at times approaches having an official status—indeed, after Belshazzar's feast he is appointed to rank third in the kingdom (Dan. 5:16, 29), though unfortunately the kingdom of Belshazzar has by then only a few hours to run.

The kings about and to whom Daniel speaks share certain features in common. Like the rulers of the world in typical prophetic oracles against the nations, they suffer from hubris, an exaggerated sense of their own importance, which is offensive to God:

> At the end of twelve months he [Nebuchadnezzar] was walking on the roof of the royal palace of Babylon, and the king said, 'Is this not magnificent Babylon, which I have built as a royal capital by my mighty power and for my glorious majesty?' While the words were still in the king's mouth, a voice came from heaven: 'O King Nebuchadnezzar, to you it is declared: The kingdom has departed from you! You shall be driven away from human society, and your dwelling shall be with the animals of the field. You shall be made to eat grass like oxen, and seven times shall pass over you, until you have learned that the Most High has sovereignty over the kingdom of mortals and gives it to whom he will.' (Dan. 4:29–32)

Kings think they can do just as they like, proclaiming themselves gods (6:7). They have to learn that only the true God has sovereignty over the world. And Daniel is commissioned to make this clear to them, so that they can be 'converted', as we might put it: not actually becoming Jews, but certainly learning to worship the God whom Jews worship as the only true God and imposing that worship on their subjects:

> Therefore I make a decree: Any people, nation, or language that utters blasphemy against the God of Shadrach, Meshach, and Abednego shall be torn limb from limb, and their houses laid in ruins; for there is no other god who is able to deliver in this way. (Dan. 3:29)

Consistently with this, the God of Israel is not referred to by his own name by these foreign rulers, as though that God were alien to them, but is given titles that express their own sense that that God is supreme over the whole world: 'the Most High God' (4:2), 'the Most High' (4:34), 'the King of heaven' (4:37), 'the living God' (6:20, 26), 'God of gods and Lord of Kings' (2:47). In the same way, when speaking to the kings Daniel himself uses terms that stress his God's power over all things: 'the God of heaven' (2:37, 44), 'the great God' (2:45), and 'Heaven' (4:26). As is well known, the name YHWH, in fact, occurs only in chapter 9, a very striking fact when one realises how much of the book is concerned with loyalty precisely to the God of the Jews. Throughout the book the emphasis lies on God as the ruler of the whole world, and it is taken for granted that all earthly kings should acknowledge him and recognize his sovereignty. It is as bad for them to worship 'the gods of gold and silver, bronze, iron, wood, and stone' (5:4) as it would be for Jews to do so: the fact that they are pagans does not exonerate them from guilt for thus worshipping 'the creature rather than the Creator', as Paul puts it in Rom. 1:25.

Thus Daniel treats non-Jewish rulers as subject to the authority of his own God—a clear indication of the advanced state of Jewish monotheism by this time. There is only one God, and all humankind should acknowledge his controlling power and respect his sovereign rule. It is not for pagan kings to set themselves up as gods, nor to require anyone—whether Jew or Gentile—to worship any god other than the 'God of heaven', who is known specially to the Jews but can be acknowledged in reverence by anyone, whatever their nation or race. This is a position found also in the books of the Prophets, where it is taken for granted that foreign rulers owe a debt of humility to God and that he can rightly punish them if they are insubordinate. This can already be seen as early as the time of Isaiah, who foretells that the Assyrians are to be punished for failing to see that they are only a tool in YHWH's hand (Isa. 10:12–16). It becomes a common theme in the various oracles against the nations in a number of prophetic books (for example, Jeremiah 50–51; Ezekiel 38–39). Daniel is thus continuing a tradition already well established in the literature of ancient Israel when he castigates foreign rulers for their pride and self-assertion. The underlying assumption must be that they can have enough knowledge of the true God for them to be culpable when they arrogate to themselves the sovereignty over the world which belongs only to him.

SUBMISSION TO GOD

Now, it seems to me that the ethical obligations binding on Jews and on Gentiles are certainly, at a superficial level, very different. On the Jew is laid the obligation to keep 'the law of Moses'; to acknowledge the sovereignty of YHWH by prayer and by refusing all respect to other supposed gods, or to human beings however exalted; and to be diligent in observing such regulations as the food laws, even when to do so is difficult and dangerous. So far as pagans are concerned, it is only rulers who are discussed at all, and their obligations consist wholly in the avoidance of insubordination to 'the God of heaven'. They must eschew hubris and recognize themselves as no more than servants in relation to the God who is the true and only ruler of the world. Yet there are points of contact between the two. The need to *acknowledge* God as the supreme power seems to unite what is said about both Jew and Gentile. Idolatry is a sin for both (3:18; 5:4). Both need to place themselves under the authority of God, claiming nothing for themselves by way of supernatural endowment (2:30; 4:30); both need to recognize that they are 'only human' (cf. Ps. 9:20). For the Jew, this is accomplished by putting the whole of life under God's authority as expressed in regular prayer and overt acknowledgement of him; for pagan kings, it consists in making no exaggerated claims and living in humility. But both have an obligation to know their place in the scheme of things and not to usurp the place that belongs to God alone.

All in all, we may say that the book of Daniel works with an idea of *submission* to God: that is its theological ethic. Everything must be done to leave decisions and outcomes to God alone. This kind of belief also undergirds the eschatological material in the second half of the book. It is probably fair to describe Daniel as deterministic in its attitude to history, as is generally the case in apocalyptic writings. The outcome of history does not depend on human decisions but is already fixed in God's purposes. But this does not lead to the conclusion that it does not matter what human beings do. On the contrary, there is a clear imperative to cooperate in God's purposes by submission to his will. For the Jew, submission to God means obedience to the law, and it is expressed in such actions as insistence on prayer and refusal to worship any other gods, even if the penalty is a terrible death—because no other course of action is appropriate if God is truly being submitted to. For pagan kings, submission to God's control of history means a recognition that God 'changes times and seasons, deposes kings and sets up kings' (Dan 2:21). The assumption of total divine control, endemic in apocalypticism, here has clear ethical correlates: everything should be done to stand out of God's way and to allow his purposes to prevail.[3] Those not doing so risk finding themselves on the wrong side when the end comes.[4]

In speaking of 'submission' I am aware of using a term which is associated more with Islam than with Judaism or Christianity, but I use it deliberately because it seems to me that the ethic of Daniel does indeed have something in common with certain Islamic ideas. There is not any thought that human obedience to divine law helps in bringing forward God's purposes; all it does is to avoid hindering them. The end of all human activity is the acknowledgement of the God who has his own way in the world, and this function is served by obedience to the law, just as by humility in the political sphere. It is nowhere clearer than in the three young men's insistence:

> If our God whom we serve is able to deliver us from the furnace of blazing fire and out of your hand, O king, let him deliver us. *But if not*, be it known to you, O king, that we will not serve your gods and we

will not worship the golden statue that you have set up. (3:17–18, emphasis added)

It is for God to do as he chooses; it is not for human beings to make nice calculations of probability about what he will do: their sole task is to remain true and loyal to him.

How far does this particular kind of ethic mark Daniel off from other texts in the Hebrew Bible? It is hard to think of any other text in which the emphasis is so strongly on absolute submission to God without any calculation of the possible outcome. Nearest to this is perhaps Hab. 3:17–18:

> Though the fig tree does not blossom,
>   and no fruit is on the vines;
> though the produce of the olives fails,
>   and the fields yield no food;
> though the flock is cut off from the fold,
>   and there is no herd in the stalls,
> yet I will rejoice in the LORD;
>   I will exult in the God of my salvation.

The framing narrative of the book of Job also provides an example of purely disinterested piety, for that is precisely what the Satan claims is impossible and what God seeks to show to be possible by allowing him to 'test' Job. But it is rare in the Hebrew Bible to find such sentiments expressed, and much more normal for ethics to be based on the assumption that God will reward the righteous who obey his will. Pure submission is seldom encountered.

The idea that there are ethical obligations incumbent on other nations than Israel is much more common. Later Judaism elaborated such an idea into the concept of the Noachide commandments, the laws which are valid for all the descendants of Noah (in other words, for everyone) as contrasted with those that are binding on Israel alone. The notion that nations other than Israel should acknowledge bounds to acceptable behaviour is already explicit in Amos 1:3–2:3, where there is felt to be a general obligation to eschew what we should nowadays call war crimes. But even if this is not closely paralleled in other Prophetic books, the abhorrence of hubris that we find in Daniel is certainly common, and is the normal justification alleged for the overthrow of foreign nations:

> Your wisdom and your knowledge
>   led you astray,
> and you said in your heart,
>   'I am, and there is no one besides me.'
> But evil shall come upon you,
>   which you cannot charm away;

disaster shall fall upon you,
  which you will not be able to ward off;
and ruin shall come on you suddenly,
  of which you know nothing. (Isa. 47:10–11)

Here Babylon utters words which are proper to YHWH alone: 'I am, and there is no one besides me'. For this it is to be annihilated because only YHWH is entitled to make such a claim of uniqueness. The obligation to acknowledge only one God who determines the destiny of kingdoms is central to all that Deutero-Isaiah has to say about the fate of the Babylonians. Nor does it sound as if the prophet is here bringing forward some surprising new teaching. He is merely reiterating what had long been believed in Hebrew tradition, that 'pride goes before a fall' in the affairs of nations as well as in those of individuals. All nations stand under the judgement of the God who refuses to be mocked by people claiming the authority which is God's prerogative. On this topic Daniel has nothing original to say, though the book is unusual in the extent to which it structures its stories about foreign rulers so exclusively around this theme.

CONCLUSION

In many ways, then, this representative of early Jewish apocalypticism continues ethical themes which were the common property of Israelite tradition and does not show many signs of the 'sectarian' style of ethics which might be expected of a book widely thought to come from a small group of pious people separate from the great bulk of the people of Judah in its day. Its determinism certainly leads this book to make more of the theme of submission to the divine will than most other Hebrew literature. However, it is part of a tradition in regarding both Jews and Gentiles as obliged to acknowledge the God of Israel, and in seeing the great sin of pagans as their hubris towards the one 'God of heaven'. In its moral concerns for Israel, the book emphasizes themes which were central for all Jews, such as prayer and the observance of the food laws, rather than concentrating on the requirements of a particular sectarian community. There is no trace of an *Interimsethik* appropriate specifically to those who believe that the end is nigh; on the contrary, those who live in hope and expectation of an imminent divine intervention are all the more obliged to take on themselves the usual obligations of the Jew and thus to bear witness to the majesty and power of the God who is also Lord of the nations.

Conclusion

The Future of Old Testament Ethics

At the end of this book it is appropriate to reflect on the present state of the study of Old Testament ethics and to speculate on where it might go in the future. Nearly all the essays collected in the present volume were written before the publication of what will surely become the classic work of our generation, Eckart Otto's *Theologische Ethik des Alten Testaments*.[1] I shall thus begin by commenting at length on his project before looking at a couple of more recent works and then turning to some thoughts of my own on possible directions for the discipline in the next few years.

Though many people have written on ethical questions in the study of the Old Testament, before the 1990s there were only two full-length studies of the first rank. Johannes Hempel's *Das Ethos des Alten Testaments*, published in 1938 and reissued in a revised edition in 1964, was an attempt to synthesize the entire world of ethics in ancient Israel using sophisticated categories from philosophy, systematic theology, and anthropology.[2] Walther Eichrodt devoted a lengthy section of his great *Theology of the Old Testament* to the subject of 'Old Testament Ethics', trying to do justice to what we might now call both diachronic and synchronic aspects and producing a study which still illuminates and clarifies.[3] Until recently there had been no successor to these great works from before the Second World War, despite the fact that they have clear flaws and belong to a phase of Old Testament study which is no longer ours.

Eckart Otto's work is in my view the first full-length book that belongs in the same class as those two studies. I shall suggest that it, too, has major flaws, especially in what it omits. But it deserves to take its place as the principal late twentieth-century contribution to a field that has proved extraordinarily difficult for Old Testament scholars to cope with—so much so that one sometimes wonders whether there is some basic but as yet undetected incoherence

162

in the very idea of Old Testament ethics. Otto's work, conceived as a textbook like other books in the Kohlhammer series, Theologische Wissenschaft, represents a rich and fertile source for anyone wanting to understand the contribution made by the Old Testament to the history of human ethical systems.

I

In a brief programmatic statement of his working assumptions (p. 10), Otto discusses the difficulty of separating out Old Testament ethics as a field of enquiry from the larger contexts of the history of Israelite religion and the theology of the Old Testament. To prevent its simply collapsing into one or another of these, he proposes that it is essential to concentrate only on the *explicit* systems of norms attested in the Old Testament. This means that the book limits itself to a consideration of legal and Wisdom sections of the text. Prophecy is almost wholly omitted, and the narrative books are not discussed at all (the index of biblical references reveals only nine references to the histories). As I shall argue, this decision is a fateful one which severely limits, even cripples, the book. But it does have the merit of clarity and ensures that we know from the outset exactly what 'Old Testament ethics' is held to cover. Against some recent works, such as Christopher Wright's impressive though lighter-weight *Living as the People of God*,[4] Otto also eschews any attempt at 'application'. He considers that Old Testament ethics remains relevant today because it is part of the Judaeo-Christian tradition of faith and action, but he is sceptical of attempts to draw direct lines from the world of the ancient Israel to the ethical dilemmas of modern industrial societies. For example, much of Israelite sexual ethics is concerned with ensuring the continuation of the family and, through it, of the human race; it is a simple error to suppose that laws formulated with this imperative in mind can be transferred to our situation, in which underpopulation is not the primary thing to be feared. Nevertheless, Otto does permit himself the occasional sideways glance at modern resonances of Old Testament teaching, and especially at its emphasis on human solidarity across boundaries of class, wealth, and even nationality. And I enjoyed the suggestion (on p. 133) that the modern equivalent of Egyptian ma^cat is the laws of the market.

The structure of the book is simple. First there is an analysis of the oldest Israelite law code, the Book of the Covenant (Exod. 21–23) in its various editions (which Otto is confident of being able to reconstruct, a point to which I shall return). From its very beginning this code had as one major concern the rights and needs of the weak in society, a concern which it shares with many other ancient Near Eastern codes but in a somewhat higher degree.

Gemeinschaft rather than *Herrschaft* is what the Book of the Covenant protects. It shares this concern with the Pentateuchal J source (one of the very few narrative texts Otto discusses), which in its portrayal of Adam and Eve sees marriage as a partnership rather than a relationship of dominance and subjugation. Justice in Exodus 21–23 is primarily *iustitia connectiva* rather than the enforcement of an abstract code. This is apparent even in the earliest edition, where the maintenance of society through the containing of conflict predominates over any desire to enforce specific legal principles. As the Book of the Covenant developed, it moved from the sphere of *Recht* into that of *Ethos*, understood as the realm of unenforceable ethical principles. This can already be seen in the inclusion of apodictic commands among the casuistic material which has been recognized, since the work of Alt, as the normal ancient Near Eastern legal form, and is also seen in the addition of motive clauses which reason with the readers in an attempt to persuade them to engage in moral activity that goes beyond the bounds of what could even in principle be enforced (see esp. pp. 82–86, and p. 213). Thus pragmatic means of containing conflict pass into law, and law passes into ethics.

Second, Otto considers the other great Old Testament section of ethical teaching, the Wisdom literature. There is a massive discussion of the ethics of wisdom in Egypt and Mesopotamia (pp. 117–52), which is fascinating in itself though not closely integrated with the treatment of Old Testament Wisdom that follows. The Wisdom ethic is seen as an ethic of the natural order. It is linked to creation rather than to historical experience (Otto is critical of Schmid's interpretation of Egyptian wisdom as historically rooted[5]), and its concern is with what makes a successful life (*gelingendes Leben*). 'Successful' here is not necessarily to be understood in crudely materialistic terms: the vision of Psalm 73, for example, can also be described as that of a 'successful' life, that is, one lived in conscious fellowship with God. But the emphasis in Wisdom—early Wisdom at least—is on what can be achieved by living in conformity with the orders of nature and society.

At this point Otto makes a move which is highly characteristic of his understanding of ethics. He introduces the idea of the *Scheitern*, the inevitable failure, of both the ethical imperatives of early law and the human attempts to live successfully that are commended by wisdom. During the later monarchic period, and in some way associated with the age of Josiah, the idea arose that ethics would need to be much more radically theologized if it was to provide a true way for human beings to walk with God. In the sphere of law, this expressed itself in the increasing integration of legal codes into Israel's *Heilsgeschichte*, a trend seen for the first time in Deuteronomy (though then reflected back on to the Book of the Covenant in its final redaction, in which it was brought into connection with the Decalogue just as the Deuteronomic laws had been). In Wisdom, it was seen in the identification of wisdom with Torah that we meet in Ben Sira (Sir. 24).

Deuteronomy and the Priestly Code represent, to quote the title of chapter 4 (p. 175), 'Die Begründung von Recht und Ethos durch die Offenbarung Gottes in der Geschichte' ['The grounding of law and ethics through the revelation of God in history']. For Deuteronomy, law and ethics alike are a response to the grace of God in guiding Israel through its long history. For P, even the possibility of faithful response is seen as problematic because of the human propensity to sin, and the system of sacrificial atonement is erected, and attributed to Moses, to show that God takes the initiative in enabling life to be lived in a way pleasing to God. Atonement proceeds essentially from God, not from any human initiative (cf. p. 239), and it represents, in a way, the final triumph of ethics over law, of the unenforceable over legal constraint, as human conduct prescribed by God becomes a divinely given means of grace rather than a response to implacable demand. It shows God's acceptance of the fact that human beings are and always will be sinners: 'Der Redaktor weiss, dass der Mensch immer wieder hinter den Forderungen des Gotteswillens zurückbleibt und sündig wird' ('The redactor knows that human beings always fall behind the demands of the divine will and become sinful') (p. 248).

Otto's answer to more pessimistic evaluations of the possibility of writing an 'Old Testament Ethics' (such as my own evaluation in 'Understanding Old Testament Ethics', reprinted in the present volume) is thus to say that there is a clear line of development attested in the Old Testament, as a result of which 'the unity of Old Testament ethics is its history' (p. 12). It proceeds from tentative beginnings in the Book of the Covenant and early Wisdom, which already express rather distinctive approaches to the human ethical task, through the experience of failure, *Scheitern*, to the sophisticated systems of Deuteronomy, P, and Ben Sira, in which Torah and wisdom are integrated and God himself meets human failure with grace abounding. The whole enterprise can be summed up in some characteristic words from Deuteronomy, taken from its latest portion, chapter 4:

> Keep them [sc. the 'statutes and ordinances'] and do them; for that will be your wisdom and your understanding in the sight of the peoples, who, when they hear all these statutes, will say, 'Surely this great nation is a wise and understanding people.' For what great nation is there that has a god so near to it as the LORD our God is to us, whenever we call upon him? And what great nation is there, that has statutes and ordinances so righteous as all this law which I set before you this day?

II

There are many virtues in Otto's work, which is already becoming definitive. It presents Old Testament ethics in a clear historical framework; it has a positive attitude towards law, on which Hempel and Eichrodt were more ambiguous—in that respect Otto has thrown off the old Lutheran anxiety about law and has embraced the view of Torah as gift, which both Jewish and Christian commentators have insisted on in recent years; it treats Law and Wisdom as equally central to the Old Testament, another recent insight; and it works with a clear definition of 'ethics'. It has the virtues of a textbook (comprehensiveness in it coverage) and of an original monograph (a stimulating new approach). I should like now to pick out a number of features which may enable us to form a more nuanced picture of its strengths and weaknesses.

1. Otto is encyclopedically well informed about earlier attempts to produce an Old Testament ethics and provides the most excellent bibliographies for every topic he deals with. Read together with his survey of Old Testament ethics in *Verkündigung und Forschung* for 1991,[6] this book provides everything the student of Old Testament ethics could wish for in the way of bibliographical help. At the same time, he also *analyses* earlier work; he does not simply report on it neutrally. I found particularly helpful his analysis of Eichrodt as representing a compromise between liberal and dialectical theology. Eichrodt, says Otto, accepted the early Israelite ethic as one of a 'healthy, unspoiled peasant people' (p. 13, with strong echoes of Wellhausen), yet wanted to show how this ethic became increasingly theologized as the word of God (in which Eichrodt also fervently believed) supervened upon it to produce something highly distinctive by comparison with its ancient Near Eastern context. He shows, similarly, how the study of the Decalogue has owed much to the influence of dialectical theology on a basically liberal substratum. Alt's famous form-critical distinction of apodictic from casuistic law, in which apodictic formulations such as the Decalogue represent the distinctively Israelite contribution to ethics and hence are genuinely early, owes much to a theology of revelation against the older liberal assumption that the Decalogue represents a comparatively late distillation of the teaching of the prophets. Yet the liberal agenda is not contradicted head on but allowed to remain in place as an explanation of casuistic laws, and there is no crude or fundamentalistic insistence on Mosaic origins. Thus 'der Offenbarungscharakter des Dekalogs war gesichert, ohne dass es noch der Verbindung des Dekalogs mit Mose und der Sinaimotivik bedurfte. Als sich Literarkritik und Formgeschichte methodisch vereinten, konnte der Geist liberalen Exegese auch mit der die Herrschaft in der protestantischen Theologie antretenden Wort-Gottes-Theologie eine

Ehe eingehen' ('The revealed character of the Decalogue was secured without any need to appeal to a link between the Decalogue and Moses, or the Sinai theme. Once literary and form criticism had combined, the spirit of liberal exegesis was able to be married to the "Word of God" theology then gaining ground in Protestant theology') (p. 209).

It is only fair to ask whether Otto may not also have theological commitments which partly condition his own account of Old Testament ethics. The theme of the *Scheitern* of human efforts at self-improvement through law and wisdom looks familiar to me from Protestant systematics, and one might wonder whether the Old Testament really recognizes it as centrally as Otto implies. The theme of human moral impotence is undoubtedly present in the Old Testament, but to make it the central thread on which the whole development of Israelite ethics hangs strikes me as rather too much of a good thing—especially in view of the essential optimism of much Old Testament anthropology which he also stresses, and to which I shall return. The person who offers sacrifices of atonement in P, on Otto's reading, is *simul iustus et peccator* and deeply aware that no works can make people righteous before God. Zimmerli is quoted with approval: '"Heiligkeit ist . . . eine nicht zuerst vom Volke oder den Priestern zu erwebende Eigenschaft, sondern eine zuvor durch Jahwes Tat der Herausführung seines Volkes . . . selbst geschaffene Qualität Israels und seiner Priester"' ('Holiness is . . . not in the first instance a characteristic to be developed by the people or the priests, but a quality of Israel and its priests created by Yahweh through his act of delivering the people from Egypt') (p. 239). While not wishing to argue that such themes are absent, I wonder whether a Jewish or indeed a Catholic scholar would have picked them out in quite this way.

2. One theme which Otto adopts from Hempel is that of ethics as imitation of God, and this seems to me important and perhaps neglected in discussions of Old Testament ethics. Hempel stressed that God did not issue demands out of *blanke Willkür* (mere arbitrary will) but bound himself to essentially the same ethical commitments that he laid upon his human subjects (see p. 15). Otto develops this idea at some length. He argues, for example, that it is central to Hosea, for whom the way God acts towards Israel is presented as a model for how Israelites (or even human beings in general) should relate to each other (p. 111). He finds the same theme clearly present in Deuteronomy, which grounds its social programme of care for the Levite, orphan, widow, and stranger in the way Yahweh treated Israel when the people were slaves in Egypt (pp. 183–84). And imitation of God emerges as one of the more distinctive features of Israel's ethic when compared with other ancient Near Eastern systems, for in most of these the gods are indeed the source of ethical obligation, but they themselves do not at all exemplify the conduct they command. 'Können in Mesopotamien Recht und Gerechtigkeit nur durch eine zeitweise

Ausserkraftsetzung des Rechts miteinander vermittelt werden, so begründet in Juda das Handeln Gottes als des Barmherzigen mit den Menschen ein Ethos der Barmherzigkeit' ('If justice in Mesopotamia could be mediated only by suspending the law from time to time, in Judah on the other hand the action of God the merciful founds an ethic of mercy') (p. 89).

3. No less than scholars like Eichrodt, Hempel, or Alt, who drew part of their inspiration according to Otto from dialectical theology, Otto himself is deeply interested in the *distinctiveness* of Old Testament ethics. Three features may be mentioned in particular.

First, Old Testament law is much more concerned than the laws of Mesopotamia with what we might call the sanctity of human life. It has often been observed that the Old Testament is unique in the ancient world in allowing no punishment for murder except the death of the offender: fines or compensation are regarded as taking insufficient account of the fundamental nature of the crime. In principle, the same law applies irrespective of the status or even the nationality of the victim. Otto indeed makes much of the tendency to encourage love of foreigners and, in effect, of all human beings *qua* human, which he sees as a highly distinctive feature of Old Testament law and as pointing forward to Jesus' ethics of the kingdom. The stringency of the laws about murder is an early illustration of the underlying belief in human life as an absolute value, regardless of whose life it is.

Second, and rather paradoxically, murder is the only case in which Old Testament law requires a talionic punishment. Otto's discussion of the laws of talion is sophisticated and, to my mind, convincing. Rather than following the common apologetic idea that 'an eye for an eye' represents a limitation of vengeance and so is to be saluted as a moral advance, Otto thinks that it originally expressed a literal tit-for-tat response to assaults on the person, just as people innocent of biblical studies think it does. But, he argues, it became a dead letter in Israel as soon as the administration of justice passed out of the hands of the local community into more centralized control, and the very codes which contain it show in their detailed provisions that they had set it aside, for it is *only* in the case of murder that talion operates. No other crime is punished talionically in any of the biblical codes whereas in Mesopotamian law it can be found quite often, usually as a way of safeguarding the special status of the upper classes. Fines were seen as adequate when members of the lower classes were assaulted, but for the aristocracy only talionic punishment could expunge the insult of assault. Israel had no class ethic and, consequently, also no talionic punishments (see p. 81). This argument needs to be carefully weighed and represents a substantial contribution to establishing what is original in the Old Testament's understanding of ethics.

Third, Israelite ethics rests on an optimistic anthropology in which the human race is created as something good and is seen as capable of living in fellowship with God, whereas in Mesopotamia the creation of humans is an aspect of the chaotic in the world. The vision of Psalm 8 is not shared by other ancient Near Eastern cultures (see p. 93), for which the human race is irredeemably unsatisfactory or even evil. This has implications for how the state is understood: in Mesopotamia, as a necessary evil, the only bulwark against disaster and the resurgence of chaos (see pp. 90–92); but in Israel, as an aspect of the cooperation between people, and between people and God, which was part of the divine intention from the first. This inevitably leads to a different way of thinking about society and about moral norms, and leads to that stress on human solidarity which is inimical to the idea of domination by one person over others and was bound to lead to a cautious attitude to the institution of absolute monarchy. Otto even goes so far as to suggest that the Old Testament's positive anthropology implies a stress on individual conscience (p. 115)— which will, I suspect, strike many readers as anachronistic. Still, the conviction that ethics is about living well with God rather than about salvaging the best that can be salvaged from cosmic disaster does do justice to one important strand in Old Testament thought and is to be welcomed. I am not sure it is the whole truth (what about the ethics of apocalyptic, for example?), and it is not fully clear to me that it fits with Otto's emphasis on the *Scheitern* of human moral effort, but it is certainly one truth and deserves its place in his system.

4. It is worth noting that Otto's analysis, like any attempt at a historical treatment of ethics in ancient Israel, inevitably depends on detailed datings of documents and events, none of which is uncontroversial, especially in the present climate. Here he perhaps falls between two stools. On the one hand, there is a great deal more on questions of 'introduction' than the average reader interested in the theological ethics of the Old Testament will probably want to plough through. But, on the other, his conclusions on matters of redaction of texts and, indeed, the history of Israel, are often stated in a summary form and not argued for in detail, so that highly vexed questions become matters of mere assertion. The most striking case of the latter tendency is on p. 212: 'The Decalogue arose in the exilic period.' Maybe it did, but more argumentation is needed. Again, passages from the Book of the Covenant or Deuteronomy are often printed in extenso with this or that verse in italics, representing a later addition, but we are seldom told how Otto knows that it is an addition. There is thus sometimes an air of rabbits being produced from hats. Otto has, in fact, argued for the details of the redaction of Old Testament law codes in a series of impressive articles, but in this textbook a lot has to be taken on trust.

Where the history of Israel is concerned, Otto has a particular interest in the late monarchy as the time when many of the foundations of Israelite ethics were laid. Sometimes this produces what seem rather strained conclusions.

Because much ethical material in Mesopotamia was attributed to Shamash, Otto often argues that it was the prevalence of a solar cult in preexilic Jerusalem that resulted in the prominence of particular distinctive ethical features, such as concern for the weaker members of society, even at a time when the cohesion of Judaean society was breaking down under the influence of urbanization and secularization. On the other hand, some ethical movements can also be seen as opposed to solar and astral tendencies in the official cult. Traditional arguments about the origins of Deuteronomy in Josiah's reformation are often brought in alongside these points, and the result is an impression that we know a great deal about life in seventh- and sixth-century Judah. One does not have to be a devotee of New Historicism to wonder if this is all really so firmly grounded as Otto seems to think.

5. I turn finally to a feature of Otto's work that I find really puzzling. He makes a great deal of the distinction between *Recht* and *Ethos*, and, as we have seen, argues that the redactional development of the Book of the Covenant shows a clear shift from the first to the second. (His chapter on the Book of the Covenant is entitled 'Vom Recht zum Ethos' (p. 18).) Ethics, that is, can be defined as the obligations human beings are, or feel themselves to be, under, which presuppose but are not exhausted by legal provisions. Ethics begins to operate when one reaches the bounds of the legally enforceable. Yet such a definition is sharply at odds with Otto's actual practice, for nearly all of his book is taken up with detailed analysis of law codes, so much so that (were it not for the long chapter on Wisdom) one might well say that, on *his* definition of ethics, the book is an account of the theological law of the Old Testament *rather than* of its theological ethics.

It would be defensible to argue that ethics is centrally concerned with what is enforceable, and certainly most people would think that what is enforceable is at least part of ethics, so that Otto's practice is perfectly reasonable: only, not on his own definition. Given the way *he* thinks of ethics, one would expect, on the contrary, a detailed analysis of the Prophets and of the implicit ethical standards to be found in narrative. Yet, as we have seen, these two areas are scarcely mentioned. And on most practical working definitions, one might look for a treatment of both *Recht* and *Ethos* in Otto's sense. It is, to me, very disappointing that the book is so one-sidedly focused on the explicit and leaves no room for the discussion of the ethics that lies beneath the surface, but it is nothing short of astonishing that it does so when *Ethos* is defined as Otto defines it. This is a shortcoming which severely limits the work's usefulness.

That a useful distinction along his lines can be drawn seems to me evident, but in drawing it, one would want to investigate the 'ethical' every bit as much as the legal side of the line. A recent study which adopts a similar definition to Otto's is Gordon Wenham's 'The Gap between Law and Ethics in the Bible'.[7]

Wenham argues precisely that the ethical interest of biblical prophecy and narrative often begins at the point where what can be enforced legally runs out. He is interested in the moral *ideals* of Israelite writers and thinkers, what they regard as truly desirable in a society, as opposed to the minimum standards that can be the subject of legislation. 'In three areas', he writes, 'idolatry, homicide, and adultery . . . the biblical writers hoped for much more than the mere avoidance of these offences. Their ideal was whole-hearted commitment to and intimacy with God, a love for the life with which the creator had endowed his creation, and total faithfulness between monogamous spouses. . . . This ideal is summed up in the imitation of God. "Be holy for I the LORD your God am holy" is not simply the motto of Leviticus, but the key to biblical ethical theory' (p. 27). Otto would surely agree. But, if so, why does he relegate such questions to the periphery of his study and concentrate instead on law? I can see no explanation.

Wenham has developed his ideas further in a full-length treatment, *Story as Torah*.[8] Studies of ethics in the Old Testament, he argues, have generally concentrated predominantly on legal and Wisdom literature: Otto is simply the most recent example of this tendency. Narrative texts have been widely neglected. Although traditional Judaism and Christianity alike have appealed to incidents and characters in the 'historical' books to justify moral precepts, modern biblical scholarship has shied away from this. It has been felt that the ethical standards appealed to in biblical narrative are too oblique or obscure to make using them sensible in any attempt at a synthesizing 'Old Testament Ethics'.

Wenham seeks to reinstate narrative as a source for ethical judgements based on the Old Testament. Like many recent biblical scholars, he eschews any interest in the underlying sources of biblical narrative and focuses instead on the 'final form' of the text, read through the techniques of rhetorical criticism as a persuasive whole. By emphasizing the place of the *implied* author, he tries to deflect attention from any concern with the real biblical writers and thus make his readings 'text-immanent' and secure from attack on source-critical grounds. Supposed stages in the growth of particular stories, or alleged interpolations or marginal comments, are ruled out: the interpretation is based on the existing form of the story. This, however, does not mean that the task of the interpreter is simple or obvious, as there remains much room for dispute about the intentions of the implied author. (There is a good illustration of this in Wenham's careful adjudication between two readings of Genesis 34 [the rape of Dinah] by Sternberg on the one hand,[9] and Fewell and Gunn on the other.[10]) It is simply that concentration is on the text's communicative intent, not on what may or may not lie behind it.

Most of Wenham's examples are taken from Genesis and Judges—an interesting pair because, in the first, there is so much that the implied author is shown to be commending and, in the second, so much that is being deplored. Lengthy chapters on the 'rhetorical function' of these two books set the scene for the ethical analysis that follows. In this, though many moral questions are addressed, two themes predominate.

The first repeats the point made in his article, that the biblical writers distinguish between the 'floor' and the 'ceiling' of ethical conduct. As we have seen, laws and wisdom precepts often set the basic minimum that is required for an action to be safe from actual legal process or overt condemnation: thus it is *illegal* to commit murder or adultery and *deplorable* to consort with prostitutes or to oppress the poor. But it is primarily the narrative texts that make it clear that basic minimal compliance is not regarded as the same as the ideal for which people should strive, which is set much higher. Adultery is banned; polygamy permitted; yet having more than one wife is shown to fall far short of the ideal proposed in Genesis, which is lifelong monogamous marriage, and those who practise bigamy, such as Jacob or Lamech, have a far from easy time of it.

Second, it is possible to distinguish between the moral attitudes of characters in the stories, who are frequently lacking in moral perception, and those of the narrators, at least so long as these are understood to be the *implied* authors and are not confused with the actual ancient Israelites who wrote the stories—these are inaccessible to us. Thus the often-expressed pessimism about whether we can really tell whether the actions of, say, the patriarchs are told with approval or disapproval is shown to be excessively cautious. There is no doubt, for example, that Joseph is presented as a model to be imitated and Esau as a type to be shunned. Sometimes Wenham may be too confident about this point. Gunkel's suggestion that the trickery of Jacob was regarded as admirable rather than deplorable by early readers is elided rather too easily by deploying the argument that we are not concerned with such 'pre-historic' readers, only with the implied audience of the finished narratives. After all, actual readers of those narratives have sometimes also reacted with a certain admiration to Jacob's exploits, and it is hard to be sure that the implied author's implied audience was actually different from such readers. Nevertheless, the point is in general a fair one: we frequently do come away from reading biblical narrative with a clear sense of what constitutes good and bad conduct, as generations of Bible readers have discovered.

This book is a considerable contribution to the study of biblical ethics and goes a long way to making good the lack of material about narrative in Otto's important work. A final chapter on the relation between Old and New Testament ethics provides, additionally, some reflections on how the Old Testament story may have continued to function ethically for the New Testament writers. Contrasts between the Testaments are played down, and continuity stressed, in a way consonant with Reformed readings of the Bible—to my taste making rather too little of the sense of newness found in New Testament writings, but always quite defensibly. A conclusion expresses the hope that the work will help ethicists to see the continuing relevance of the Old Testament, and I hope and believe this will indeed be so.

III

Where should the study of Old Testament ethics go next? I hope that it will follow Otto's lead in aiming primarily to present a descriptive, historical account of ethical beliefs and practices in ancient Israel as evidenced in the Old Testament, rather than attempting to systematize what is in the Old Testament in a synchronic way. There is nothing to prevent scholars from noting continuities and coherence within the different moral approaches to which the Old Testament bears witness, nor (like Otto) from pointing out things that are distinctive and potentially fruitful for ethics today in what the Old Testament has to say. But, to me, any attempt deliberately to read the text 'flat', as it were, ignoring historical variations and developments, is simply to return to precritical perceptions. Even Otto's careful developmentalism is a little too teleological for my taste, and I am concerned that he is so focused on continuities between Old Testament ethics and the 'ethics of the kingdom' in Christianity and gives so little space to any discussion of continuities or discontinuities with postbiblical Judaism. Nevertheless, his basic model is a historical one, which seems to me important.

From my last comments, on the lack of interest in prophecy and narrative, it is obvious that I would like to see those two great blocks of material (approximately two-thirds of the Old Testament) more strongly represented in an 'Old Testament Ethics'. Indeed, what I should like to see is a kind of second volume of Otto's work. What he has given us is an excellent first volume on what may be called explicit or overt ethical teaching in the Old Testament in its historical development. There is room for a volume on implicit ethics: the ethical norms that are implied by the prophets' criticisms of contemporary society and by the way narratives are constructed about the deeds of Israelite and pre-Israelite characters from the past. One of the deficiencies of Eichrodt's ethical studies is that, in handling narrative, he tends to look for evidence of very early attitudes to ethics *underlying* the stories of, say, the patriarchs or the early kings, and pays too little attention to the narratives themselves as the products of later periods in the history of Israel, for whose moral attitudes they may be very good evidence. This deficiency is partly made good in Wenham's work, but there is more work to be done here.

Nowadays, to be interested in the narratives as such seems to signal a primarily 'synchronic' and antihistorical concern, but that need not be so. The narratives were written by Israelites or Judaeans or Jews during what we may loosely call the Old Testament period, and they are primary evidence for what people thought about ethical questions in the period in which they were written. If the latest theories are correct, according to which all Old Testament narrative is postexilic, then we lack evidence for implicit moral attitudes in the preexilic age but have it in abundance for the Persian or Hellenistic periods; but even then it would still be *historical* evidence. There is no necessary connection between very late datings and synchronic readings. If, as I still believe to be the case, at least some Old Testament narrative material is earlier than this, then it makes sense to analyse it alongside the books of the Prophets, for example, and to ask about the ethical stance of authors in the preexilic age. Such a study would be just as dependent as Otto's on disputed datings and theories of redaction, but that is not to be avoided when one is dealing with endlessly rewritten texts such as so many of the Old Testament documents are.

It might still be the case that certain continuities or similarities of approach were to be found, even over texts widely separated in time. At all events, the quest for the more implicit types of ethical attitude is not doomed to failure from the start, and I cannot see that it is ruled out on Otto's own principles: his insistence on looking only at the explicit is a self-denying ordinance that has no necessary connection with his desire to establish 'ethics of the Old Testament' as a separate discipline from 'history of Israelite religion' or 'Old Testament theology', even though he seems to think it has.

Even in looking at the ethics of narrative texts—in which we could profit by some of the distinctions made by Wenham between ethical minima as against moral ideals—there is an important sociological dimension which ought not to be overlooked. Sociology has been part of the study of Old Testament ethics at least since the work of Hempel, which in many ways was ahead of its time in this regard. We need continually to ask whose ethics we are discovering—meaning by that not simply 'people of which period?' but also 'people of which class?' and 'people in which social situation?' It is important that Old Testament scholars take account of the style of ethical study pioneered by Wayne Meeks in New Testament scholarship and ask about the 'moral world' of the Israelite thinkers and writers to whom we owe the Old Testament, as well as the moral world of those on whose moral standards and achievements they were commenting.[11] Otto, of course, is strongly aware of sociological issues himself, as can be seen, for example, in his analysis of Wisdom ethics as the ethics of a particular social class. But sometimes perhaps he rushes past social questions rather quickly in the search for what is theologically significant, and that certainly should be avoided.

While insisting on the primacy of historical questions in the study of Old Testament ethics, then, I do not mean that we should limit ourselves to 'history' in an old-fashioned sense that excludes social or literary history. Both have a vital role to play in reconstructing ethical ideas in ancient Israel. I personally find the study of what is implicit in some ways more interesting than what is made explicit in law codes and wisdom teaching, and from that point of view feel that Otto's meticulous spade work on the latter leaves the route to discovering the former much more clear of stones and debris than it was before. The implicit in narrative is well served by Wenham's work, but it seems obvious that prophetic ethics would benefit from the same kind of treatment. Some of the essays in the present volume lay the foundations for a consideration of what is implied about ethical matters by the teaching of the prophets, but a full-length volume on prophetic ethics remains to be written. It would perhaps be the logical next step in what is a growing body of material on ethics in the Old Testament.

Notes

Notes for Introduction: The Moral Vision of the Old Testament

1. E. Otto, *Theologische Ethik des Alten Testaments* (Stuttgart: Kohlhammer, 1994), 62.
2. For a more detailed discussion of Otto see the Conclusion.
3. The ethics of the narrative books is now the subject of an extended study by G. J. Wenham, *Story as Torah: Reading the Old Testament Ethically* (Edinburgh: T. & T. Clark, 2000).
4. A. S. Byatt, *Elementals* (London: Vintage, 1998), 200.
5. See my discussion of this point in chap. 1, 'Understanding Old Testament Ethics', in this volume.
6. On this again see chap. 1, 'Understanding Old Testament Ethics'.
7. See R. E. Friedman, *The Hidden Book in the Bible* (London: Profile Books, 1998).
8. See chap. 4, 'Reading for Life', in this volume, and also my *Ethics and the Old Testament* (London: SCM, 1998).
9. Friedman, *The Hidden Book*, 56.
10. D. Reimer, 'The Apocrypha and Biblical Theology: The Case of Interpersonal Forgiveness', in *After the Exile: Essays in Honor of Rex Mason* (Macon, Ga.: Mercer University Press, 1996), 259–82.
11. See M. C. Nussbaum, *Love's Knowledge: Essays on Philosophy and Literature* (Oxford: Oxford University Press, 1990). See the discussion in chap. 4, 'Reading for Life', in this volume.
12. This idea is already developed in detail in H. C. Pyper, *David as Reader: 2 Samuel 12:1–15 and the Poetics of Fatherhood* (Leiden: Brill, 1996), to which I am greatly indebted.

Notes for Chapter 1: Understanding Old Testament Ethics

1. Cf. R. E. Clements, *A Century of Old Testament Study* (London, 1976), 107: '[T]he subject of Old Testament ethics has proved to be a most difficult one to deal with . . . the literature devoted to it has been surprisingly sparse . . . it has been difficult to avoid the merely superficial'.
2. BZAW 67 (Berlin, 1938; 2d ed., 1964). The more recent work of H. Van Oyen, *Die Ethik des Alten Testaments* (Gütersloh, 1967), is useful but in no way a replacement of Hempel. (This paper was of course written before the publication of E. Otto's *Theologische Ethik des Alten Testaments*, on which see the Conclusion.)
3. BWA(N)T 3:3 (Stuttgart, 1936).

4. W. Eichrodt, *Theologie des Alten Testaments*, vol. 2 (Leipzig, 1935); *Theology of the Old Testament*, vol. 2 (London, 1967). References are to the English version (=*Theology*).

5. SBT 1:4 (London, 1951).

6. *Theology* 2, 322–3.

7. Hempel's *Ethos* begins (p. 1), 'Das Ethos Israels ist keine Einheit, die sich auf Formeln bringen oder in Begriffe fassen liesse, welche durch die Jahrhunderte hin konstant geblieben wären' ('The ethics of Israel is *not a unity* such as could be summarized in a formula or captured in concepts that remained constant through the centuries'). But this is said (p. 2) primarily to stress that *actual ethical conduct* in Israel included wide divergences—that ancient Israelite life was 'kein Heiligenleben, auf Goldgrund gemalt' ('no life of the saints, painted on a golden background'). It is clear that Hempel is here thinking mainly of 'popular morality' in very early times, and that so far as ethical *norms* are concerned he does think in terms of a unified system which gradually supplanted the customs of an earlier time: see especially his discussion of Israelite sexual ethics, pp. 165ff.

8. *Theology* 2, 351.

9. See for example the discussion in D. S. Spriggs, *Two Old Testament Theologies* (London, 1975).

10. For this point cf. the arguments of J. W. Rogerson, 'The Old Testament view of nature: some preliminary questions', in *Instruction and Interpretation*, *OtSt* 20 (1977): 67–84.

11. *Theology* 2, 319–20.

12. Eichrodt at one point concedes the principle (*Theology* 2, 370): 'It must also of course be remembered that the degree to which the people were sensitive to the impact of the presence and intervention of the divine sovereign was not the same at all periods, nor was its effect the same on all sections of the nation'. But nothing seems to come of this.

13. *Theology* 2, 335.

14. Ibid., 329.

15. Ibid., 316.

16. *Ethos*, 189–92.

17. *Gott und Mensch*, passim.

18. *Man in the Old Testament*, 29.

19. In *Festschrift Otto Procksch* (Leipzig, 1934), 45–70.

20. This assumption may be found underlying even the much more open-minded article of F. Horst, 'Naturrecht und Altes Testament', *EvT* 10 (1950–51): 253–73 = *Gottes Recht*, ed. H. W. Wolff (1961), 235–259. Horst isolates a number of examples of 'natural law' in the Old Testament—e.g., the 'self-evident' laws of responsibility towards guests; he then argues that they are not 'secular' laws, but theological; and he concludes, on general grounds, that they are *therefore* a matter of obedience to the will of God. Both stages in this argument, it seems to me, need to be justified, and in each case with detailed evidence rather than with general principles of Old Testament theology. It may be that the theologizing of 'obvious' moral norms *logically* implies that they are commands of God; it does not follow that the Old Testament writers themselves saw the implication. Cf. Van Oyen, *Die Ethik*, and his 'Biblische Gerechtigkeit und weltliches Recht', *TZ* 6 (1950): 270–92.

21. Cf. Eichrodt, *Theology* 2, 349.

22. Ibid., 318.
23. Glencoe, Ill., 1952.
24. *Ancient Israel, its life and institutions*, 2d ed. (London, 1961).
25. Cf. W. McKane, *Prophets and Wise Men*, SBT 1:44 (London, 1965); R. N. Why-bray, *The Intellectual Tradition in Ancient Israel*, BZAW 135 (1974).
26. Cf. G. von Rad, *Studies in the Book of Deuteronomy*, SBT 1:9 (London, 1958); M. Weinfeld, *Deuteronomy and the Deuteronomic School* (Oxford, 1972); J. Wein-green, *From Bible to Mishna* (Manchester, 1976).
27. Eichrodt, *Theology* 2, 317–18.
28. Ibid., 317.
29. *Ethos*, 1–2.
30. See the list illustrating the humanness and variety of ethical ideals and attitudes in early Israel on pp. 2–4 of *Ethos*.
31. T. L. Thompson, *The Historicity of the Patriarchal Narratives*, BZAW 133 (1974); J. Van Seters, *Abraham in History and Tradition* (New Haven and London, 1975).
32. K. J. Dover, *Greek Popular Morality in the Time of Plato and Aristotle* (Oxford, 1974).
33. Ibid., 13.
34. Demosthenes, 59:22, cited in Dover, 14.
35. Dover, *Greek Popular Morality*, 14.
36. Ibid., 18.
37. H. W. Wolff, 'Das Zitat im Prophetenspruch', BeiEvTh 4 (1937): 3–112 = *Gesammelte Studien* (Munich, 1964), 36–129.
38. See chap. 6: 'Amos's Oracles against the Nations'.
39. The image of Yahweh as Israel's husband probably carries the implication that she owes him obedience (though of course it also expresses the conviction of his love for her).
40. *Ethos*, 189ff.
41. See chap. 2 in this volume.
42. Cf. von Rad, *Wisdom in Israel* (London, 1972), 62–63.
43. M. Buber, *Kampf um Israel* (Berlin, 1933), chapter 'Nachahmung Gottes', 75.
44. *Theology* 2, 373.

Notes for Chapter 2: Natural Law
and Poetic Justice in the Old Testament

1. F. Horst, 'Naturrecht und Altes Testament', *EvT* 10 (1950–51): 253–73 = *Gottes Recht*, ed. H. W. Wolff (1961), 235–59. H. S. Gehman, 'Natural Law and the Old Testament', in *Biblical Studies in Honour of H. C. Alleman*, ed. J. M. Myers et al. (New York, 1960), 109–22, provides an exception to the general neglect of natural law in Old Testament scholarship, but his conclusions are mainly negative.
2. Ed. J. Macquarrie (London, 1967); see 'Natural Law' by V. J. Bourke.
3. Cited by Aquinas *In IV Sent.*, d33 q1 a1 ad 4um (see C. E. Curran, 'Absolute Norms in Moral Theology', in *Norm and Context in Christian Ethics*, ed. Outka and Ramsey (London, 1969), 143).
4. e.g., Deut. 24:17–18.
5. J. L. Mays, *Amos* (London, 1969), ad loc., cf. W. Eichrodt, *Theology of the Old Testament* II (London, 1967), 333.
6. C. S. Rodd, 'Shall not the Judge of All the Earth do what is just? (Gen. xviii. 25)', *ExpTim* 83 (1972): 137–39. See now Rodd's detailed discussion in *Glimpses of a Strange Land: Studies in Old Testament Ethics* (Edinburgh: T. & T. Clark, 2001).

7. J. Fichtner, 'Jesaja unter den Weisen', *TLZ* 74 (1949): cols. 75–80.
8. J. W. Whedbee, *Isaiah and Wisdom* (Nashville, 1971).
9. Ibid., 317–19.
10. *ZTK* 52 (1955): 1–42.
11. Ed. K. Koch (Darmstadt, 1972); the article referred to in note 10 is reprinted in this collection.
12. K. Fahlgren, *Sedaqa* (Diss. Uppsala, 1932); extracts appear in *Um das Prinzip der Vergeltung* (= *Prinzip*).
13. J. Pedersen, *Israel* I & II (London, 1926).
14. G. von Rad, *Wisdom in Israel* (London, 1972).
15. H. Graf Reventlow, 'Sein Blut komme auf sein Haupt', *VT* 10 (1960): 311–27; reprinted in *Prinzip*.
16. See H. Gunkel, 'Vergeltung im Alten Testament', *RGG* 5 (1931): 1529–33; also in *Prinzip*.
17. Cf. H. van Oyen, *Die Ethik des Alten Testaments* (Gütersloh, 1967), 68; R. Knierim, *Die Hauptbegriffe für Sünde im Alten Testament* (Gütersloh, 1965), 73 ff.
18. J. Scharbert, 'ŠLM im Alten Testament', in *Lex tua veritas* (H. Junker Festschrift; Trier, 1961), 209–29; also in *Prinzip*.

Notes for Chapter 3:
The Basis of Ethics in the Hebrew Bible

1. W. H. Schmidt, 'Zu diesem Heft', *VF* 36, no. 1 (1991): 1–2, introducing the article by E. Otto, 'Forschungsgeschichte der Entwürfe einer Ethik im Alten Testament', 3–37.
2. Ibid.
3. R. Smend, 'Ethik III: Altes Testament', *TRE* 10 (1995): 423–35.
4. See chap. 1 in this volume.
5. See N. J. Biggar, *The Hastening that Waits: Karl Barth's Ethics* (Oxford: Oxford University Press, 1993).
6. Mic. 6:6.
7. Otto, 'Forschungsgeschichte', 19.
8. Ibid.
9. See p. 29 above.
10. Cf. Otto, 'Forschungsgeschichte', 29–30.
11. W. Eichrodt, *Man in the Old Testament* (London: SCM Press, 1951), 29.
12. See M. Greenberg, 'Some Postulates of Biblical Criminal Law', *Yehezkel Kaufmann Jubilee Volume*, ed. M. Haran (Jerusalem: Magnes, 1960), 5–28, reprinted in *The Jewish Expression*, ed. J. Goldin (New Haven and London: Yale University Press, 1976), 18–37; J. J. Finkelstein, *The Ox that Gored* (Transactions of the American Philosophical Society 71/2; Philadelphia: The American Philosophical Society, 1981); M. Douglas, *Purity and Danger* (London: Routledge & Kegan Paul, 1966).
13. J. Barr, *Biblical Faith and Natural Theology: The Gifford Lectures for 1991* (Oxford: Clarendon Press, 1993).
14. See chap. 6, 'Amos's Oracles against the Nations'.
15. Otto, 'Forschungsgeschichte', 17–18.
16. John Rogerson has suggested instead the term 'natural morality', and this seems to me entirely satisfactory as an alternative; see J. W. Rogerson, 'Old Testament Ethics', in *Text in Context*, ed. A. D. H. Mayes (Oxford: Oxford University Press, 2000), 116–37.

17. Otto, 'Forschungsgeschichte', 19.
18. Ibid.
19. Ibid., 20.
20. See C. S. Rodd, 'Shall not the Judge of All the Earth do what is just?', *ExpTim* 83 (1972): 137–39. In his recent book on Old Testament ethics, *Glimpses of a Strange Land: Studies in Old Testament Ethics* (Edinburgh: T. & T. Clark, 2001), Rodd sharply rejects the interpretation of any of the material surveyed here in terms of 'imitation of God'; see especially 65–76. I do not find his arguments entirely convincing.
21. Otto, 'Forschungsgeschichte'.
22. W. H. Schmidt, *Die Zehn Gebote im Rahmen alttestamentlicher Ethik* (Erträge der Forschung 281; Darmstadt: Wissenschaftliche Buchgesellschaft, 1993).
23. Cf. Biggar, *The Hastening*.
24. E. Jacob, 'Les bases théologiques de l'éthique de l'Ancien Testament', VTSup 7 (1960): 39–51.
25. W. Eichrodt, *Theology of the Old Testament*, vol. 2 (London: SCM Press, 1967).

Notes for Chapter 4: Reading for Life: The Use of the Bible in Ethics

1. M. C. Nussbaum, *The Fragility of Goodness* (Cambridge: Cambridge University Press, 1986).
2. Ibid., 300–301.
3. Pindar, *Nemean*, viii; cited in Nussbaum, *Fragility*, vi.
4. *By Blue Ontario's Shore*; cited in M. C. Nussbaum, *Love's Knowledge: Essays on Philosophy and Literature* (Oxford: Oxford University Press, 1990), 54.
5. Nussbaum, *Fragility*, 314–15.
6. Compare my 'Understanding Old Testament Ethics', 'Natural Law and Poetic Justice in the Old Testament', and 'Ethics in Isaiah of Jerusalem': chaps. 1, 2, and 7 in the present volume.
7. J. Magonet, *Bible Lives* (London: SCM, 1992).
8. See note 4. I am greatly indebted to Dr. Tal Goldfajn for introducing me to *Love's Knowledge* and for helping me to see the fruitfulness of Nussbaum's approach.
9. Nussbaum, *Love's Knowledge*, 345–46.
10. J. Cheryl Exum, *Tragedy and Biblical Narrative: Arrows of the Almighty* (Cambridge: Cambridge University Press, 1992).

Notes for Chapter 5: Virtue in the Bible

1. For a survey, see R. Crisp and M. Slote, eds., *Virtue Ethics* (Oxford: Oxford University Press, 1977).
2. See, classically, Alisdair MacIntyre, *After Virtue* (London: Duckworth, 1981); also J. Kotva, *The Christian Case for Virtue Ethics* (Washington, D.C.: University of Georgetown Press, 1996).
3. See the discussion in G. Meilaender, *The Theory and Practice of Virtue* (Notre Dame, Ind.: University of Notre Dame Press, 1984).
4. See especially M. C. Nussbaum, *The Fragility of Goodness* (Cambridge: Cambridge University Press, 1986) and *Love's Knowledge* (Oxford and New York: Oxford University Press, 1990).
5. See Stanley Hauerwas, *Vision and Virtue* (Notre Dame, Ind.: University of Notre Dame Press, 1981).

6. See E. P. Sanders, *Paul and Palestinian Judaism: A Comparison of Patterns of Religion* (Philadelphia: Fortress Press, 1977) and *Paul, the Law, and the Jewish People* (Philadelphia: Fortress Press, 1983).
7. On 'natural law' in the Old Testament see my 'Natural Law and Poetic Justice in the Old Testament', chap. 2 in this volume.
8. E. W. Heaton, *Solomon's New Men* (London: Thames & Hudson, 1974), 124–26.
9. Ambrose, *De mysteriis* 1 *(Sources Chrétiennes* 25bis), 156.
10. See the discussion in R. N. Whybray, *The Succession Narrative: A Study of II Samuel 9–20, I Kings 1 and 2* (London: SCM Press, 1968).
11. D. M. Gunn, *The Story of King David* (Sheffield: JSOT Press, 1978).
12. See 'Reading for Life: The Use of the Bible in Ethics', chap. 4 in this volume.
13. *Vision and Virtue*, 14.
14. This paper was read at the meeting of the Society for the Study of Christian Ethics at Wycliffe Hall, Oxford, on 11 September 1998. I am greatly indebted to Professor Oliver O'Donovan for help and advice during its preparation.

Notes for Chapter 6: Amos's Oracles against the Nations

Section I

1. For an important discussion of the principle involved here see C. B. Macpherson, *The Political Theory of Possessive Individualism* (Oxford, 1962), especially 6–7.

Section II

1. R. E. Clements, *Prophecy and Tradition* (Oxford, 1975), 60–61.
2. N. K. Gottwald, *All the Kingdoms of the Earth* (New York and London, 1964).
3. J. H. Hayes, 'The Usage of Oracles against Foreign Nations in Ancient Israel', *JBL* 87 (1968): 81–92.
4. Cf. R. Bach, *Die Aufforderung zur Flucht und zum Kampf im alttestamentlichen Prophetenspruch* (WMANT 9; 1962).
5. On taunts against individuals see R. de Vaux, 'Single Combat in the Old Testament', in *The Bible and the Ancient Near East* (London, 1972), 122–35.
6. Gottwald, *All the Kingdoms*, 48; see his note 14 for bibliography.
7. Which, however, need not be intended to be heard by him; it may be a 'word of power', cf. G. Fohrer, 'Prophetie und Magie', in *Studien zur alttestamentlichen Prophetie* (1949–65) (BZAW 99; 1967), 242–64 (reprinted from *ZAW* 78 (1966)); cf. also Clements, *Prophecy and Tradition*, 62.
8. See Gottwald, *All the Kingdoms*, 47–50; W. F. Albright, 'The Oracles of Balaam', *JBL* 63 (1944): 207–33; F. M. Cross and D. N. Freedman, 'The Blessing of Moses', *JBL* 67 (1948): 191–210, for further discussion of the linguistic and orthographical criteria involved.
9. See especially G. von Rad, *Der heilige Krieg im alten Israel* (Zurich, 1951), and *Old Testament Theology*, vol. 2 (London, 1965), 159ff.; E. Würthwein, 'Jesaja 7, 1–9. Ein Beitrag zu dem Thema "Prophetie und Politik,"' in *Theologie als Glaubenswagnis* (Festschrift for Karl Heim; Tübingen and Hamburg, 1954), 47–63; R. Bach, *Die Aufforderung*; H. Wildberger, '"Glauben" im Alten Testament', *ZTK* 65 (1968): 129–59.
10. See, inter alia, G. Dossin, 'Sur le prophétisme à Mari' in *La divination en Mésopotamie ancienne et dans les régions voisines* (14e rencontre assyriologique internationale, Strasbourg 2–6 July, 1965; Paris, 1966), 77–86; F. Ellermeier,

Prophetie in Mari und Israel (Theologische und orientalische Arbeiten 1; Hertzberg, 1968); A. Malamat, 'Prophetic Revelations in New Documents from Mari and the Bible', VTSup 15 (1966): 214–19; W. L. Moran, 'New Evidence from Mari on the History of Prophecy', *Biblica* 50 (1969): 15–56; J. H. Hayes, 'Prophetism at Mari and Old Testament Parallels', *AThR* 49 (1967): 397–409.

11. G. Fohrer, 'Remarks on Modern Interpretations of the Prophets', *JBL* 80 (1961): 309–19.

12. Both arguments are rightly used by Clements, *Prophecy and Tradition*, 71.

13. This point is well made by Gottwald, *All the Kingdoms*, 109–10. But see below, pp. 94 and 110, for attempts to see a crime against Israel here.

14. S. Herrmann, *A History of Israel in Old Testament Times* (London, 1975), 233–34, notes recent cautions against the 'Indian summer' or 'lull before the storm' view of the reigns of Jeroboam II and Uzziah; nevertheless, it remains implausible to think of Israel as surrounded by enemies in this period. See below, chapter 4.

15. Clements, *Prophecy and Tradition*, 60, 65.

16. Ibid., 71–72.

17. See F. Stolz, *Interpreting the Old Testament* (London, 1975), 60–62, and bibliography there.

18. See S. Mowinckel, *The Psalms in Israel's Worship* (Oxford, 1962), I:217–18 and II:58–61.

19. See H. J. Kraus, *Psalmen* (BK XV; 1966), ad loc.

20. Ibid.; cf. also J. Begrich, 'Das priesterliche Heilsorakel', *ZAW* 52 (1934): 81–92.

21. E. Würthwein, 'Amosstudien', *ZAW* 62 (1949): 10–52.

22. See J. Gray, *I & II Kings* (OTL; 1964), ad loc.; B. S. Childs, *Isaiah and the Assyrian Crisis* (SBT II.3; 1967), 103.

23. See E. Würthwein, 'Der Ursprung der prophetischen Gerichtsrede' in *Wort und Existenz: Studien zum Alten Testament* (Göttingen, 1970), 111–28 (= *ZTK* 49 (1952): 1–16). For an exhaustive discussion of the origin of *Gerichtsreden*, see E. von Waldow, *Der traditionsgeschichtliche Hintergrund der prophetischen Gerichtsreden* (BZAW 85; 1963).

24. This theory is discussed at length by G. H. Jones in his unpublished Ph.D. dissertation 'An Examination of Some Leading Motifs in the Prophetic Oracles against Foreign Nations' (Bangor: University College of North Wales, 1970). He sees as early as Gressmann the implication that 'the oracles against foreign nations pronounce judgment on the nations, which meant salvation for Israel'. He adds, 'That the oracles against foreign nations were intentionally salvation oracles in this way is very unlikely' (4).

25. H. Graf Reventlow, *Das Amt des Propheten bei Amos* (Göttingen, 1962); *Wächter über Israel: Ezechiel und seine Traditionen* (BZAW 82; 1962); *Liturgie und prophetisches Ich bei Jeremia* (Gütersloh, 1963).

26. A. Bentzen, 'The Ritual Background of Amos 1:2–2:16' (OS 8; 1950) 85–99; see also A. S. Kapelrud, *Central Ideas in Amos* (Oslo, 1961).

27. See below, pp. 95–6.

28. M. Weiss, 'The Pattern of the "Execration Texts" in the Prophetic Literature', *IEJ* 19 (1969): 150–57.

29. For this point cf. also S. M. Paul, 'Amos 1:3–2:3: A Concatenous Literary Pattern', *JBL* 90 (1971): 397–403. I do not, however, think that his own attractive alternative theory of a catchword or cyclic arrangement in the oracles has any

more power to tip the scales against the probable deletions discussed in section 2.

30. Fohrer, 'Prophetie und Magie', 40–42.
31. Cf. K. Tallquist, *Himmelsgegenden und Winde* (Studia Orientalia 2; Helsinki, 1928), 118–19. Weiss ('The Pattern', 156) prefers this to the explanation offered by H. W. Wolff) *Joel and Amos* [Philadelphia, 1977], 145–46)—following W. Helck, *Die Beziehungen Ägyptens zu Vorderasien im 3. und 2. Jahrtausend vor Chr.* (Ägyptologische Abhandlungen 5; Wiesbaden, 1962), 62–63, that the order of naming of countries in Egyptian texts follows the major trading routes from Egypt.
32. See below, p. 111.
33. Wolff, *Joel and Amos*, 145–47.
34. In *Das Amt des Propheten bei Amos*.
35. Gottwald, *All the Kingdoms*, 104.
36. See below, p. 106.
37. Gottwald, *All the Kingdoms*, 105.
38. Ibid., 106.
39. Clements, *Prophecy and Tradition*, 65.
40. Wolff, *Joel and Amos*, 138; cf. the same author's *Amos' geistige Heimat* (Neukirchen-Vluyn, 1964), 26–29.
41. Cf. W. M. W. Roth, 'The Numerical Sequence x/x + 1 in the Old Testament', *VT* 12 (1962): 300–11, and 'Numerical Sayings in the Old Testament', VTSup 13 (1965).
42. Gottwald adds another argument, that Amos appears to have been familiar with 'an ancient prophetic scroll which was apparently also employed in Joel 3:16–18'. In this he draws on Y. Kaufmann, *A History of the Religion of Israel* (tr. M. Greenberg; London, 1961), III.1: 61–62. But few commentators regard Amos 1:2 as part of the oracles against the nations in any case; frequently it is taken to be inauthentic. Other explanations than a common source are available for the literary connection with Joel.
43. Clements, *Prophecy and Tradition*, 72.
44. 'Die Bedrohung von Feinden mochte man zu jeder Zeit gern hören': author's own translation from Wolff, *Dodekapropheton 2: Joel und Amos*, 181 (see note 31 above); cf. Wolff, *Joel and Amos*, 149.

Section III

1. H. W. Hogg, 'The Starting Point of the Religious Message of Amos' in *Transactions of the 3rd International Congress for the History of Religions*, ed. P. S. Allen and J. de M. Johnson (Oxford, 1908), I: 325–27; cited in R. S. Cripps, *A Critical and Exegetical Commentary on the Book of Amos*, 2d ed. (London, 1955); cf. K. Budde, 'Zu Text und Auslegung des Buches Amos', *JBL* 43 (1924): 46–131.
2. A. Néher, *Amos* (Paris, 1950).
3. J. Morgenstern, 'Amos Studies IV', *HUCA* 32 (1961).
4. Wolff, *Joel and Amos*, ad loc.; A. Weiser, *Das Buch der zwölf kleinen Propheten* (ATD; 1967), ad loc.
5. Budde, 'Zu Text'.
6. V. Maag, *Text, Wortschatz und Begriffswelt des Buches Amos* (Leiden, 1951), 5.
7. T. H. Robinson, *Die zwölf kleinen Propheten* (HAT; 1938).
8. There is some evidence of links between Phoenicia and Edom as early as the Ras Shamra texts: cf. Keret III.5, where Keret undertakes a journey to *udm*.
9. W. Nowack, *Die kleinen Propheten* (Göttingen, 1897).

10. Weiser, *Das Buch der zwölf kleinen Propheten*, ad loc.
11. W. R. Harper, *Amos and Hosea* (ICC; London, 1905).
12. E. A. Edghill, *The Book of Amos* (London, 1914).
13. Cited ibid.
14. VTE 7:545f.
15. See A. Malamat, 'Amos 1:5 in the Light of the Til Barsip Inscriptions', *BASOR* 129 (1953): 25f.
16. M. Haran, 'The Rise and Decline of the Empire of Jeroboam ben Joash', *VT* 17 (1967): 266–97.
17. Gottwald, *All the Kingdoms*, 95 (footnote).
18. See J. A. Fitzmyer, *The Aramaic Inscriptions of Sefire* (Biblica et Orientalia 19; Rome, 1967); cf. *KAI* 224:2–3.
19. Cf. Deut. 21:10; 2 Sam. 12:31; and CH 280f. (*ANET* 177).
20. M. Fishbane, 'The Treaty Background of Amos 1:11', *JBL* 89 (1970): 313–18. Cf. also J. Priest, 'The Covenant of Brothers', *JBL* 84 (1965): 400–406.
21. If Israel is indeed meant, we may recall 2 Sam. 5:11 and 1 Kgs. 5:15ff. Cripps's suggestion that the covenant thus infringed was between Edom and the state to which the slaves belonged (Israel, he thought) could be right, but does not seem a natural interpretation.
22. Fishbane has since modified his position slightly and now holds that *rḥmyw* and *ra'amu* are translation equivalents, though deriving ultimately from different Semitic roots: see his 'Additional Remarks on RḤMYW (Amos 1:11)' (*JBL* 91 [1972]: 391–93). This point about the semantic as opposed to etymological equivalence of the two roots had been made by G. Schmuttermayr, 'RḤM— eine lexikalische Studie' (*Biblica* 51 [1970]: 499–532).
23. G. R. Driver ('Linguistic and Textual Problems—Minor Prophets II', *JTS* 39 [1938]: 260–73) argues that this crime could have nothing to do with enlarging one's borders, and so that the passage is best understood as 'because they broke through into the plateau' (*bwh* interpreted from an Arabic analogue). Of the atrocity against pregnant women he says 'being an incident in all ancient campaigns, [it] was unlikely to be the subject of a special denunciation by the prophet'—cf. Budde, 'Zu Text'. This begs a number of questions!
24. Würthwein, 'Amosstudien', 10–52.
25. N. H. Torczyner, *hallason we hassepher* (Jerusalem, 1948), I.66.
26. J. R. Bartlett, 'The Moabites and Edomites' in *Peoples of Old Testament Times*, ed. D. J. Wiseman (Oxford, 1973), 228–58—for this suggestion see note 84 on p. 254.
27. K. Marti, 'Zur Komposition von Amos 1:3–2:3', *BZAW* 33 (1917): 323–30.
28. H. E. W. Fosbroke, *Amos* (IB VI; New York, 1956).
29. J. L. Mays, *Amos* (OTL; 1969).
30. Wolff, *Joel and Amos*, 140–41.
31. Cf. the defences by K. Cramer, *Amos—Versuch einer theologischen Interpretation* (BWA(N)T III.15; 1930); Priest, 'The Covenant'; Fishbane, 'The Treaty Background'; M. A. Beek, 'The Religious Background of Amos 2:6–8' (OS 5; 1948), 132–41; and many of the older commentators.
32. W. Rudolph ('Die angefochtenen Völkersprüche in Amos 1 und 2' in *Schalom (Studien zu Glaube und Geschichte Israels, A. Jepsen zum 70. Geburtstag dargebracht)*, ed. K. H. Bernhardt [Stuttgart, 1971]) argues that the sin of abandoning the law contains all the other sins with which Amos might have charged Judah, so that this objection does not stand; though he accepts the deletion of

v. 4b (the condemnation of idols). There are, however, no other examples of such an attitude to 'the Torah' in Amos. Rudolph also denies that the small formal variations noted by Wolff can be used to support deletions, since other variations are ignored—e.g., *wĕḥiṣattî* for *wĕšilaḥtî* in 1:14. But it must be said that the allegedly significant variations noted above are more substantial than this.

33. Marti, 'Zur Komposition'.
34. B. Duhm, 'Anmerkungen zu den zwölf Propheten', *ZAW* 31 (1911): 1–43 (especially 8–9).
35. Marti, 'Zur Komposition'.
36. See above, pp. 86–8.

Section IV

1. The dating followed in this chapter is that of K. T. Andersen, 'Die Chronologie der Könige von Israel und Juda', *ST* 23 (1969): 69–114.
2. See Weiser, *Das Buch der zwölf kleinen Propheten* (ATD; Göttingen, 1967), and cf. J. Bright, *A History of Israel* (London, 1966), 252.
3. Clements, *Prophecy and Tradition*, 65.
4. In a private communication.
5. Wolff, *Joel and Amos*, 148–51.
6. Herrmann, *A History of Israel*, part II, chapters 6 and 7.
7. On Aramaean history see E. G. H. Kraeling, *Aram and Israel* (New York, 1918); A. Malamat, 'The Arameans' in *Peoples of Old Testament Times*, ed. D. J. Wiseman, and bibliography there.
8. Herrmann, *A History of Israel*, 213.
9. Reading the verbs in 1 Kgs. 11:24 as singular, with Gray, *I & II Kings* (OTL), ad loc.
10. See Herrmann, *A History of Israel*, 176; Bright, *A History*, 193.
11. Bright, *A History*, 224.
12. See Malamat, 'The Arameans'.
13. J. M. Miller, 'The Elisha Cycle and the Accounts of the Omride Wars', *JBL* 85 (1966): 441–54, following A. Jepsen, 'Israel und Damaskus', *AfO* 14 (1942): 153–72, and ultimately A. Kuenen (*Historisch-kritische Einleitung in die Bücher des Alten Testaments*, 1:2, p. 83 note 13) and G. Hölscher (*Eucharisterion*, 185–91). Cf. also Miller's 'The Fall of the House of Ahab', *VT* 17 (1967): 307–24. Miller's arguments are summarized in his *The Old Testament and the Historian* (London, 1976), chapter 2.
14. See Jepsen, 'Israel und Damaskus'. A common explanation has been that 'Benhadad' was a 'throne name': cf. M. Unger, *Israel and the Aramaeans of Damascus* (London, 1957), 70, and Kraeling, *Aram and Israel*, chap. 9.
15. Incidentally, this is another argument against supposing that Amos is here selecting from much older oracles, as Kaufmann thinks (*History of the Religion of Israel*, III.1, 61–62); the oracle cannot antedate the accession of the sole Benhadad, in the time of Jehu at the earliest.
16. *ANET* 279–80; cf. Malamat, 'The Arameans'.
17. Miller argues (*VT* 17:313–14, and *JBL* 85:444–45) that the discrepancy between this passage and 1 Kings 22 is evidence for the 'double redaction' of the Deuteronomic History rejected by M. Noth in *Überlieferungsgeschichtliche Studien*, vol. 1 (Halle, 1943), especially 45–64. This is too large a question to enter into here.

18. Unless we take seriously the account in 2 Kings 6 of a siege of Samaria by 'Benhadad' in the reign of Joram, a little before this. But see below.
19. Malamat, 'The Arameans', 145. Wolff (*Joel and Amos*, 150) identifies Adadnirari III with the 'saviour' of 2 Kgs. 13:5 (thus also Gottwald, *All the Kingdoms*, 82), though Herrmann (*A History of Israel*, 228) thinks that this refers to an earlier and very temporary check to the Aramaean advance by an unnamed charismatic leader in Israel itself. There seems little to be said for the Jerusalem Bible's suggestion that Jeroboam II is meant, by anticipation. There have been many other suggested identifications, including Elisha (thus Miller, 'The Elisha Cycle', 442–43). J. A. Soggin ('Amos VI.13–14 und I:3 auf dem Hintergrund der Beziehungen zwischen Israel und Damaskus im 9. und 8. Jahrhundert' in *Near Eastern Studies in Honor of W. F. Albright*, ed. H. Goedicke [Baltimore and London, 1971], 433–41) comments ruefully 'quot capita, tot sententiae'.
20. Herrmann, *A History of Israel*, 232.
21. This represents a return to the views of Miller's predecessors, such as Jepsen ('Israel und Damaskus').
22. 2 Kgs. 6:8–23 represents a separate problem: another account from the days of Ben-hadad, but impossible to date.
23. Compare Gray, *I & II Kings*, 404.
24. Haran, 'The Rise and Decline', 266–97.
25. On the meaning of 'Lebo-hamath' see K. Elliger, 'Die Nordgrenze des Reiches Davids', *PJB* 32 (1936): 34–73 (especially 42). Haran ('The Rise and Decline', 282–84) argues that, whatever its exact meaning, the general sense of the stereotyped phrase is that Jeroboam had free access to the Euphrates, i.e., had restored in principle the northern holdings of Solomon.
26. Wolff, *Joel and Amos*, 150.
27. The Sefire treaties provide evidence for the relative independence of the Aramaean states at this time; see Fitzmyer, *The Aramaic Inscriptions of Sefire*, and M. Noth, 'Der historische Hintergrund der Inschriften von sefire', *ZDPV* 77 (1961): 138–45.
28. See Soggin, 'Amos VI.13–14'.
29. S. Cohen ('The Political Background of the Words of Amos', *HUCA* 36 [1965]: 153–60) argues strongly for this: even if Karnaim and Lo-debar are recent *victories*, 4:10f. and 5:15 probably point to recent setbacks.
30. Cf. above, p. 93.
31. On *sgr* see above, p. 93.
32. Kaufmann, *History of the Religion of Israel*, II.1, 61ff.
33. Cf. Gray, *I & II Kings*. For counterarguments see R. E. Murphy, 'Israel and Moab in the Ninth Century B.C.', *CBQ* 15 (1953): 409–17.
34. K.-H. Bernhardt, 'Der Feldzug der drei Könige' in *Schalom*. Festschrift for A. Jepsen, 11–22.
35. See above, p. 101.
36. Gottwald, *All the Kingdoms*, 70–74, sees this as a 'Holy War'. Even if this is so, it conflicts just as strongly with the presentation of the campaign, in 3:7, as the reconquest of a rebellious vassal.
37. Thus Bartlett, 'The Moabites and Edomites', 238.
38. This was suggested by Wellhausen, though it is dismissed as too speculative by M. Noth ('Eine palästinische Lokalüberlieferung in 2 Chron. 20' *ZDPV* 67 [1944]: 45–71), who prefers to see it as a reminiscence of a small local con-

frontation much nearer to the Chronicler's day; and by W. Rudolph, *Chronikbücher* (HAT 21; 1955), ad loc.

39. It may be noted that the Lucianic recension of the LXX reads 'Ahaziah' for 'Jehoshaphat' in this chapter—see J. R. Bartlett, 'The Rise and Fall of the Kingdom of Edom', *PEQ* 104 (1972): 26–37; cf. also J. D. Shenkel, *Chronology and Recensional Development in the Greek Text of Kings* (Cambridge, 1968), 93–108.

Section V

1. Thus Weiser in *Das Buch der zwölf kleinen Propheten* and in *Die Profetie des Amos* (BZAW 53; 1929); Edghill, *The Book of Amos*; J. Marsh, *Amos and Micah* (London, 1959); S. Lehming, 'Erwägungen zu Amos', *ZTK* 55 (1958): 145–69; Cripps, *Commentary*; P. Humbert, *Un béraut de la justice—Amos* (Lausanne, 1917); J. Vollmer, *Geschichtliche Rückblicke und Motive in der Prophetie des Amos, Hosea und Jesaja* (BZAW 119; 1971); E. Hammershaimb, *The Book of Amos* (Oxford, 1970); Wolff, *Joel and Amos*.

2. 'Musik für die Ohren der lauschenden Israeliten' ('Music to the ears of the listening Israelites'; Weiser, *Die Profetie des Amos*, 102).

3. Cf. H. W. Wolff, 'Das Zitat im Prophetenspruch' in *Gesammelte Studien* (Munich, 1964), 36–129 (= EvT Beiheft 4 [1937], 3–112).

4. Würthwein, 'Amosstudien'; cf. the same author's 'Der Ursprung der prophetischen Gerichtsrede'.

5. Weiser (*Die Profetie des Amos*, 21) makes a strong case for deliberate dramatic effect here. Much the same point about Yahweh's patience is made in 4:6–12, though there the 'chances' have been provided by awful warnings rather than by acts of obvious mercy.

6. Wolff, 'Das Zitat'.

7. See J. W. Whedbee, *Isaiah and Wisdom* (Nashville, 1971), 47.

8. See S. Terrien, 'Amos and Wisdom', in *Israel's Prophetic Heritage*, ed. B. W. Anderson and W. Harrelson (New York, 1962); J. Lindblom, 'Wisdom in the Old Testament Prophets' in *Wisdom in Israel and in the Ancient Near East*, ed. M. Noth (VTSup 3; 1960); and H. W. Wolff, *Amos' geistige Heimat*.

9. See Wolff's comments, *Joel and Amos*, 312–14.

10. See above p. 86, for discussion of the view that oracles against the nations imply victory for Israel.

11. Cf. the similar criticisms by Lehming, 'Erwägungen zu Amos'.

12. See p. 86 above.

13. Kapelrud, *Central Ideas in Amos*.

Section VI

1. See above, p. 85.

2. Haran, 'Jeroboam ben Joash', 273–74.

3. This is also the explanation given by Haran.

4. Weiser, *Die Profetie des Amos*, 112.

5. F. C. Fensham, 'Common Trends in Curses of the Near Eastern Treaties and *kudurru*-Inscriptions compared with Maledictions of Amos and Isaiah', *ZAW* 75 (1957): 155–75.

6. R. E. Clements, *Prophecy and Covenant*, SBT 1:43 (1965). Clements's more recent work (*Prophecy and Tradition*) seriously modifies this conclusion.

7. Mays, *Amos* (OTL); cf. Wolff, *Joel and Amos*, 106.

8. Weiser, *Die Profetie des Amos*, 104.

9. Cf. E. Baumann, *Der Aufbau der Amosreden*, BZAW 7 (1903).
10. Cf. Wolff, *Joel and Amos*, 101: 'That Yahweh is the only God of Israel and of the world of nations is not a theme of his message but its self-evident presupposition.'
11. Thus Cramer, *Amos*, 156ff.
12. Cf. Beek, 'The Religious Background', 132, and Nowack, *Die kleinen Propheten*.
13. J. Lindblom, *Prophecy in Ancient Israel* (Oxford, 1962), 335 (footnote).
14. Cf. Kapelrud, *Central Ideas in Amos*, 17ff.
15. Humbert, *Un héraut de la justice*, 22 and 27 respectively; cf. also F. Nötscher, *Die Gerechtigkeit Gottes bei den vorexilischen Propheten* (Münster-i.-W., 1915), 79: 'Es ist für Jahwes Strafe nach Amos ohne Belang, ob die Sünden gegen sein Volk gerichtet sind oder nicht; die Verletzung der rechten sittlichen Ordnung an sich ist strafbar' ('According to Amos it is unimportant for Yahweh's punishment whether the sins are directed against his people or not; damage to the correct moral order is culpable in itself'). Cf. ibid., 85: 'Die Schuld der Heiden liegt meist in einer ihnen wohl zurechenbaren Überschreitung der rechten Ordnung' ('The guilt of the heathen mostly lies in a transgression of the right order which can certainly be laid to their account').
16. H. S. Gehman, 'Natural Law and the Old Testament', in *Biblical Studies in Memory of H. C. Alleman*, ed. J. M. Myers, O. Reimherr and H. N. Bream (New York, 1960), 109–22.
17. Ibid., 113. Cf. Clements, *Prophecy and Tradition*, 65, and the discussion in Jones, 'Some Leading Motifs', 156ff.
18. M. Weber, *Ancient Judaism* (Glencoe, Ill., 1952), 302.
19. Jones, 'Some Leading Motifs', 156.

Section VII

1. See above, p. 111.
2. Weiser, *Die Profetie des Amos*, 112.
3. E. W. Heaton, *The Hebrew Kingdoms* (Oxford, 1968), 266.

Appendix: International Law in the Ancient Near East

1. W. Preiser, 'Zum Völkerrecht der vorklassischen Antike', *Archiv des Völkerrechts* 4 (1954): 257–88.
2. Cf. T. J. Lawrence, *The Principles of International Law* (London, 1895), especially 26; E. von Ullmann, 'Völkerrecht' in *Das öffentliche Recht der Gegenwart*, vol. 3, 12th ed., ed. G. Jellinek et al. (Tübingen, 1935).
3. Full details in A. Poebel, 'Der Konflikt zwischen Lagas und Umma z. Z. Enannatums I und Entemenas' in *Oriental Studies* (Festschrift for Paul Haupt), ed. C. Adler and A. Ember (Baltimore, 1926), 220–67.
4. Cf. A. Nussbaum, *A Concise History of the Law of Nations*, 2d ed. (New York, 1962), 1. There is a possible example of mediation between two *sovereign* states by Zimri-lim in the Mari letters, discussed by J. M. Munn-Rankin in her 'Diplomacy in Western Asia in the Early Second Millennium B.C.' (*Iraq* 18 [1956]: 68–110; esp. 78f.).
5. Text in E. F. Weidner, *Politische Dokumente aus Kleinasien* (Leipzig, 1923), 112–23.
6. W. Mettgenberg, 'Vor mehr als 3000 Jahren—ein Beitrag zur Geschichte des Auslieferungsrechts', *Zeitschrift für Völkerrecht* 23 (1939): 23–32. The existence of extradition treaties may be attested by 1 Kgs. 2:39 and 18:10; see K. A. Kitchen, 'The Philistines' in *Peoples of Old Testament Times*, ed. D. J. Wiseman, 65.

7. Sections 17 and 18.
8. D. J. Wiseman, *The Alalakh Tablets* (London, 1953), 30.
9. Ibid., 29.
10. Ibid.
11. See V. Korošec, *Hethitische Staatsverträge* (Leipziger rechtswissenschaft-liche Studien 60; Leipzig, 1931).
12. On this point cf. A. Wegner, *Geschichte des Völkerrechts* (Stuttgart, 1936); vassal treaties stand 'erst auf der Schwelle der Rechtsgeschichte' ('only on the threshold of the history of law'), when 'weder VR noch Staatsrecht voll ausgebildet sind' ('neither international nor state law are yet fully formed'; p. 3).
13. Weidner, *Politische Dokumente*, 17ff.
14. Cf. in this connection the letter of accusation from Arnuwandaš to Madduwattaš, which complains that extradition arrangements have been allowed to lapse. See A. Götze, *Madduwattaš*, MVAG 32, no. 1 (1927): 146–47.
15. Noth ('Der historische Hintergrund') thinks they are, in fact, one half of a parity treaty.
16. See Fitzmyer, *The Aramaic Inscriptions of Sefire*.
17. Ibid.
18. J. Knudtzon, *Die el-Amarna Tafeln* (Leipzig, 1907–8) (= EA).
19. Munn-Rankin, 'Diplomacy'.
20. ARMT II. 24.
21. ARMT I. 15.
22. ARMT V. 11.
23. ARMT VI. 15, 7–9.
24. ARMT II. 73.
25. J. Pirenne, 'Le droit international sous la XVIIIe dynastie égyptienne aux Xve et XVIe siècles av. J.-C.', *Revue internationale des droits de l'antiquité* 5 (1958): 3–19.
26. Cf. Munn-Rankin, 'Diplomacy', 96–99.
27. EA 42. The same order is to be found in the Mari letters.
28. EA 34.
29. EA 81 and 189.
30. EA 55 and 140.
31. EA 89, 122, and 123.
32. Deut. 27:17, etc., and all the *kudurru*-inscriptions. Cf. *KAI* 259.
33. *KAI* 1; cf *KAI* 14, also translated in G. A. Cooke, *A Text-Book of North Semitic Inscriptions* (Oxford, 1903), 31: *KAI* 9, 13, 79, 191 and 225; Livy, *Ab urbe condita* XXXI. 30:2–7.
34. VTE 545f., cf. 449–50, and see D. J. McCarthy, *Treaty and Covenant* (Rome, 1963), 201ff. See also Lev. 26:29; Deut. 28:53ff.; 2 Kgs. 6:28f.; Jer. 19:9; Lam. 2:20; 4:10; Ezek. 5:10.
35. EA 74; cf. EA 62, 75 and 142.
36. Quoted by Wolff (*Joel and Amos*, 161) from U. Schmökel, *Ur, Assur, und Babylon* (Stuttgart, 1955), 114.
37. *Iliad* 6. 57f. ('We are not going to leave a single one of them alive, down to the babies in their mothers' wombs—not even they must live. The whole people must be wiped out of existence': E. V. Rieu, *Homer: The Iliad* [London: Penguin Classics, 1950]).
38. The annals of the Assyrian and Neo-Babylonian kings abound in gloating accounts of horrible tortures inflicted on captured enemies and rebellious vassals; and compare some of the scenes in the Nimrud wall reliefs. For a

classic series of atrocities see D. D. Luckenbill, *The Annals of Sennacherib* (Chicago, 1924), 5f.

39. Thus J. A. Montgomery and H. S. Gehman, *The Books of Kings* (ICC, 1951), ad loc.

40. Thus Gray, *I & II Kings* (OTL), 515.

41. 2 Sam. 3:34 might be of interest here. When David laments that Abner was not fettered or manacled, he is presumably saying first that his murder was an act of treachery, as in the passage just discussed; but there does seem to be a clear implication that those who have been fettered may be killed. But if, as H. W. Hertzberg maintains (*I & II Samuel* OTL, 1964, ad loc.), the reference is not to an enemy taken in war but to a criminal awaiting execution, the verse is not relevant to our purposes.

42. See A. Götze, *Kleinasien*, 2d ed., part III.1 of *Kulturgeschichte des alten Orients* (Munich, 1957), 122ff., and especially 127. This is my chief source for what follows, but for some discussion of evidence for these points from the original texts see the Additional Note, pp. 60–61.

43. A. Alt, 'Hethitische und ägyptische Herrschaftsordnung in unterworfenen Gebieten' in *Kleine Schriften zur Geschichte des Volkes Israel*, vol. 3 (Munich, 1953), 99–106 (= *Forschungen und Fortschritte* 25 [1949]: 249–51) argues against too great an emphasis on the humanitarianism of the Hittites; still, the differences from their neighbours are striking.

44. Text and translation in A. Götze, *Die Annalen des Muršiliš* (MVAG 38, no. 6; 1933). The original publications of the annals are referred to by somewhat complicated abbreviations; see the List of Abbreviations for their explanation.

45. Ibid., 47; *KBo* III (= 2*BoTU* 48 (II)), 9–14. This is effectively a trial by battle (see p. 126 above). For a complicated challenge of this sort from Roman times cf. Livy, *Ab urbe condita* I. 32:6–14. The practice of issuing an ultimatum is well attested in the ancient Near East; cf. the Epic of Tukulti-Ninurta, in R. C. Thompson, 'The Excavations on the Temple of Nabu at Nineveh', *Archaeologia* 79 (1929): 126–33 (French translation in J. Harvey, *Le plaidoyer prophétique contre Israël après la rupture de l'alliance* [Studia 22; Bruges, 1967]); the Indictment of Iarîm-Lim of Alep, Mari letter A1314, in G. Dossin, 'Une lettre de Iarîm-Lim, roi d'Alep, à Iasub-Iahad, roi de Dîr', *Syria* 33 (1956): 63–9; the Ultimatum to Milavata, in F. Sommer, *Die Aḫḫiyava-Urkunden* (Munich, 1932), 65–6; and the accusation of Madduwattaš, cited on p. 189 in note 14. And compare Judg. 11:12–29.

46. See above p. 126.

47. *KBo* III 4 (= 2*BoTU* 48 (IX)), 43–8 (Götze, *Die Annalen des Muršiliš*, 37); *BoTU* II 43 (II), 23; *KBo* III 4 (=2*BoTU* 48 (II)), 6: *KBo* III 4 (= 2*BoTU* 48 (IV)), 28.

48. *KUB* XIV 15 (= 2*BoTU* 51A), 7–23.

49. *KUB* XIV 15 (= 2*BoTU* 51A), 45–50. See above, p. 127.

50. *KBo* III 4 (= 2*BoTU* 48 (III)), 11–20 (Götze, *Die Annalen des Muršiliš*, 71).

51. *KUB* XIX 37 (= 2*BoTU* 60 (III)), 41–48. Many more details of the practice of war in the ancient Near East, most of them not directly relevant to our limited purposes, are to be found in *Iraq* 25 (1963), which was devoted to the subject. The points we have made about Hittite rules of war will be found in A. Götze, 'Warfare in Asia Minor' (124–30); and V. Korošec, 'The Warfare of the Hittites— from the Legal point of View' (159–66). W. von Soden, 'Die Assyrer und der Krieg' (131–44) questions how aggressive the Assyrians really were and emphasises that the trait becomes apparent only well into the first millennium, though

even so, he concedes superiority to the Hittites; and H. W. F. Saggs, 'Assyrian Warfare in the Sargonid Period' (145–54) doubts whether they were really exceptional in their brutality. That Hittites were less ferocious than Assyrians has long been a received opinion: see O. Gurney, *The Hittites* (London, 1952), 115.

Notes for Chapter 7: Ethics in Isaiah of Jerusalem

1. On this see my 'Natural Law and Poetic Justice in the Old Testament', chap. 2 in the present volume.
2. A major exception, to be discussed below, is H. H. Schmid, *Gerechtigkeit als Weltordnung* (Tübingen, 1968).
3. A classic attempt is that of E. Troeltsch, 'Das Ethos der hebräischen Propheten', *Logos* 6 (1916–17): 1–28; the most thorough recent study is that of H. J. Kraus, 'Die prophetische Botschaft gegen das soziale Unrecht Israels', *EvT* (1955): 295–307. There is useful material also in J. Lindblom, *Prophecy in Ancient Israel* (Oxford, 1962); A. Phillips, *Ancient Israel's Criminal Law* (Oxford, 1970); and N. W. Porteous, 'The Care of the Poor in the Old Testament', in his *Living the Mystery* (Oxford, 1967). Two important attempts to relate the prophets' moral teaching to specific aspects of the social organization of ancient Israel are H. Donner, 'Die soziale Botschaft der Propheten im Lichte der Gesellschaftsordnung in Israel', *Oriens Antiquus* 2 (1963): 229–45, and A. Alt, 'Micah 2. 1–5–ΓΗΣ ΑΝΑΔΑΣΜΟΣ in Juda', in *Interpretationes ad vetus testamentum pertinentes S. Mowinckel missae* (Oslo, 1955), 13–23, reprinted in his *Kleine Schriften* 3 (Munich, 1959), 373–81.
4. See, for example, L. Dürr, 'Altorientalisches Recht bei Amos und Hosea', *BZ* 23 (1935–36): 150–57; M. A. Beek, 'The Religious Background of Amos II. 6–8', *OtSt* 5 (1948): 132–41; R. Bach, 'Gottesrecht und weltliches Recht in der Verkündigung des Propheten Amos', in *Festschrift für Günther Dehn*, ed. W. Schneemelcher (Neukirchen-Vluyn, 1957), 23–34; R. E. Clements, *Prophecy and Covenant*, SBT 1:43 (London, 1965); N. W. Porteous, 'The Care of the Poor', and W. Eichrodt, 'Prophet and Covenant—some observations on the exegesis of Isaiah', in *Proclamation and Presence*, ed. J. I. Durham and J. R. Porter (London, 1970). For a survey of scholarly opinion about the prophets' reliance on legal traditions see the chapter 'Prophecy and Law' by A. Phillips in *Prophecy and Tradition: Essays in Honour of Peter Ackroyd*, ed. R. J. Coggins, M. A. Knibb, and A. Phillips (Cambridge, 1982).
5. Thus E. Würthwein, 'Der Ursprung der prophetischen Gerichtsrede', *ZTK* 49 (1952): 1–16; H. J. Kraus, 'Die prophetische Verkündigung des Rechts in Israel', *ThSt* 51 (1957); and E. Hammershaimb, 'On the Ethics of the Old Testament Prophets', VTSup 7 (1960): 75–101. N. W. Porteous, 'The Prophets and the Problem of Continuity', in *Israel's Prophetic Heritage* (ed. B. W. Anderson and W. Harrelson [New York, 1962]), discusses the possibility cautiously, but regards the prophets themselves as the main tradents of the ethical tradition in Israel.
6. See J. Fichtner, 'Jesaja unter den Weisen', *TLZ* 78 (1949): cols. 75–80; R. T. Anderson, 'Was Isaiah a Scribe?', *JBL* 79 (1960): 57–58; J. Lindblom, 'Wisdom in the Old Testament Prophets', in *Israel's Prophetic Heritage*; J. W. Whedbee, *Isaiah and Wisdom* (Nashville, 1971); H. W. Wolff, *Amos' geistige Heimat* (Neukirchen-Vluyn, 1964) (translated as *Amos the Prophet: the Man and his Background* [Philadelphia, 1973]).
7. Whedbee (*Isaiah and Wisdom*, 93–94), argues that Isaiah is here appealing simply to general ancient Near Eastern tradition deploring *seizure* of land and

boundary breaking, well attested in treaties and *kudurru* inscriptions as well as in wisdom and legal texts throughout the area. However, there is no reason to suppose that those condemned by Isaiah were simply *seizing* land without observing even the form of law, and it seems to many commentators more likely that Isaiah is here implicitly appealing to the more specifically Israelite tradition of the inalienability of the family inheritance, which is being transgressed through compulsory purchase of land from poor debtors.

8. On the other hand, it could well be argued that 10:5–15 represents a sophisticated theological rationalization of an Israelite chauvinism that was the very reverse of internationalist.

9. Whedbee, *Isaiah and Wisdom*, 98 ff.

10. Cf. the work of R. R. Wilson, *Prophecy and Society in Ancient Israel* (Philadelphia, 1980).

11. See G. von Rad, *Old Testament Theology*, vol. 2 (London, 1965), 135–38, 149–55, 212–17.

12. J. Hempel, *Das Ethos des Alten Testaments*, 2d ed. (BZAW 67; 1964), 109–35, 194–203.

13. W. Eichrodt, *Theology of the Old Testament*, vol. 2 (London, 1967), 365–400.

14. H. Wildberger, *Jesaja 1–12* (BKAT 10; Neukirchen, 1972), 15–17, 201 ff. There is much useful material on this subject in U. Türck, *Die sittliche Forderung der israelitischen Propheten des 8. Jahrhunderts* (Göttingen, 1935), an undeservedly neglected work. N. W. Porteous's article 'The Basis of the Ethical Teaching of the Prophets', in his *Living the Mystery*, is not (as might appear) on this subject, but is concerned with the sources of the prophets' moral teaching and the urgency with which they present it. E. Jacob ('Les bases théologiques de l'éthique de l'ancien testament', VTSup 7 [1960]: 39–51) has little to say about the prophets.

15. It will be apparent that these categories do not correspond to any form-critical distinctions, but cut across differences of *Gattung*. The possible objection that this renders the investigation somewhat unscientific is discussed in section IV.

16. Here, as generally with the preexilic prophets, the question arises of how far this is condemned in itself and how far it is regarded merely as an illicit attempt to avert the consequences of other sins.

17. W. Eichrodt, *Der Heilige in Israel (Jes. 1–12)* (Stuttgart, 1960), 56.

18. R. Lowth, *Isaiah* (London, 1778), ad loc.

19. K. Budde, 'Zu Jesaja 1–5', *ZAW* 69 (1931): 197.

20. See the discussion by H. Wildberger, *Jesaja 1–12*, 100 f., 113–14; he himself accepts the authenticity of the material about idols.

21. See my 'Natural Law and Poetic Justice in the Old Testament', chap. 2 in this volume.

22. It will be seen from this that the analysis presented here is quite compatible with the contention that Isaiah drew on the moral teaching of the law and believed that it was being infringed; see above, p. 133, on the distinction between the *source* and the *basis* of ethical norms appealed to by the prophets.

23. Classic studies of this are R. Anthes, *Die Maat des Echnaton von Amarna*, Suppl. *JAOS* 14 (1952); *Lebensregeln und Lebensweisheit der alten Ägypter*, AO 32, no. 2 (1933); see also S. Morenz, *Gott und Mensch im alten Ägypten* (Heidelberg, 1965); *Ägyptische Religion*, vol. 8 of *Die Religionen der Menschheit*, ed. C. M. Schröder (Stuttgart, 1960); H. Gese, *Lehre und Wirklichkeit in der alten Weisheit* (Tübingen, 1958).

24. *Gerechtigkeit als Weltordnung*, esp. 23–66. Schmid contends that *ṣedeq* and *ṣĕdaqâ* are often distinguished: *ṣedeq* is the abstract quality which produces specific acts that can be described as *ṣĕdaqâ*. But whichever word is used, the idea of cosmic order is always implicit, in his view.

25. In the passages with which we are concerned, the root *ṣdq* occurs in 1:21, 26, and 27; 5:7, 16, and 23; 10:22; and 28:17. *mišpāṭ* and *ṣĕdaqâ* together seem to function as general terms for 'well-doing', but it is difficult to see how one could establish that a particular view of ethics lay behind them. There is now a large body of critical literature on both terms, most of it reviewed in Schmid's work.

26. For example, Eichrodt stresses that ethical obligation does *not* (in his view) stem from 'natural' or rational considerations but only from the absolute will of Yahweh, which brooks no rational probing, by speaking of 'the Unconditional Ought' (*Man in the Old Testament*, SBT 1, no. 4 (London, 1951). Whether or not this is a fair way of describing Old Testament attitudes to morality, it clearly comes under the same condemnation as the present paper in respect of its use of nonbiblical terminology.

27. Hence the approach adopted by C. Westermann, *Basic Forms of Prophetic Speech* (London, 1967). A detailed statement of the belief that exegesis must always begin from a (structural) form-critical approach is to be found in K. Koch et al., *Amos untersucht mit den Methoden einer strukturalen Formgeschichte* (Neukirchen-Vluyn, 1976).

28. This is most clearly expressed in Schmid's article 'Schöpfung, Gerechtigkeit und Heil' (*ZTK* 70 [1973]: 1–19). Against von Rad, he argues that creation is the central theme of the Old Testament, and he makes it clear that by 'creation' he understands the existence of order and pattern in the world, not just the idea that it had a beginning. Thus 'wenn auch die Art des Auftretens der Propheten . . . ohne altorientalische Parallele dasteht . . . , so bleibt doch das Material, der Horizont und sogar die Logik ihrer Verkündigung die gemeinorientalische (Schöpfungs-) Ordnungsvorstellung' (p. 8: 'even if the way the prophets appeared . . . is without ancient Near Eastern parallels, still the material, the horizon, and even the logic of their proclamation remains the universal ancient Near Eastern idea of (creation) order'); and again 'Der Schöpfungsglaube, das heisst der Glaube, dass Gott die Welt mit ihren mannigfaltigen Ordnungen geschaffen hat und erhält, ist nicht ein Randthema biblischer Theologie, sondern im Grunde ihr Thema schlechthin' (p.15: 'Belief in creation—that is, the belief that God made and sustains the world with its manifold orders—is not a marginal theme in biblical theology, but basically its whole theme').

29. See R. P. Carroll (*When Prophecy Failed* [London, 1979], 12–15) for the application of this term to the Prophets.

Notes for Chapter 8: Ethics in the Isaianic Tradition

1. For this trend, see especially E. W. Conrad, *Reading Isaiah* (OBT 27; Minneapolis: Fortress Press, 1991); M. A. Sweeney, 'The Book of Isaiah in Recent Research' in *Currents in Research: Biblical Studies*, vol. 1, ed. A. J. Hauser and P. Sellew (Sheffield: JSOT Press, 1993), 141–62; R. Rendtorff, 'The Book of Isaiah: A Complex Unity: Synchronic and Diachronic Reading', in *Society of Biblical Literature 1991 Seminar Papers*, ed. E. H. Lovering, Jr. (SBLSP 30; Atlanta: Scholars Press, 1991), 8–20; and already W. L. Holladay, *Isaiah, Scroll of a Prophetic Heritage* (Grand Rapids: Eerdmans, 1978).

2. See C. R. Seitz, 'Isaiah 1–66: Making Sense of the Whole,' in *Reading and Preaching the Book of Isaiah*, ed. C. R. Seitz (Philadelphia: Fortress Press, 1988).

3. H. G. M. Williamson, *The Book Called Isaiah: Deutero-Isaiah's Role in Composition and Redaction* (Oxford: Oxford University Press, 1994).
4. See J. Barton, 'Ethics in Isaiah of Jerusalem', chapter 7 in this volume.
5. See O. Kaiser, *Isaiah 1–12* (London: SCM Press, 1972 [2d, completely revised ed., 1983]); *Isaiah 13–19* (London: SCM Press, 1974 [2d ed., 1980]).
6. On this, see R. E. Clements, *Isaiah and the Deliverance of Jerusalem: A Study of the Interpretation of Prophecy in the Old Testament* (JSOTSup 13; Sheffield: JSOT Press, 1980).

Notes to Chapter 9: Theological Ethics in Daniel

1. A classic study of ethics and eschatology can be found in L. Couard, *Die religiösen und sittlichen Anschauungen der alttestamentlichen Apokryphen und Pseudepigraphen* (Gütersloh, 1907). To be noted among the sparse modern literature dealing with the ethics of apocalypticism is L. H. Silberman, 'The Human Deed in a Time of Despair: The Ethics of Apocalyptic', in *Essays in Old Testament Ethics: In Memoriam J. Philip Hyatt*, ed. J. L. Crenshaw and J. T. Willis (New York: Ktav, 1974), 191–202.
2. Cf. W. L. Humphreys, 'A Life-Style for Diaspora: A Study of the Tales in Esther and Daniel', *JBL* 92 (1973): 211–23.
3. See W. Schrage, *The Ethics of the New Testament* (Edinburgh: T. and T. Clark, 1988), esp. 22, who argues that apocalyptic writers believed individuals must be *prepared* for the coming end by ethical conduct.
4. Cf. J. G. Gammie ('Spatial and Ethical Dualism in Jewish Wisdom and Apocalyptic Literature', *JBL* 93 [1974]: 356–85), who stresses the contrast between the eschatological fate of the righteous and the wicked. See also C. Münchow, *Ethik und Eschatologie: Ein Beitrag zum Verständnis der frühjüdischen Apokalyptik mit einem Blick auf das Neue Testament* (Göttingen: Vandenhoeck & Ruprecht, 1981).

Notes for Conclusion: The Future of Old Testament Ethics

1. E. Otto, *Theologische Ethik des Alten Testaments* (Stuttgart: Kohlhammer, 1994). See my review in *TRE* 64:4 (1999): 425–31.
2. J. Hempel, *Das Ethos des Alten Testaments* (BZAW 67; Berlin, 1938; 2d ed., 1964).
3. W. Eichrodt, *Theologie des Alten Testaments*, vol. 2 (Leipzig, 1935); *Theology of the Old Testament*, vol. 2 (London, 1967). For critical comments on both Hempel and Eichrodt see my 'Understanding Old Testament Ethics', chap. 1 in this volume.
4. C. J. H. Wright, *Living as the People of God: The Relevance of Old Testament Ethics* (Leicester: InterVarsity Press, 1983).
5. See H. H. Schmid, *Wesen und Geschichte der Weisheit: Eine Untersuchung zur altorientalischen und israelitischen Weisheitsliteratur* (BZAW 101; Berlin: de Gruyter, 1966).
6. E. Otto, 'Forschungsgeschichte der Entwürfe einer Ethik im Alten Testament', *Verkündigung und Forschung* 36 (1991): 3–37.
7. G. J. Wenham, 'The Gap between Law and Ethics in the Bible', *Journal of Jewish Studies* 48 (1997): 17–29.
8. G. J. Wenham, *Story as Torah: Reading the Old Testament Ethically* (Edinburgh: T. & T. Clark, 2000). A 'narrative' approach to Old Testament ethics can also be found in W. Janzen, *Old Testament Ethics: A Paradigmatic Approach* (Louisville, Ky.: Westminster John Knox Press, 1994).

9. Ibid., 109–19. See M. Sternberg, *The Poetics of Biblical Narrative* (Bloomington: Indiana University Press, 1985).
10. See D. N. Fewell and D. M. Gunn, 'Tipping the Balance: Sternberg's Reader and the Rape of Dinah', *JBL* 110 (1991): 193–211.
11. See W. A. Meeks, *The Moral World of the First Christians* (Philadelphia: Westminster Press, 1986); *The Origins of Christian Morality: The First Two Centuries* (New Haven: Yale University Press, 1993). For a highly stimulating example of what could be attempted along these lines in Old Testament studies, see A. Mein, *Ezekiel and the Ethics of Exile* (Oxford: Clarendon Press, 2001).

Bibliography

Albright, W. F. 'The Oracles of Balaam'. *JBL* 63 (1944): 207–33.
Alt, A. 'Hethitische und ägyptische Herrschaftsordnung in unterworfenen Gebieten'. In *Kleine Schriften zur Geschichte des Volkes Israel*. Vol. 3. Munich: 1953, 99–106 (= *Forschungen und Fortschritte* 25 (1949): 249–51).
———. 'Micah 2. 1–5—ΓΗΣ ΑΝΑΔΑΣΜΟΣ in Juda'. In *Interpretationes ad vetus testamentum pertinentes S. Mowinckel missae*. Oslo, 1955, 13–23. Reprinted in his *Kleine Schriften* 3. Munich: 1959, 373–81.
Andersen, K. T. 'Die Chronologie der Könige von Israel und Juda'. *ST* 23 (1969): 69–114.
Anderson, R. T. 'Was Isaiah a Scribe?' *JBL* 79 (1960): 57–58.
Anthes, R. *Die Maat des Echnaton von Amarna*. Suppl. *JAOS* 14 (1952).
———. *Lebensregeln und Lebensweisheit der alten Ägypter*. *AO* 32, no. 2 (1933).
Bach, R. *Die Aufforderung zur Flucht und zum Kampf im alttestamentlichen Prophetenspruch*. WMANT 9. Neukirchen-Vluyn: Neukirchener Verlag, 1962.
Bach, R. 'Gottesrecht und weltliches Recht in der Verkündigung des Propheten Amos'. In *Festschrift für Günther Dehn*. Ed. W. Schneemelcher. Neukirchen-Vluyn: Neukirchener Verlag, 1957, 23–34.
Barr, J. *Biblical Faith and Natural Theology: The Gifford Lectures for 1991*. Oxford: Clarendon Press, 1993.
Bartlett, J. R. 'The Moabites and Edomites'. In *Peoples of Old Testament Times*. Ed. D. J. Wiseman. Oxford: Oxford University Press, 1973, 228–58.
Bartlett, J. 'The Rise and Fall of the Kingdom of Edom'. *PEQ* 104 (1972): 26–37.
Baumann, E. *Der Aufbau der Amosreden*. BZAW 7. Berlin: W. de Gruyter, 1903.
Beek, M. A. 'The Religious Background of Amos 2:6–8'. *OtSt* 5 (1948): 132–41.
Begrich, J. 'Das priesterliche Heilsorakel'. *ZAW* 52 (1934): 81–92.
Bentzen, A. 'The Ritual Background of Amos 1:2–2:16'. *OtSt* 8 (1950): 85–99.
Bernhardt, K.-H. 'Der Feldzug der drei Könige'. In *Schalom (Studien zu Glaube und Geschichte Israels, A. Jepsen zum 70. Geburtstag dargebracht)*. Ed. K.-H. Bernhardt. Stuttgart: Calwer, 1971, 11–22.
Biggar, N. J. *The Hastening that Waits: Karl Barth's Ethics*. Oxford: Oxford University Press, 1993.
Bourke, V. J. 'Natural Law'. In *Dictionary of Christian Ethics*. Ed. J. Macquarrie. London: SCM Press, 1967.
Bright, J. *A History of Israel*. London: SCM Press, 1966.
Buber, M. *Kampf um Israel*. Berlin: Schocken, 1933.
Budde, K. 'Zu Text und Auslegung des Buches Amos'. *JBL* 43 (1924): 46–131.
Budde, K. 'Zu Jesaja 1–5'. *ZAW* 69 (1931): 197.
Carroll, R. P. *When Prophecy Failed*. London: SCM Press, 1979.

Childs, B. S. *Isaiah and the Assyrian Crisis.* SBT 2, no. 3. London: SCM Press, 1967.

Clements, R. E. *Prophecy and Covenant,* SBT 1, no. 43. London: SCM Press, 1965.

———. *A Century of Old Testament Study.* London: Lutterworth Press, 1976.

———. *Isaiah and the Deliverance of Jerusalem: A Study of the Interpretation of Prophecy in the Old Testament.* JSOTSup 13. Sheffield: JSOT Press, 1980.

———. *Prophecy and Tradition.* Oxford: Blackwell, 1975.

Cohen, S. 'The Political Background of the Words of Amos'. *HUCA* 36 (1965): 153–60.

Conrad, E. W. *Reading Isaiah.* OBT 27. Minneapolis: Fortress Press, 1991.

Cooke, G. A. *A Text-Book of North Semitic Inscriptions.* Oxford: Oxford University Press, 1903.

Couard, L. *Die religiösen und sittlichen Anschauungen der alttestamentlichen Apokryphen und Pseudepigraphen.* Gütersloh: 1907.

Cramer, K. *Amos—Versuch einer theologischen Interpretation.* BWA(N)T 3.15. Stuttgart: Kohlhammer, 1930.

Cripps, R. S. *A Critical and Exegetical Commentary on the Book of Amos.* 2d ed. London: SPCK, 1955.

Crisp, R. and M. Slote, eds. *Virtue Ethics.* Oxford: Oxford University Press, 1977.

Cross, F. M. and Freedman, D. N. 'The Blessing of Moses'. *JBL* 67 (1948): 191–210.

Curran, C. E. 'Absolute Norms in Moral Theology', in *Norm and Context in Christian Ethics.* Ed. Outka and Ramsey. London: SCM Press, 1969.

Donner, H. 'Die soziale Botschaft der Propheten im Lichte der Gesellschaftsordnung in Israel'. *Oriens Antiquus* 2. Rome: Centro per le artichità e la storia dell'arte del vicino Oriente, 1963, 229–45.

Dossin, G. 'Une lettre de Iarîm-Lim, roi d'Alep, à Iasub-Iahad, roi de Dîr', *Syria* 33 (1956): 63–69.

———. 'Sur le prophétisme à Mari' in *La divination en Mésopotamie ancienne et dans les régions voisines.* 14e rencontre assyriologique internationale. Strasbourg 2–6 July 1965. Paris: 1966, 77–86.

Douglas, M. *Purity and Danger.* London: Routledge & Kegan Paul, 1966.

Dover, K. J. *Greek Popular Morality in the time of Plato and Aristotle.* Oxford: Oxford University Press, 1974.

Driver, G. R. 'Linguistic and Textual Problems—Minor Prophets II'. *JTS* 39 (1938): 260–73.

Duhm, B. 'Anmerkungen zu den zwölf Propheten'. *ZAW* 31 (1911): 1–43.

Dürr, L. 'Altorientalisches Recht bei Amos und Hosea'. *BZ* 23 (1935–36): 150–57.

Edghill, E. A. *The Book of Amos.* London: 1914.

Eichrodt, W. 'Vorsehungsglaube und Theodizee im Alten Testament'. In *Festschrift Otto Procksch.* Leipzig: 1934, 45–70.

———. *Der Heilige in Israel (Jes. 1–12).* Stuttgart: Calwer Verlag, 1960.

———. *Man in the Old Testament.* London: SCM Press, 1951.

———. 'Prophet and Covenant—some observations on the exegesis of Isaiah'. In *Proclamation and Presence.* Ed. J. I. Durham and J. R. Porter. London: 1970.

———. *Theology of the Old Testament.* Vol. 2. London: SCM Press, 1967.

Ellermeier, F. *Prophetie in Mari und Israel.* Theologische und orientalische Arbeiten 1. Hertzberg: Jungfer, 1968.

Elliger, K. 'Die Nordgrenze des Reiches Davids'. *PJ* 32 (1936): 34–73.

Fahlgren, K. *'sedaqa'.* Ph.D. Diss. Uppsala: 1932.

Fensham, F. C. 'Common Trends in Curses of the Near Eastern Treaties and *kudurru*-Inscriptions compared with Maledictions of Amos and Isaiah'. *ZAW* 75 (1957): 155–75.

Fewell, D. N. and D. M. Gunn. 'Tipping the Balance: Sternberg's Reader and the Rape of Dinah'. *JBL* 110 (1991): 193–211.

Fichtner, J. 'Jesaja unter den Weisen'. *TLZ* 78 (1949): cols. 75–80.

Finkelstein, J. J. *The Ox that Gored*. Transactions of the American Philosophical Society 71/2. Philadelphia: The American Philosophical Society, 1981.

Fishbane, M. 'Additional remarks on RḤMYW (Amos 1:11)'. *JBL* 91 (1972): 391–93.

———. 'The Treaty Background of Amos 1:11'. *JBL* 89 (1970): 313–18.

Fitzmyer, J. A. *The Aramaic Inscriptions of Sefire*. Biblica et Orientalia 19. Rome: Pontifical Biblical Institute, 1967.

Fohrer, G. 'Prophetie und Magie'. In *Studien zur alttestamentlichen Prophetie (1949–65)*. BZAW 99. Berlin: 1967, 242–64. Reprinted from *ZAW* 78 (1966).

Fohrer, G. 'Remarks on Modern Interpretations of the Prophets'. *JBL* 80 (1961): 309–19.

Fosbroke, H. E. W. *Amos*. IB VI. New York: Abingdon-Cokesbury Press, 1956.

Friedman, R. E. *The Hidden Book in the Bible*. London: Profile Books, 1998.

Gammie, J. G. 'Spatial and Ethical Dualism in Jewish Wisdom and Apocalyptic Literature'. *JBL* 93 (1974): 356–85.

Gehman, H. S. 'Natural Law and the Old Testament'. In *Biblical Studies in Memory of H. C. Alleman*. Ed. J. M. Myers, O. Reimherr, and H. N. Bream. New York: J. J. Augustin, 1960, 109–22.

Gese, H. *Lehre und Wirklichkeit in der alten Weisheit*. Tübingen: Mohr, 1958.

Gottwald, N. K. *All the Kingdoms of the Earth*. New York and London: Harper & Row, 1964.

Götze, A. *Die Annalen des Muršiliš*. MVAG 38, no. 6. Leipzig: 1933. *Kleinasien* 2d ed., part 3.1 of *Kulturgeschichte des alten Orients*. Munich: Beck, 1957.

———. *Madduwattaš*. MVAG 32, no. 1. Leipzig: J. C. Hinrichs, 1927.

———. 'Warfare in Asia Minor'. *Iraq* 25. London: British School of Archaeology in Iraq, 1963, 124–30.

Gray, J. *I & II Kings*. OTL. London: SCM, 1964.

Greenberg, M. 'Some Postulates of Biblical Criminal Law'. In *Yehezkel Kaufmann Jubilee Volume*. Ed. M. Haran. Jerusalem: Magnes, 1960, 5–28. Reprinted in *The Jewish Expression*. Ed. J. Goldin. New Haven: Yale University Press, 1976, 18–37.

Gunkel, H. 'Vergeltung im Alten Testament'. *RGG* 5 (1931): 1529–33.

Gunn, D. M. *The Story of King David*. Sheffield: JSOT Press, 1978.

Gurney, O. *The Hittites*. London: Penguin, 1952.

Hammershaimb, E. *The Book of Amos*. Oxford: Blackwell, 1970.

———. 'On the Ethics of the Old Testament Prophets'. VTSup 7 (1960): 75–101.

Haran, M. 'The Rise and Decline of the Empire of Jeroboam ben Joash'. *VT* 17 (1967): 266–97.

Harper, W. R. *Amos and Hosea*. ICC. Edinburgh: T. & T. Clark, 1905.

Harvey, J. *Le plaidoyer prophétique contre Israël après la rupture de l'alliance*. Studia 22. Bruges: Desdee de Brouwer, 1967.

Hauerwas, S. *Vision and Virtue*. Notre Dame, Ind.: University of Notre Dame Press, 1981.

Hayes, J. H. 'Prophetism at Mari and Old Testament Parallels'. *AThR* 49 (1967): 397–409.

Hayes, J. H. 'The Usage of Oracles against Foreign Nations in Ancient Israel'. *JBL* 87 (1968): 81–92.

Heaton, E. W. *The Hebrew Kingdoms*. Oxford: Oxford University Press, 1968.

————. *Solomon's New Men*. London: Thames & Hudson, 1974.

Helck, W. *Die Beziehungen Ägyptens zu Vorderasien im 3. und 2. Jahrtausend vor Chr.* Ägyptologische Abhandlungen 5. Wiesbaden: D. Harrassowitz, 1962.

Hempel, J. *Das Ethos des Alten Testaments*. BZAW 67. 1938. 2d ed., 1964.

Herrmann, S. *A History of Israel in Old Testament Times*. London: SCM, 1975.

Hertzberg, H. W. *I & II Samuel*. OTL. London: SCM, 1964.

Hogg, H. W. 'The Starting Point of the Religious Message of Amos'. In *Transactions of the 3rd International Congress for the History of Religions*. Ed. P. S. Allen and J. de M. Johnson. Oxford: Oxford University Press, 1908, 1:325–7.

Holladay, W. L. *Isaiah, Scroll of a Prophetic Heritage*. Grand Rapids: Eerdmans, 1978.

Hölscher, G. *Eucharisterion*. Festschrift for H. Gunkel. Göttingen: Vandenhoeck & Ruprecht, 1923.

Horst, F. 'Naturrecht und Altes Testament'. *EvT* 10 (1950–51): 253–73 = *Gottes Recht*. ed. H. W. Wolff. 1961, 235–59.

Humbert, P. *Un héraut de la justice—Amos*. Lausanne: 1917.

Humphreys, W. L. 'A Life-Style for Diaspora: A Study of the Tales in Esther and Daniel'. *JBL* 92 (1973): 211–23.

Jacob, E. 'Les bases théologiques de l'éthique de l'Ancien Testament'. VTSup 7 (1960): 39–51.

Janzen, W. *Old Testament Ethics: A Paradigmatic Approach*. Louisville, Ky.: Westminster John Knox Press, 1994.

Jepsen, A. 'Israel und Damaskus'. *AfO* 14 (1942): 153–72.

Jones, G. H. 'An Examination of Some Leading Motifs in the Prophetic Oracles against Foreign Nations'. PhD. Diss. (unpublished). Bangor: University College of North Wales, 1970.

Kaiser, O. *Isaiah 1–12*. London: SCM Press, 1972. 2d, completely revised ed., 1983.

————. *Isaiah 13–39*. London: SCM Press, 1974. 2d ed., 1980.

Kapelrud, A. S. *Central Ideas in Amos*. Oslo: Oslo University Press, 1961.

Kaufmann, Y. *A History of the Religion of Israel*. Tr. M. Greenberg. London: Allen & Unwin, 1961.

Kitchen, K. A. 'The Philistines'. In *Peoples of Old Testament Times*. Ed. D. J. Wiseman. Oxford: Oxford University Press, 1973, 53–78.

Knierim, R. *Die Hauptbegriffe für Sünde im Alten Testament*. Gütersloh: G. Mohn, 1965.

Knudtzon, J. *Die el-Amarna Tafeln*. Leipzig: J. C. Hinrichs, 1907–08.

Koch, K., ed. *Um das Prinzip der Vergeltung in Religion und Recht des Alten Testaments*. Darmstadt: Wissenschaftliche Buchgesellschaft, 1972.

Koch, K., et al. *Amos untersucht mit den Methoden einer strukturalen Formgeschichte*. Neukirchen-Vluyn: Neukirchener Verlag, 1976.

Koch, K. 'Gibt es ein Vergeltungsdogma im Alten Testament?' *ZTK* 52 (1955): 1–42.

Korošec, V. *Hethitische Staatsverträge*. Leipziger rechtswissenschaftliche Studien 60. Leipzig: T. Weicher, 1931.

————. 'The Warfare of the Hittites—from the Legal Point of View'. *Iraq* 25. London: British School of Archaeology in Iraq, 1963, 159–66.

Kotva, J. *The Christian Case for Virtue Ethics*. Washington, D.C.: University of Georgetown Press, 1996.

Kraeling, E. G. H. *Aram and Israel*. New York: Columbia University Press, 1918.

Kraus, H. J. *Psalmen*. BK XV. Neukirchen-Vluyn: Neukirchener Verlag, 1966.

Kraus, H. J. 'Die prophetische Botschaft gegen das soziale Unrecht Israels'. *EvT* (1955): 295–307.

Kraus, H. J. 'Die prophetische Verkündigung des Rechts in Israel'. ThSt 51 (1957).

Kuenen, A. *Historisch-kritische Einleitung in die Bücher des Alten Testaments*. 3 vols. Leipzig: 1885–94.

Lawrence, T. J. *The Principles of International Law*. London: 1895.

Lehming, S. 'Erwägungen zu Amos'. *ZTK* 55 (1958): 145–69.

Lindblom, J. *Prophecy in Ancient Israel*. Oxford: Blackwell, 1962.

Lindblom, J. 'Wisdom in the Old Testament Prophets'. In *Wisdom in Israel and in the Ancient Near East*. Ed. M. Noth. VTSup 3. Leiden: Brill, 1960.

Lowth, R. *Isaiah*. London: 1778.

Luckenbill, D. D. *The Annals of Sennacherib*. Chicago: University of Chicago Press, 1924.

Maag, V. *Text, Wortschatz und Begriffswelt des Buches Amos*. Leiden: Brill, 1951.

MacIntyre, A. *After Virtue*. London: Duckworth, 1981.

Macpherson, C. B. *The Political Theory of Possessive Individualism*. Oxford: Oxford University Press, 1962.

Malamat, A. 'Amos 1:5 in the Light of the Til Barsip Inscriptions'. *BASOR* 129 (1953): 25f.

Malamat, A. 'Prophetic Revelations in New Documents from Mari and the Bible'. VTSup 15 (1966): 214–19.

Malamat, A. 'The Arameans' in *Peoples of Old Testament Times*. Ed. D. J. Wiseman. Oxford: Oxford University Press, 1973, 134–55.

Marsh, J. *Amos and Micah*. London: SCM, 1959.

Marti, K. 'Zur Komposition von Amos 1:3–2:3'. BZAW 33 (Berlin, 1917): W. de Gruyter, 323–30.

Mays, J. L. *Amos*. OTL. London: SCM, 1969.

McCarthy, D. J. *Treaty and Covenant*. Rome: Pontifical Biblical Institute, 1963.

McKane, W. *Prophets and Wise Men*. SBT 1:44. London: SCM, 1965.

Meeks, W. A. *The Moral World of the First Christians*. New Haven, Conn.: Yale University Press, 1993.

———. *The Origins of Christian Morality: The First Two Centuries*. New Haven, Conn.: Yale University Press, 1993.

Meilaender, G. *The Theory and Practice of Virtue*. Notre Dame, Ind.: University of Notre Dame Press, 1984.

Mein, A. *Ezekiel and the Ethics of Exile*. Oxford: Clarendon Press, 2001.

Mettgenberg, W. 'Vor mehr als 3000 Jahren—ein Beitrag zur Geschichte des Auslieferungsrechts'. *Zeitschrift für Völkerrecht* 23. Breslau: J. Kern, 1939, 23–32.

Miller, J. M. 'The Elisha Cycle and the Accounts of the Omride Wars'. *JBL* 85 (1966): 441–54.

———. 'The Fall of the House of Ahab'. *VT* 17 (1967): 307–24.

———. *The Old Testament and the Historian*. London: SPCK, 1976.

Montgomery, J. A. and Gehman, H. S. *The Books of Kings*. ICC. Edinburgh: T. & T. Clark, 1951.

Moran, W. L. 'New Evidence from Mari on the History of Prophecy'. *Biblica* 50. Rome: Pontifical Biblical Institute, 1969, 15–56.

Morenz, S. *Ägyptische Religion*. Vol. 8 of *Die Religionen der Menschheit*. Ed. C. M. Schröder. Stuttgart: Kohlhammer, 1960.

———. *Gott und Mensch im alten Ägypten*. Heidelberg: Lambert Schneider, 1965.

Morgenstern, J. 'Amos Studies IV'. *HUCA* 32 (1961).

Mowinckel, S. *The Psalms in Israel's Worship*. Oxford: Blackwell, 1962.

Münchow, C. *Ethik und Eschatologie: Ein Beitrag zum Verständnis der frühjüdischen Apokalyptik mit einem Blick auf das Neue Testament*. Göttingen: Vandenhoeck & Ruprecht, 1981.

Munn-Rankin, J. M. 'Diplomacy in Western Asia in the Early Second Millennium B.C.'. *Iraq* 18 (1956): 68–110.

Murphy, R. E. 'Israel and Moab in the Ninth Century B.C.'. *CBQ* 15 (1953): 409–17.

Néher, A. *Amos.* Paris: J. Vrin, 1950.

Noth, M. 'Der historische Hintergrund der Inschriften von Sefire'. *ZDPV* 77 (1961): 138–45.

Noth, M. 'Eine palästinische Lokalüberlieferung in 2 Chron. 20'. *ZDPV* 67 (1944): 45–71.

Noth, M. *Überlieferungsgeschichtliche Studien.* Halle: Niemeyer, 1943.

Nötscher, F. *Die Gerechtigkeit Gottes bei den vorexilischen Propheten.* Münster-i.-W.: 1915.

Nowack, W. *Die kleinen Propheten.* Göttingen: 1897.

Nussbaum, A. *A Concise History of the Law of Nations.* 2d ed. New York: Macmillan, 1962.

Nussbaum, M. C. *Love's Knowledge.* Oxford and New York: Oxford University Press, 1990.

———. *The Fragility of Goodness.* Cambridge: Cambridge University Press, 1986.

Otto, E. 'Forschungsgeschichte der Entwürfe einer Ethik im Alten Testament', *VF* 36, no. 1 (1991): 3–37.

———. *Theologische Ethik des Alten Testaments.* Stuttgart: Kohlhammer, 1994.

Oyen, H. van. *Die Ethik des Alten Testaments.* Gütersloh: G. Mohn, 1967.

Paul, S. M. 'Amos 1:3–2:3: A Concatenous Literary Pattern'. *JBL* 90 (1971): 397–403.

Pedersen, J. *Israel I & II.* London: Oxford University Press, 1926.

Phillips, A. In *Prophecy and Tradition: Essays in Honour of Peter Ackroyd.* Ed. R. J. Coggins, M. A. Knibb, and A. Phillips. Cambridge: Cambridge University Press, 1982.

———. *Ancient Israel's Criminal Law.* Oxford: Blackwell, 1970.

Pirenne, J. 'Le droit international sous la XVIIIe dynastie égyptienne aux Xve et XVIe siècles av. J.-C.', *Revue internationale des droits de l'antiquité* 5 (1958): Brussels, 3–19.

Pleins, J. D. *The Social Visions of the Hebrew Bible: A Theological Introduction.* Louisville and London: Westminster John Knox Press, 2000.

Poebel, A. 'Der Konflikt zwischen Lagas und Umma z. Z. Enannatums I und Entemenas'. In *Oriental Studies.* Festschrift for Paul Haupt, Johns Hopkins University. Ed. C. Adler and A. Ember. Baltimore: 1926, 220–67.

Porteous, N. W. 'The Care of the Poor in the Old Testament'. In *Living the Mystery.* Oxford: Blackwell, 1967.

———. 'The Prophets and the Problem of Continuity'. In *Israel's Prophetic Heritage.* Ed. B. W. Anderson and W. Harrelson. New York: Harper, 1962.

Preiser, W. 'Zum Völkerrecht der vorklassischen Antike'. *Archiv des Völkerrechts* 4. Tübingen: J. C. B. Mohr, 1954, 257–88.

Priest, J. 'The Covenant of Brothers'. *JBL* 84 (1965): 400–406.

Pyper, H. C. *David as Reader: 2 Samuel 12:1–15 and the Poetics of Fatherhood.* Leiden: Brill, 1996.

Rad, G. von. *Studies in the Book of Deuteronomy.* SBT 1:9. London: SCM, 1958.

———. *Wisdom in Israel.* London: SCM, 1972.

———. *Der heilige Krieg im alten Israel.* Zurich: Zwingli-Verlag, 1951.

———. *Old Testament Theology.* London: T. & T. Clark, 1965.

Reimer, D. 'The Apocrypha and Biblical Theology: The Case of Interpersonal Forgiveness'. In *After the Exile: Essays in Honor of Rex Mason.* Macon, Ga.: Mercer University Press, 1996, 259–82.

Rendtorff, R. 'The Book of Isaiah: A Complex Unity: Synchronic and Diachronic Reading'. In *Society of Biblical Literature 1991 Seminar Papers*. Ed. E. H. Lovering, Jr. SBLSP 30. Atlanta: Scholars Press, 1991, 8–20.

Reventlow, H. Graf. *Liturgie und prophetisches Ich bei Jeremia*. Gütersloh: G. Mohn, 1963.

———. *Wächter über Israel. Ezechiel und seine Traditionen*. BZAW 82. Berlin: W. de Gruyter, 1962.

———. 'Sein Blut komme auf sein Haupt'. *VT* 10 (1960).

———. *Das Amt des Propheten bei Amos*. Göttingen: Vandenhoeck & Ruprecht, 1962.

Robinson, T. H. *Die zwölf kleinen Propheten*. HAT. Tübingen: 1938.

Rodd, C. S. *Glimpses of a Strange Land: Studies in Old Testament Ethics*. Edinburgh: T. & T. Clark, 2001.

———. 'Shall not the Judge of All the Earth do what is just? (Gen. xviii. 25)'. *ExpTim* 83 (1972): 137–39.

Rogerson, J. W. 'Old Testament Ethics'. In *Text in Context*. Ed. A. D. H. Mayes. Oxford: Oxford University Press, 2000, 116–37.

———. 'The Old Testament view of nature: some preliminary questions'. In *Instruction and Interpretation*. OS 20. Leiden: Brill, 1977, 67–84.

Roth, W. M. W. *Numerical Sayings in the Old Testament*. VTSup 13. Leiden: Brill, 1965.

———. 'The Numerical Sequence x/x + 1 in the Old Testament'. *VT* 12 (1962): 300–11.

Rudolph, W. 'Die angefochtenen Völkersprüche in Amos 1 und 2'. In *Schalom (Studien zu Glaube und Geschichte Israels, A. Jepsen zum 70. Geburtstag dargebracht)*. Ed. K.-H. Bernhardt. Stuttgart: Calwer, 1971.

———. *Chronikbücher*. HAT 21. Tübingen: Mohr (Paul Siebeck), 1955.

Saggs, H. W. F. 'Assyrian Warfare in the Sargonid Period'. *Iraq* 25 (1963): 145–54. London: British School of Archaeology in Iraq, 1963, 145–54.

Sanders, E. P. *Paul and Palestinian Judaism: A Comparison of Patterns of Religion*. Philadelphia: Fortress Press, 1977.

———. *Paul, the Law, and the Jewish People*. Philadelphia: Fortress Press, 1983.

Scharbert, J. 'ŠLM im Alten Testament'. In *Lex tua veritas*. H. Junker Festschrift. Trier: Paulinus-Verlag, 1961.

Schmid, H. H. *Gerechtigkeit als Weltordnung*. Tübingen: Mohr, 1968.

———. 'Schöpfung, Gerechtigkeit und Heil'. *ZTK* 70 (1973): 1–19.

———. *Wesen und Geschichte der Weisheit: Eine Untersuchung zur altorientalischen und israelitischen Weisheitsliteratur*. BZAW 101. Berlin: de Gruyter, 1966.

Schmidt, W. H. 'Zu diesem Heft'. *VF* 36, no. 1 (1991): 1–2.

———. *Die Zehn Gebote im Rahmen alttestamentlicher Ethik*. Erträge der Forschung 281. Darmstadt: Wissenschaftliche Buchgesellschaft, 1993.

Schmökel, H. *Ur, Assur, und Babylon*. Stuttgart: Gustav Kilpper, 1955.

Schmuttermayr, G. 'RHM—eine lexikalische Studie'. *Biblica* 51 (1970): 499–532.

Schrage, W. *The Ethics of the New Testament*. Edinburgh: T. and T. Clark, 1988.

Seitz, C. R. 'Isaiah 1–66: Making Sense of the Whole.' In *Reading and Preaching the Book of Isaiah*. Ed. C. R. Seitz. Philadelphia: Fortress Press, 1988.

Shenkel, J. D. *Chronology and Recensional Development in the Greek Text of Kings*. Cambridge, Mass.: Harvard University Press, 1968.

Silberman, L. H. 'The Human Deed in a Time of Despair: The Ethics of Apocalyptic'. In *Essays in Old Testament Ethics: In Memoriam J. Philip Hyatt*. Ed. J. L. Crenshaw and J. T. Willis. New York: Ktav, 1974, 191–202.

Smend, R. 'Ethik III: Altes Testament'. *TRE* 10 (1995): 423–35.

Soden, W. von. 'Die Assyrer und der Krieg'. *Iraq* 25 (1963): 131–44.

Soggin, J. A. 'Amos VI.13–14 und I:3 auf dem Hintergrund der Beziehungen zwischen Israel und Damaskus im 9. und 8. Jahrhundert'. In *Near Eastern Studies in Honor of W. F. Albright*. Ed. H. Goedicke. Baltimore and London: Johns Hopkins Press, 1971, 433–41.

Sommer, F. *Die Aḫḫiyava-Urkunden*. Munich: Verlag der bayerischen Akademie der Wissenschaften, 1932.

Spriggs, D. C. *Two Old Testament Theologies*. London: SCM, 1975.

Sternberg, M. *The Poetics of Biblical Narrative*. Bloomington: Indiana University Press, 1985.

Stolz, F. *Interpreting the Old Testament*. London: SCM, 1975.

Sweeney, M. A. 'The Book of Isaiah in Recent Research'. In *Currents in Research: Biblical Studies*. Vol. 1. Ed. A. J. Hauser and P. Sellew. Sheffield: JSOT Press, 1993, 141–62.

Tallquist, K. *Himmelsgegenden und Winde*. Studia Orientalia 2. Helsinki: Finnish Oriental Society, 1928.

Terrien, S. 'Amos and Wisdom'. In *Israel's Prophetic Heritage*. Ed. B. W. Anderson and W. Harrelson. New York: Harper, 1962.

Thompson, R. C. 'The Excavations on the Temple of Nabu at Nineveh'. *Archaeologia* 79 (1929).

Thompson, T. L. *The Historicity of the Patriarchal Narratives*. BZAW 133. 1974.

Torczyner, N. H. *hallason we hassepher*. Jerusalem: Mosad Byalik, 1948.

Troeltsch, E. 'Das Ethos der hebräischen Propheten'. *Logos* 6 (1916–17).

Türck, U. *Die sittliche Forderung der israelitischen Propheten des 8. Jahrhunderts*. Göttingen: Vandenhoeck & Ruprecht, 1935.

Ullmann, E. von. 'Völkerrecht'. In *Das öffentliche Recht der Gegenwart*. Ed. G. Jellinek et al. Vol. 3, 12th ed. Tübingen: J. C. B. Mohr (P. Siebeck), 1935.

Unger, M. *Israel and the Aramaeans of Damascus*. London: J. Clarke & Co., 1957.

Van Seters, J. *Abraham in History and Tradition*. New Haven and London: Yale University Press, 1975.

Vaux, R. de. *Ancient Israel, its life and institutions*. 2d ed. London: Darton, Longman & Todd, 1961.

———. 'Single Combat in the Old Testament'. In *The Bible and the Ancient Near East*. London: Darton, Longman & Todd, 1972, 122–35.

Vollmer, J. *Geschichtliche Rückblicke und Motive in der Prophetie des Amos, Hosea und Jesaja*. BZAW 119. Berlin: W. de Gruyter, 1971.

Waldow, E. von. *Der traditionsgeschichtliche Hintergrund der prophetischen Gerichtsreden*. BZAW 85. Berlin: W. de Gruyter, 1963.

Weber, M. *Ancient Judaism*. Glencoe, Ill.: Free Press, 1952.

Wegner, A. *Geschichte des Völkerrechts*. Stuttgart: Kohlhammer, 1936.

Weidner, E. F. *Politische Dokumente aus Kleinasien*. Leipzig: J. C. Hinrichs, 1923.

Weinfeld, M. *Deuteronomy and the Deuteronomic School*. Oxford: Oxford University Press, 1972.

Weingreen, J. *From Bible to Mishna*. Manchester: Manchester University Press, 1976.

Weiser, A. *Das Buch der zwölf kleinen Propheten*. ATD. Göttingen: Vandenhoeck & Ruprecht, 1967.

———. *Die Profetie des Amos*. BZAW 53. Berlin: 1929.

Weiss, M. 'The pattern of the 'Execration Texts' in the Prophetic Literature'. *IEJ* 19 (1969): 150–57.

Wenham, G. J. 'The Gap between Law and Ethics in the Bible'. *Journal of Jewish Studies* 48 (1997): 17–29.

———. *Story as Torah: Reading the Old Testament Ethically*. Edinburgh: T. & T. Clark, 2000.

Westermann, C. *Basic Forms of Prophetic Speech*. London: Lutterworth Press, 1967.

Whedbee, J. W. *Isaiah and Wisdom*. Nashville: Abingdon, 1971.

Whybray, R. N. *The Intellectual Tradition in Ancient Israel*. BZAW 135. 1974.

———. *The Succession Narrative: A Study of II Samuel 9–20, I Kings 1 and 2*. London: SCM Press, 1968.

Wildberger, H. 'Glauben' im Alten Testament'. *ZTK* 65 (1968): 129–59.

———. *Jesaja 1–12*. BK10. Neukirchen-Vluyn: Neukirchener Verlag, 1972.

Williamson, H. G. M. *The Book Called Isaiah: Deutero-Isaiah's Role in Composition and Redaction*. Oxford: Oxford University Press, 1994.

Wilson, R. R. *Prophecy and Society in Ancient Israel*. Philadelphia: Fortress, 1980.

Wiseman, D. J. *The Alalakh Tablets*. London: British Institute of Archaeology at Ankara, 1953.

———, ed. *Peoples of Old Testament Times*. Oxford: Oxford University Press, 1973.

Wolff, H. W. *Joel and Amos*. Philadelphia: Fortress, 1977 (translation of *Dodekapropheton 2: Joel und Amos*. BK XIV. Neukirchen-Vluyn: Neukirchener Verlag, 1969).

———. *Amos' geistige Heimat*. Neukirchen-Vluyn: Neukirchener Verlag, 1964. Translated as *Amos the Prophet: the Man and his Background*. Philadelphia: Fortress, 1973.

———. 'Das Zitat im Prophetenspruch'. BeiEvTh 4 (1937): 3–112 = *Gesammelte Studien*. Munich: C. Kaiser, 1964, 36–129.

Wright, C. J. H. *Living as the People of God: The Relevance of Old Testament Ethics*. Leicester: InterVarsity Press, 1983.

Würthwein, E. 'Amosstudien'. ZAW 62 (1949): 10–52.

———. 'Jesaja 7, 1–9. Ein Beitrag zu dem Thema "Prophetie und Politik."' In *Theologie als Glaubenswagnis*. Festschrift for Karl Heim. Tübingen and Hamburg: Furche-Verlag, 1954, 47–63.

———. 'Der Ursprung der prophetischen Gerichtsrede'. In *Wort und Existenz: Studien zum alten Testament*. Göttingen: 1970, 111–28 (= *ZTK* 49 (1952), 1–16).

Index of Biblical Passages

Index of Modern Authors

209